Urban Living

Urban Living

D. J. Walmsley

URBAN LIVING
The individual in the city

Longman Scientific & Technical

Copublished in the United States with
John Wiley & Sons, Inc., New York

Longman Scientific & Technical,
Longman Group UK Limited,
Longman House, Burnt Mill, Harlow,
Essex CM20 2JE, England
and Associated Companies throughout the world.

Copublished in the United States with
John Wiley & Sons, Inc., 605 Third Avenue, New York, NY 10158

First published 1988

British Library Cataloguing in Publication Data
Walmsley, D. J.
    Urban living: the individual in the city.
    1. Sociology, Urban
    I. Title
    307.7'6   HT151
    ISBN 0-582-30167-X

Library of Congress Cataloging-in-Publication Data
Walmsley, D. J.
    Urban living.

    Bibliography: p.
    Includes indexes.
    1. City and town life. 2. Sociology, Urban.
3. Spatial behaviour. I. Title.
HT231.W36 1988   307.7'6   87-2944
ISBN 0-470-20863-5 (Wiley, USA only).

Set in 10/11pt Ehrhardt Roman
Produced by Longman Group (FE) Limited
Printed in Hong Kong

Contents

List of figures

List of tables

Preface

There exists a vast literature in the field of urban studies. However, despite the fact that the range of topics that has been written about is enormous, three areas seem to be of particular concern. The first is the whole question of the spatial organization of urban society, including discussion of housing, residential segregation, and social areas. The second area of concern involves political issues, planning, and the question of how cities are managed and governed. The third area centres on the study of individual urban dwellers and how they cope with city living. These three areas have long preoccupied commentators on urban affairs. In recent years, however, the tenor of urban studies has changed somewhat as there has emerged a general willingness to focus research efforts away from traditional topics and towards what are perceived to be pressing contemporary problems. Often this redirection has involved a challenge to established methodology, philosophy, and ideology. Thus the study of the spatial organization of society has come to examine 'who gets what where' from the standpoint of equity and justice. Similarly, an interest in 'structuralism' and neo-marxism has encouraged a reappraisal of urban politics and fostered new insights into the role of the state in urban affairs. Both of these initiatives have been well explored in a number of books. The same cannot be said about recent work on how individuals cope with urban living. Such work has in fact received very little attention from book writers, despite the great volume of research that is being undertaken. The present book seeks to rectify this shortcoming.

This is not to say that the book attempts to provide coverage of everything that has been written about the behaviour of city dwellers. Such a task would be nightmarish. Instead the book focusses on just four main issues: how individuals come to know the city in which they live; how they feel about the urban environment; the extent of their travel patterns within the city; and the influence of place on behaviour. In seeking to explore these issues the book addresses a number of important questions. How well do people know the urban environment? How do they find their way around? What makes a city memorable? How do people feel about the city in which they live? Are there basic human needs that city living is expected to fulfill? Why do city dwellers develop a sense of emotional attachment to particular places? What makes certain urban landscapes appealing? How extensive are people's travel patterns within the city? To what extent are urban dwellers territorial animals? What effect does the character of the local neighbourhood have on its inhabitants? Does high density living create stress and social problems? Do certain sorts of urban environment foster crime, delinquency, and vandalism?

Unfortunately it is impossible to give categorical answers to some of these questions because of gaps in the present state of our understanding of how individuals cope with city living. To some extent, therefore, the book aims to do no more than suggest how answers might be found. The book does not however push one particular theoretical orientation. Rather it covers both research in 'mainstream' social science and newer initiatives that are commonly described as 'humanistic'. Implicit in the text, therefore, is the view that a great many different approaches can provide insights into the behaviour of city dwellers and that the student of urban affairs needs to take stock of all these different approaches. Hopefully, undergraduates in courses concerned with environment and behaviour will find that, by reading the book, their knowledge of what it means to be an urban dweller will be enhanced. Hopefully, too, the book will help planners prepare for the daunting task of providing liveable urban environments.

Several people have helped immensely with the preparation of this book. Many colleagues and friends have assisted, often unwittingly, in the shaping of my ideas. However, I owe a special debt of gratitude to Chris Cunningham, Don Perlgut and Wendy Sarkissian for their advice and comments on a draft manuscript. Rudi Boskovic produced the illustrations in his usual efficient manner and Denise Cumming, Carmen Jones, Bev Waters and Megan Wheeler provided a secretarial team that was unsurpassed in terms of both friendliness and performance. My sincere thanks to them all. Above all, though, I would like to thank Jenny, Adam and Rachel for their continuing support and, in particular, for the endless hours they have spent trudging around cities I have wanted to visit.

D J Walmsley
Armidale
January 1987

Acknowledgements

We are grateful to the following for permission to reproduce copyright material:

Edward Arnold (Publishers) Ltd for figs 2.4 from fig 2 (Golledge 1978) and 5.2 from fig 2 (Boots 1979); Association of American Geographers for figs 2.10 from fig 1 (Walmsley 1982a), 3.1 from fig 36, p 221 (Ley 1974), 3.2 from fig 1 (Pred 1984) and 4.7 from fig 2 (Desbarats 1983); Australian Bureau of Statistics for table 5.2 (Australian Bureau of Statistics 1979); Cambridge University Press for table 3.1 from table D.3, p 281 (Csikszentmihalyi & Rochberg-Halton 1981); Economic Geography for fig 4.4 from figs 7 & 9 (Janelle & Goodchild 1983); the author, H. W. Faulkner for table 3.2 from table 2.2, p 62 (Faulkner 1978); Geografiska Annaler for fig 2.6 from fig 2 (Potter 1979); the author, J. R. Gold for fig 3.3 from fig 8.1, p 124 (Gold 1980); the author, R. G. Golledge for table 1.1 from table 2.2, p 33 (King & Golledge 1978); the author, P. Gould for fig 2.1 from figs 5.2 & 5.12 (Gould & White 1974); Institute of British Geographers for fig 2.2 from fig 1 (Matthews 1984b); Methuen & Co. for table 4.2 from table 2.1, pp 20–1 (Daniels & Warnes 1980); MIT Press for fig 2.8 from fig 23.2 (Appleyard 1969b); Mouton de Gruyter for table 4.3 from table 11 on p. 350 (Von Rosenbladt 1972); Plenum Publishing Corp and the author for fig 2.11 from fig 4 (Lee 1968); the author, C. Sagan for fig. 3.4 from p 59 (Sagan 1977) copyright © 1977 by Carl Sagan; Sage Publications Inc for fig 2.7 (Ladd 1970) and table 5.1 (Stokols 1976); John

Wiley & Sons Inc for fig 4.2 from fig II–I, p 33 and table 4.1 from tables VI–4 & VI–5, pp 174–7 (Chapin 1974).

Whilst every effort has been made to trace the owners of copyright, in a few cases this has proved impossible and we take this opportunity to offer our apologies to any authors whose rights may have been unwittingly infringed.

Chapter

1

Introduction

Cities evoke mixed feelings. Some people regard them as the epitome of all that is good in society. According to this view cities are seen as providing a wide variety of lifestyles, a great range of choices for both work and play, and a stimulating atmosphere. In this context it is worth noting that the very word 'city' comes from the same Latin root as the word 'civilization'. Other commentators take a less positive view. Instead of being regarded as a symbol and a manifestation of civilization, cities are viewed in more jaundiced terms as the locale for many of the problems that bedevil present-day society. The evidence for this point of view is plentiful: drug abuse, crime, mental illness, vandalism, truancy, and family breakdown are usually more prevalent in urban than in rural areas. This is not to say that there is something in the nature of the urban environment that 'causes' such problems. It may well be that cities, in concentrating vast numbers of people in relatively small areas, also serve to concentrate social problems to the point where these problems are more noticeable than they would otherwise have been.

Of course not all cities are the same and not all cities have the same effects on individual behaviour. Careful investigation has, for example, revealed significant differences in behaviour, attitudes, and outlook between residents of large cities and residents of small towns. Likewise the character of cities has changed over time and continues to change as ever increasing numbers of people become urban dwellers (Table 1.1). The widespread and large-scale growth of cities really began with the Industrial Revolution in the late eighteenth and

Table 1.1 World urban population (in millions)

Major area	1925	1950	1975	2000	2025
World total	405	701	1,548	3,191	5,713
Northern America	68	106	181	256	308
Europe	162	215	318	425	510
U.S.S.R.	30	71	154	245	318
East Asia	58	99	299	638	1,044
Latin America	25	67	196	464	819
Africa	12	28	96	312	803
South Asia	45	108	288	825	1,873
Oceania	5	8	15	26	38

Source: King and Golledge (1978)

early nineteenth centuries. Before that time society can be characterized as being 'pre-industrial'. This is a curious expression. It does
not denote, as a literal interpretation might suggest, a society in which
'industry' has yet to develop. Rather it signifies a society where
industry is a relatively small employer of labour and a society in which
the majority of people live in small, homogeneous groups based on
tightly knit primary relations usually involving family and neighbours.
Members of such a society tend to perform similar tasks and tend also
to have similar interests. This means that they tend to think and
behave alike with a result that there emerges a more or less uniform
way of life. Of course this picture of a so-called *gemeinschaft* society
(Tönnies 1887) is something of a caricature because it is overdrawn
to the extent that 'pre-industrial' life was probably far more varied
than is commonly assumed. Nevertheless it does afford a useful
comparison with the so-called *gesellschaft* society that emerged as a
result of large-scale industrialization and urbanization. Of course this
is not to say that changes in society arose simply or solely as a result
of industrialization and urbanization. Tuan (1982), for example, has
pointed out that a fundamental shift in society occurred as early as
the Renaissance as medieval society, with its emphasis on group norms
and the repression of individuality, gave way to new forms of social
organization that fostered individuality at the expense of community
allegiance. Despite this, it was not really until the twentieth century
that the true nature of *gesellschaft* society emerged. In a *gesellschaft*
society great numbers of people are agglomerated in large cities. This
agglomeration process inevitably involves much higher population
densities than are to be found in *gemeinschaft* societies. As a result
there is a massive increase in the number of people and the variety
of situations with which an individual comes into contact. At the same

time the heterogeneity of the population leads to the emergence of divergent and sometimes conflicting life styles. The sense of community that typifies *gemeinschaft* society is lost in *gesellschaft* society. No longer is there a bond of common interest to hold together people who live in close proximity to one another. Instead people are sorted out into different suburbs in accordance with their socio-economic status, their ethnic affiliation, and the stage they have reached in their life cycle. The neighbourhoods in which people live in *gesellschaft* societies are usually thought of as pale shadows of the communities that form the building blocks of *gemeinschaft* societies. As a result, a transition from *gemeinschaft* to *gesellschaft* society is usually thought of as involving a decrease in primary contacts with family and friends and a corresponding decrease in the level of social cohesion. This, of course, is every bit as much a caricature as was the description of *gemeinschaft* society presented earlier. For example, the nuclear family began to supplant the extended family to a significant extent even in so-called 'pre-industrial' society (Laslett 1965; Hareven 1982). Moreover, in the early days of industrialization, the process of urbanization possibly did little to disrupt family life because families were often recruited *in toto* to join the industrial workforce (Anderson 1971). Nevertheless the caricature is one with more than a grain of truth in it. After all, twentieth century urban living does display many of the features of *gesellschaft* society. The consequences of this are far reaching. On the one hand an individual is able to follow his or her whims and fancies free from the constraints that operate in closely knit communities. On the other hand the individual is deprived of the sense of identity and security that comes from being part of a larger group. In such cases a condition known as *anomie* may develop whereby the individual becomes disturbed by the lack of any feeling of belonging and by an inability to identify with the group among whom the individual is forced to live (Wirth 1938).

This bleak picture of the impact of urbanization on the individual had many advocates in the early years of this century (see Simmel 1905; Sumner 1906). More recently attention has turned to consideration of the coping strategies that individuals adopt in order to combat *anomie*. In such work cities are commonly viewed as providing far more stimuli than individuals can cope with. City dwellers live, in other words, in a state of *information overload*. They adapt to this situation by restricting the amount of information that they pay attention to. According to Milgram (1970) this process of adaptation to information overload can take many forms: individuals may limit the amount of time they devote to certain activities (e.g. shopping can become transformed from a social activity into a simple and impersonal exercise of replenishing stores); individuals may limit the amount of incoming information by opting out of certain types of interaction (e.g.

using unlisted phone numbers); and individuals may allow themselves only weak and relatively superficial forms of involvement with others (e.g. speaking to neighbours but not entering their houses). The upshot of these coping strategies is that individuals take little responsibility for people outside the immediate family and friends, preferring instead to leave it to institutionalized welfare agencies to cater for those swamped by the stresses of urban living. In other words, a distinction emerges between the *private* and *public* worlds of city life; although private social worlds may escape relatively unscathed from the experience of urban living, the public arena is not so fortunate (Fischer 1981). As public activities bring them into contact with unfamiliar, annoying, or even threatening situations, city dwellers express estrangement from, and sometimes even conflict with, members of unfamiliar subcultures. City dwellers, as a result, often find themselves in a position where it is difficult to know whether taking an active role is unwarranted meddling or an appropriate response to a critical situation (Milgram 1970, 1463). Nowhere is this dilemma better exemplified than in bystander apathy at the scene of a crime.

The anonymity associated with city life means that city dwellers are free from the constraints that would otherwise apply in social situations. City life is, in other words, segmented into discrete activities that take place at different locations (e.g. work, shop, home). As a result, individuals adopt formalized roles (e.g. employee, consumer, home owner) and are less likely to do personal favours than is the case in rural areas and small towns. For example, Milgram (1970) cites an experiment where researchers rang doorbells at a selection of houses and asked to use the telephone. The request was granted twice as often in country towns as in cities. This non-involvement of city dwellers in the immediate social environment has other, more far-reaching effects. For example, it may create situations that are conducive to vandalism, it may encourage the development of blasé attitudes towards deviant or bizarre behaviour, and it may legitimize selfishness in the competition for scarce resources that is part and parcel of city life (e.g. the rush for taxis, the subway rush) although, of course, none of these consequences is inevitable (Milgram 1970, 1465). Non-involvement, in other words, is a pervasive characteristic of urban living. It is important therefore to appreciate why non-involvement arises. The evidence here seems to suggest that individuals resort to non-involvement because they feel unable to cope with the vast amount of information with which they are confronted in everyday city life.

The inability of individuals to handle all the information provided in their environment means, quite obviously, that individuals cannot behave as fully rational human beings. Individuals are incapable of collecting and evaluating *all* relevant information prior to arriving at optimal decisions regarding where to go and what to do. Instead they simplify questions of spatial choice (e.g. where to spend leisure time, where to live, where to shop) by disregarding information about many alternative courses of action. In other words, individuals simplify the problem of spatial choice by concerning themselves with only a fraction of the possibilities that are on offer. This simplification process is often thought to involve the development of a cognitive image of the environment in the mind. Such an image can be thought of as a much simplified version of reality. Opinions differ as to how individuals behave in regard to such a simplified image. Boulding (1956), for example, has suggested that individuals act in a 'boundedly rational' way, that is to say they attempt to act as rational human beings albeit within a much simplified version of reality. In contrast, Simon (1957) has argued that not only are individuals incapable of handling the totality of information available to them but they are also unwilling and unable to behave rationally in regard to their simplified images of the real world. Instead, according to Simon, individuals are *satisficers* who select a satisfactory rather than an optimal or rational course of action when confronted with the problem of where to go and what to do. It is difficult to prove or disprove the ideas of Boulding and Simon because it is very difficult to identify and measure the cognitive images on which behaviour is based. Nevertheless there is evidence that individuals build up a simplified image of reality by treating particularly vivid components of the landscape as characteristic of entire areas (e.g. constructing an image of a neighbourhood on the basis of one or two buildings that may be noteworthy because of their architecture, their state of disrepair, or their occupants) (Tversky and Kahneman 1974).

The idea that there is a difference between the real world and the behavioural world is an idea that has attracted a good deal of attention in recent years. Kirk (1963) was one of the first to appreciate this distinction when he introduced the concept of a *phenomenal* and a *behavioural* environment. The former refers to the 'real' world whereas the latter refers to selectively perceived facts which are structured into patterns, imbued with values, given meaning, and interpreted in line with culture. In other words, Kirk drew attention to the difference between 'objective' reality and the partial, distorted, and value laden image of reality that individuals build up in their minds and which serves as the basis for behaviour. This distinction is widely regarded as a useful one although it is perhaps more common nowadays to use the terms *objective* and *behavioural* environments (Gold, 1980). A slightly more complex categorization along the same lines was developed by Porteous (1977) who differentiated between *phenomenal* environments (physical objects), *personal* environments (perceived images of the phenomenal environment), and *contextual* environments (culture, beliefs, and expectations that influence behaviour). This classification is important in that it emphasizes the role of *perception* as a critical component in the process whereby individuals build up simplified images of reality. There is of course nothing new in the suggestion that perception is an all-important process intervening betweeen environment and behaviour. Gestalt psychologists have argued along similar lines since the 1930s. To them, perception reflects motives, preferences, and social and cultural traditions. As a result, gestalt psychologists tend to regard people (P) and their environment (E) as inextricably linked, through the process of perception, in a 'life-space' (Lewin 1951). The manner in which behaviour (B) is a function of this life-space is commonly expressed in a simple equation:

$$B = f(P, E)$$

Obviously this equation is only notational because there is no way in which precise values can be given to each of the variables. It is not surprising therefore that gestalt psychology has made little contribution to the study of urban living. Instead the issue of perception of the environment has been taken up principally by behavioural geographers, environmental psychologists, environmental sociologists, planners and environmental designers.

The perception that a given individual has of an environment is inevitably unique because it is impossible for two persons to bring to bear on their perceptions exactly the same history, experience, outlook and motivation. Nevertheless it has been found that the behavioural environments of different people, particularly those living close to each other, are very similar. There are two reasons for this: first, all people have common and innate neurological mechanisms for handling incoming information; and secondly, people from the same area of a city tend to have similar socializing experiences imposed upon them by the situation in which they find themselves living (e.g. individual travel within the city is largely restricted to the local environment and to main thoroughfares with the result that neighbours tend to have similar activity patterns and similar experiences) (Walmsley and Lewis 1984, 4–9). In this context the term 'perception' is of course something of a misnomer. A strict definition of the term 'perception' would probably restrict its meaning to the impinging of stimuli on the human sense organs (sight, hearing, taste, touch, smell). Use of the term 'perception' to describe the development of behavioural environments involves much more than this. Most notably it involves the mental manipulation of information and the development of coherent but distorted images of reality. In the eyes of many, the process involved in the development of a behavioural environment would be more appropriately labelled 'cognition' since this term covers not merely the impinging of stimuli on the human sense organs but also the way in which individuals come to learn about the environment in which they live. It is important, therefore, to explore how individuals learn about the city.

This book begins, in Chapter 2, with a look at how individuals come to know the environment in which they live. A short, introductory discussion puts forward the proposition that environmental knowledge is not accumulated in bits and pieces but rather is 'constructed' in an individual's mind while that individual tries to make sense of the surroundings in which he or she operates. After that the Chapter is divided into four parts. The first is concerned with how young children come to know the city, and particularly with the qualitative as well as quantitative changes in environmental knowledge that occur as the child develops. Learning of the environment by young children is, of course, only one special case of how individuals come to terms with the city. Accordingly, the second part of Chapter 2 moves on to the more general issue of how adults adapt to, and learn about, new environments. In this regard, it is noted that there are different types of environmental knowledge and that acquisition of these different types of knowledge may involve different mental skills and different parts of the brain. Despite this, it is possible to develop a generalized model of environmental learning whereby individuals learn nodes, then paths, then areas. Clearly such a model only describes *what* individuals learn; it has nothing to say about *how* individuals interpret what they learn. Likewise it says nothing about the distance metrics underlying an individual's mental representation of the environment. Successful adaptation to city living is, however, dependent upon knowledge of the distance separating different places. As a result Section 2.3 examines individual impressions of distance and direction, and their use in orientation and wayfinding. It is shown that cognitive distance is usually overestimated relative to real distance, irrespective of the methodology used to measure cognitive distance, particularly in downtown and busy areas. Impressions of distance are, of course, only one element of the overall mental representation of the city that individuals build up in their minds. The nature of these overall images is considered in Section 2.4 where a good deal of attention focusses on the strengths and weaknesses of different methods of eliciting urban images. In particular, a distinction is drawn between *designative* images of what is where and *appraisive* images that reveal how individuals feel about the environment (notably their preferences for living in different areas).

Maps of residential preferences are interesting but they reveal little about the *meaning* that places have for individuals. In fact the subject of 'environmental meaning' is remarkably difficult to study by means of conventional social science methodology and, as a result, it tends to be omitted from most studies of city living. Chapter 3 rectifies this failing in that it explicitly considers the way in which individuals ascribe meaning to the urban environment. After an introductory outline of the humanistic alternatives to mainstream social science, Section 3.1 looks at the feelings that individuals have about the city. This necessitates some consideration of the role of culture in providing a frame of reference to help individuals cope with the world. In this connection particular attention is paid to the tendency of individuals to operate in a 'taken-for-granted world'. The 'lived-world' of individuals, incorporating both feelings and geographical knowledge, is also examined. Of course the feelings that an individual has towards a city are influenced by the degree to which that city fulfils the individual's needs. Accordingly, Section 3.2 examines human needs in the city. Different definitions of need are explored with special attention being focussed on Maslow's hierarchy of needs and their translation to the urban scene. One of the most fundamental of all human needs is the need for a sense of belonging. This often manifests itself in a sense of belonging to a certain place. Place identity can in fact be very important in human psychological development. Section 3.3 therefore examines how individuals come to develop a sense of place and what happens to individuals when a sense of place is lacking. Of course individuals develop affinities for large scale *spaces* as well as particular *places*. Nowhere is this better seen than in the way in which individuals demonstrate liking for certain types of landscape. Accordingly, Section 3.4 examines landscape appreciation, special attention being paid to the question of what it is that makes certain landscapes appealing. This leads on, in Section 3.5, to consideration of environmental design and to examination of the environment as a form of non-verbal communication.

The principal reason usually advanced for studying the feelings that individuals have towards different parts of the city is that such study provides a better understanding of spatial behaviour. This issue of where people go and what they do in the city is the subject of Chapter 4. The logical starting point for any study of individual mobility within the city is the individual's place of residence, and the fact that individuals identify with such places of residence immediately raises the question of whether humans are territorial animals. This question is examined in Section 4.1 which considers personal space and proxemics, the home as a territorial unit, and the bonding that develops between individuals and neighbourhoods. Of course, city dwellers do not restrict their spatial behaviour to the immediate environment. Rather they travel extensively around the city. Section 4.2 considers this question of individual mobility within the urban environment. In particular it looks at how individuals build up an 'action space' (the subset of places within the city with which the individual is familiar) and an 'activity space' (the subset of the action space with which an individual interacts on a day-to-day basis). In other words, the geographical extent of mobility is examined in order to show how different lifestyles are reflected in different patterns of spatial behaviour. It is, of course, important to remember that movement around a city involves the use of time as well as movement in space. Accordingly, Section 4.3 looks at how people in cities use their time. This section focusses on time-budget studies and on the way in which individuals describe a 'life-path' through 'time-space'. Traditional models of spatial behaviour assume, of course, that individuals decide where to go and what to do with their time in accordance with their own attitudes, values, and needs. In reality things are very different: individual city dwellers are not sovereign decision-makers; instead they are highly constrained by a large number of factors. The nature of these constraints is examined in Section 4.4.

The net effect of many of the constraints operating on an individual is to restrict much of that individual's activity to the local environment. It is not surprising, therefore, that the character of the local environment has a significant impact on behaviour. The nature of this influence is looked at in Chapter 5 which begins, in Section 5.1, with an examination of the effect of neighbourhood on well-being. The influence of the local environment on behaviour is not of course a deterministic one in the sense that a certain type of environment will always produce a certain type of behaviour. Rather it is a case of certain types of environment tending to produce (or perhaps attract) certain forms of behaviour. This is shown clearly in Section 5.2 which looks at the way in which high density and crowded environments can produce stress which sometimes results in mental health problems. This raises the question of why some environments are stressful and others are not, and why some people can cope with stress while others cannot. Mental illness in cities tends to be most pronounced in inner suburbs and the assumption is usually made that in-migrants to such areas tend to feel alienated and are therefore prone to detrimental effects of stress. The same element of alienation is often thought to underlie high crime rates in certain parts of cities. Whether or not this is true is examined in Section 5.3 where attention focusses on the link between city size and crime and on vandalism as an environmental crime.

The book concludes in Chapter 6 by reflecting on the changing nature of urban living. The Chapter stresses that the city is not an empty container within which behaviour is carried out but rather a dynamic environment that reflects the changing nature of an economy and society.

In short, then, the book is concerned, above all, with the study of how individuals cope with living in cities. In investigating this issue, the book adopts the standpoint that individuals are not automatons driven by forces such as class and culture. The book therefore holds to the point of view that very little can be learned about the behaviour of individual city dwellers by adopting one of the varieties of structuralist approach now common in social science. This is because such approaches have inherent in them the argument that social phenomena (such as the behaviour of city dwellers) can only really be understood if they are seen as part of a superstructure that is related to the material needs, or mode of production, on which society is based (Walmsley and Lewis 1984, 17). This argument is felt to be unacceptable because it ignores values, ideas, and action in favour of autonomous concepts like 'class' which are seen, often simplistically and often in the absence of other influences, as major determinants of human behaviour. Instead of such a structuralist viewpoint, the central theme of the book is that a true understanding of what it means to be a city dweller will only be achieved by looking carefully at the real world behaviour, attitudes, values, knowledge, and opinions of urban residents. The book also holds, however, that there is often not a great deal to be gained from studying behaviour in the aggregate. Although there may well be situations where it is profitable to focus on the general features that can be observed when a group of individuals interact with their environment (and a case in point is perhaps to be seen in the regular distance decay curves that commonly emerge in travel patterns irrespective of the particular identity of the individuals involved), such macro-scale analyses reveal very little about why behaviour takes the form that it does. Understanding of the causes and characteristics of behaviour can only really be achieved, it is argued, by focussing on the way in which individuals learn their way around the urban environment, ascribe meaning to their surroundings, and decide on their travel patterns, all within the context of both personal and situational constraints. It is not, of course, the intent of the book to argue that such a focus will of itself provide a total understanding of urban life. Rather, the book simply adopts the view that consideration of individual behaviour has been relatively neglected in urban studies in the past and certainly merits a position alongside the study of both the spatial organization of society and the management and government of cities.

How individuals learn about the city

Any consideration of how individuals come to learn about the city requires some attention to be paid to epistemology, that is to say the study of the nature and origins of knowledge. Three questions are particularly important: How does environmental knowledge come about? Does knowledge involve the gradual accumulation of bits of information or does it entail the 'awakening' of *a priori* structures in the brain that cause individuals to think of the environment in terms of a limited number of predetermined ways? What is the nature of the relationship between knowledge and behaviour? Many attempts have been made to answer these questions and an enormous volume of literature has resulted (see Walmsley and Lewis, 1984). The main thrust of this research has been summarized very neatly by Moore (1976) who suggested that several general principles underlie the development of environmental knowledge.

1. Environmental knowledge is 'constructed' in the sense that individuals invent *structures* – or models – that enable them to understand and cope with reality. This means that individuals do not merely accumulate bits and pieces of information. Rather they try to make sense of the world by identifying the order and the principles according to which the world is structured (see Johnson-Laird 1983). The nature of the structures or models that are developed by an individual determines what that individual 'sees' in the real world. Predictably, similar people in similar situations tend to adopt similar constructs and hence have similar levels and types of environmental knowledge.

2. Knowledge results from interaction between factors internal to the individual (needs, personality, motivation) and the demands placed on the individual by the situation in which that individual is operating. This means that knowledge is built up in a purposeful manner in that most learning takes place during goal-oriented activities (e.g shopping, journey-to-work) which are themselves constrained to that part of the urban environment which is most accessible or with which interaction is most frequent.

3. Humans are naturally inquisitive animals. They seek out and assimilate information above and beyond what is necessary for day-to-day living. This inquisitiveness enables individuals to elaborate on their model of reality as well as test its reliability.

4. It is extremely rare for an individual to encounter a type of environment with which that individual has not had some prior experience. For example, knowledge of one large city provides the individual with information about the structure and functioning of large cities *in general* with the result that a visit to a previously unknown city does not necessitate the interpretation of city structure *de novo*.

5. Environmental knowledge has different structures at different stages in an individual's intellectual development. As a result, different types of environmental knowledge are likely to be recognizable in children of different ages. It follows from this that any study of environmental knowledge must take stock of the origin and transformation of these structures.

The structures with which Moore is concerned perform the same function as Kirk's (1963) 'behavioural environment' (Chapter 1) in that they both involve a simplified image of a real world that is too complex to understand in its entirety. In this context, however, the word 'image' is somewhat misleading in so far as it implies a pictorial representation of the urban environment. Both Moore's 'structures' and Kirk's 'behavioural environment' involve far more than pictures. The complex nature of structures is in fact best appreciated by examining their origin and development in young children.

2.1 YOUNG CHILDREN AND THE CITY

The acquisition of information about the environment is an activity in which all children engage. It is also an activity that makes an important contribution to an individual's intellectual growth and development. For example, there is ample evidence to show that the environmental awareness of children (in the sense of the number of

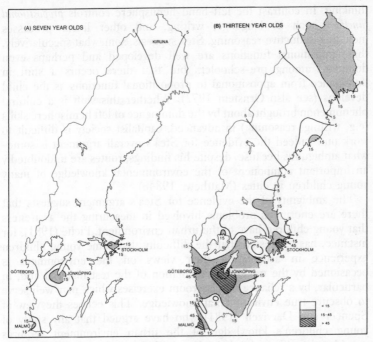

Fig. 2.1 Environmental awareness of children in Jönköping, Sweden.
Source: Gould and White (1974)

places of which they have knowledge) improves with age (Gould 1973; Siegel *et al*. 1979). Fig 2.1 clearly illustrates this, the isolines indicating the number of places listed in five minutes by a class of forty Swedish schoolchildren aged seven and thirteen. Similarly, children's understanding of the way in which the environment operates improves with age (Hart and Moore 1973). The precise nature of environmental awareness in young children is however remarkably difficult to measure. As a result it is difficult to establish precisely what level of understanding is achieved by children of different ages. Stea (1976) has argued that young children at a very early age think of their environment in holistic terms. That is to say, children do not memorize routes so much as understand how routes and landmarks 'hang together' in a coherent whole. This corroborates evidence that children under the age of eight have little difficulty with relative judgement but great difficulty with absolute values (Bryant 1974). Stea interprets this ability to accomplish holistic thinking in terms of the differences that exist between the two hemispheres of the brain. The right-hand hemisphere controls perception and spatial knowledge. These are termed *appositional functions* and are used in holistic thinking. In contrast the left-hand hemisphere controls *propositional functions* such as language, writing, and other linear processes including deductive reasoning. Stea suggests, somewhat speculatively, that appositional functions are well developed and perhaps even dominant among pre-schoolers but that there occurs a shift in dominance from appositional to propositional functions as the child develops (see also Ornstein 1972). Whether this shift is a cultural phenomenon brought about by the dominance of left hemisphere skills (e.g. writing, reasoning) in advanced, capitalist society is difficult to work out. Indeed the evidence for Stea's overall argument is somewhat ambiguous because, despite his findings, routes are undoubtedly an important component of the environmental knowledge of many young children in cities (Matthews 1984b).

The ambiguity of the evidence for Stea's argument suggests that there are enormous problems involved in measuring the awareness that young children have of the urban environment. Piché (1981), for instance, has suggested that the difficulty that some young children experience in articulating their views on the environment is occasioned by the mode of presentation of the test material and, in particular, by a reliance on classroom exercises which may well serve to obscure true environmental knowledge. This echoes the view of Spencer and Darvizeh (1981) who have argued that any study of young children's knowledge of the urban environment requires consideration of real-life behaviour in the everyday environment. To date, however, there have been few studies which adopt this methodologically difficult approach. The most notable example is probably Hart's (1979) two-year day-by-day study of the feelings, travel, and preferences of young children in the New England community of 'Innavale'. Of course this is not to say that classroom exercises have no value. When conducted properly, they can reveal a good deal about how children learn their way around the urban environment. A good case in point is the work of Matthews (1984a; 1984b).

According to Matthews there are two ways of looking at the development of environmental awareness in young children. The first is to study the quantitative accretion of environmental knowledge. This approach assumes that environments are learnt in an *incrementalist* fashion whereby bits of information are gradually pieced together over time. From such a perspective there could be expected to be a more or less linear relationship between environmental knowledge and age, assuming that children acquire information at a more or less uniform rate. The second approach is different. It attempts to discern qualitative changes in the ability of children to externalize, or put down on paper, their mental representation of the environment. This approach is *structuralist* in emphasis in that it assumes that individuals will pass through a series of distinct stages of environmental understanding, the nature of each stage being determined by the evolving structure of the brain. Matthews sought to evaluate the relative advantages of the different perspectives by asking two questions: Does age influence a child's awareness of place and macro-scale space? Does age influence the manner, style, and composition of children's representations of space? In order to answer these questions, a survey was undertaken of schoolchildren in Coventry, England. A total of 172 individuals, aged between six and eleven, were required to draw freehand maps of (1) their journey-to-school, and (2) their home area. Knowledge of home area was found to increase markedly with age, from a radius of 180 metres at the age of six to a radius of 870 metres at the age of eleven. The increasing size of the children's home area was not however a linear function of their age. Rather the pace of environmental learning was found to be distinctly stepped with noticeable differences between three groups: those aged six, seven, and eight; those aged nine and ten; and those aged eleven. For all but eleven-year olds the home area maps were much more detailed than the journey-to-school maps (although it should be stressed that all individuals had at least some ability to map both the journey-to-school and the home area at a very early stage in their intellectual development).

Maps of the journey-to-school tended to be dominated by routes whereas maps of home areas tended to be comprised very largely of landmarks. These results applied irrespective of the age of the children. This suggests that different environments are learnt in different ways, linear journeys being thought of in terms of routes and areas being remembered in terms of spatial properties like landmarks. Of the landmarks included in maps, 75% could be described as 'functional' by the age of eleven, that is to say they comprised places in the environment (e.g. shops) that performed a function in which children could participate. 'Functional' landmarks accounted for only 50% of the landmarks on the maps drawn by six-year olds, partly because this group exhibited a tendency to include other transitory features such as animals and lollipop men. This suggests that the nature of a child's understanding of the urban environment may change over time. Indeed Matthews grouped maps into three classes: *pictorial maps* in which children did little more than draw a 'picture' of the environment; *pictorial plans* in which there was some attempt made to rotate and scale the map and some attempt at symbolization; and *plans* which were based on an orthogonal transformation of space (Fig. 2.2). These classes corresponded approximately to three stages in map accuracy: the *egocentric* (where everything in the map was drawn in relation to the child); the *objective* (where maps were fairly accurate but incomplete reflections of reality); and the *abstract* (where maps demonstrated both an awareness of all parts of the environment

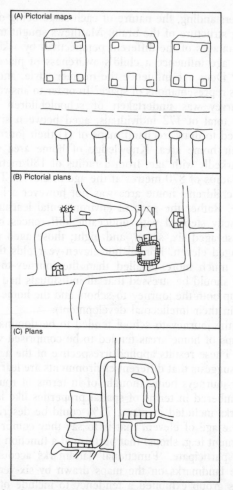

Fig. 2.2 Children's maps of the urban environment. *Source*: Matthews (1984b)

in question and a sound understanding of the relative position of elements within the environment). These three stages of map accuracy approximate a development sequence. However, they cannot be viewed in such strict terms because children of the same age do not necessarily represent all environments in the same way. Moreover, very familiar environments can be handled in a more or less objective way even by six-year-olds whereas adults, when encountering a new environment, may sometimes adopt an egocentric orientation.

Aside from the freehand maps, Matthews (1984a) also gave children air photographs and maps of the area surrounding their home. Children were then instructed to draw their home area on the air photographs and maps. Most children accomplished this task with ease and the results proved very interesting. Not only did the size of the home area interpolated on the maps and air photographs exceed the size of the area committed to paper in the freehand mapping technique, but also the evidence for distinct 'steps' in the development of environment knowledge was no longer apparent. This result has important implications. First, it suggests that the environmental knowledge demonstrated in classroom experiments is not independent of the techniques used to elicit that knowledge, and secondly, it suggests that distinct and sequential stages in a child's development of environmental knowledge may be more apparent than real and may reflect, as much as anything, stages in externalizing ability rather than stages in spatial competence (Siegel 1981).

The suggestion that there may not be distinct stages in a child's intellectual growth flies in the face of a great deal of evidence brought to light in developmental psychology, notably by Piaget (see Piaget

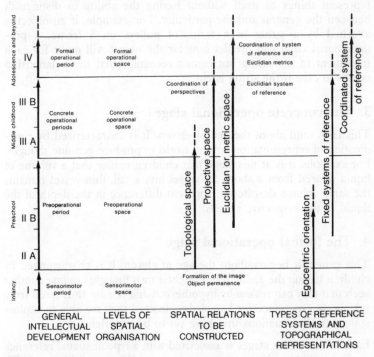

Fig. 2.3 Intellectual growth and environmental awareness. *Source:* Moore (1976)

and Inhelder 1956; Moore 1976; Hart 1984). According to this view, each child passes through a sequence of four stages (see Halford 1972) (Fig. 2.3).

1. The sensorimotor stage

This usually lasts from birth until two years of age. It is the stage where motor actions (e.g. movements of the body) are the dominant form of behaviour and where there is little thought activity. Individuals have only limited mental representations of their surroundings and the representations which they do have are based on experience. Piaget argued, for example, that it was not until towards the end of the sensorimotor stage that a child realizes that a ball which rolls under a sofa can be recovered by walking around the sofa.

2. The pre-operational stage

This lasts from the age of two to somewhere between five and eight years of age. It is characterized by a child having the ability to represent things to itself without having the ability to distinguish between the general and the particular. For example, if an object is attached by a string to a series of pulleys on a frame, a pre-operational child can predict how far the object will move for each movement of the string but cannot recognize that this relationship ceases to exist if the string is cut.

3. The concrete operational stage

This lasts until about the age of eleven. It is characterized by coordination of representations of the world to produce genuine thought. For example, it is at this stage that children realize that a volume of liquid poured from a short, fat vessel into a tall, thin vessel remains the same volume despite the apparent difference in the depth of the liquid in the respective vessels.

4. The formal operational stage

This generally begins about the age of eleven. It is characterized by children having the ability to relate their own thoughts to one another such that they can reason by hypothesis. Children are thus freed from relying on experience for knowledge. Instead they are able to explore systematically situations that have yet to be experienced.

Each of these four stages is associated with a type of spatial reference system and a particular type of geometry (Hart and Moore 1973; Moore 1976) (Fig. 2.3). For example, the sensorimotor period can be characterized by an egocentric orientation in which the environment is viewed simply in relation to the child. This egocentric orientation may persist well into the pre-operational period. Eventually it is replaced by a fixed system of reference in which the child thinks of the environment mainly in relation to fixed and known points (e.g. home, school, friends' homes). At the beginning of the pre-operational stage, the child's representation of the environment is based on simple topological geometry whereby places are thought of in terms of proximity and connectedness. This simple set of spatial relations is soon replaced by an emphasis on projective relations (where places are thought of in terms of perspectives like straight lines) and, ultimately, by an emphasis on Euclidean or metric relations (where the individual uses a system of coordinates and distance measurements to build up an overall representation of the environment). This ability to base environmental knowledge on Euclidean geometry may appear as early as the pre-operational stage but the adoption of a fully coordinated, spatial reference system is not usually apparent until well into the concrete operational stage.

Each of Piaget's stages involves a qualitative change in the organization of behaviour. Each stage also involves a qualitative change in the manner in which children construe the environment in their minds. Piaget's theory, in other words, involves far more than the mere accumulation of bits and pieces of information. In essence, it involves a qualitative shift from 'action-in-space' to 'perception-of-space' to 'conceptions-about-space' as the child develops its intellectual ability (Hart and Moore 1973, 255). There is some evidence that these stages are reflected in successive levels of mapping accuracy as individuals are able to handle first 'egocentric' spatial relations (based on self), then 'objective' spatial relations (based on objects), and finally 'abstract' spatial relations (based on coordinates). Of course not all authorities agree with this point of view and some have questioned whether young children do in fact see the world as egocentrically as Piaget suggests (Blaut *et al.* 1970; Liben 1978). The fact remains however that Piaget's views attract a wide following and many developmental psychologists would accept his propositions that adaptation to the environment is the key to knowledge and that intelligence is the key to adaptation. Intelligence itself cannot be inherited. What are inherited are particular forms of intellectual functioning, notably *assimilation* (the incorporation of new information into existing frames of reference in the mind) and *accommodation* (the readjustment of these mental frames of reference in the light of assimilation). This type of intellectual functioning is not of course limited to children. It also comes into play when adults are forced to adapt to new environments or to environmental change. The extent to which there exists a 'conceptual parallel' between the intellectual development of children and the environmental adaptation of adults can, however, only be demonstrated by looking in detail at how individuals adapt to new environments.

2.2 ADAPTATION TO, AND LEARNING OF, NEW ENVIRONMENTS

The means by which individuals adapt to new environments have been explored by a number of researchers. Predictably, a wide variety of different approaches has been adopted, ranging from a focus on the way in which humans evolved from lower primates through to consideration of precisely how learned information is stored in the brain.

Kaplan (1973; 1976) is probably the foremost advocate of the point of view that the ability to process environmental information gave *homo sapiens* an evolutionary advantage over other primates in so far as it enabled the species to cope with new, dangerous, and uncertain surroundings. Specifically, Kaplan argued that humans, in coming to terms with their environment, need to know four things: where they are; what is likely to happen; whether events will be good or bad; and what needs to be done about the unfolding sequence of events. In other words, in order to cope successfully with new environments, individuals need to be able to perceive the environment and to represent it mentally in their mind, they need to be able to predict what will happen, they need to be able to evaluate happenings, and they need to be able to adopt different courses of action. Each of these challenges involves the development of specific skills which can be labelled, respectively, recognition, anticipation, generalization, and innovation (Table 2.1). According to Kaplan, it was the development of these skills that ensured the survival of *homo sapiens* and gave the species an evolutionary advantage over many of its competitors. Particularly important was the growth of an ability to cope with *specific information* (facts about the situation with which individuals are immediately confronted) in such a way as to abstract from this in order to get *generic information* (knowledge that helps an individual to cope

Table 2.1 Kaplan's views on environmental information processing

Necessary knowledge	Response	Acquired skill
Where one is	perception	recognition
What is likely to happen	prediction	anticipation
Whether it will be good or bad	evaluation	generalization
What to do about it	action	innovation

with new surroundings on the basis of prior experience with reasonably similar surroundings).

It is, of course, very difficult to prove or disprove Kaplan's argument. Moreover, it is difficult to see the direct relevance of the argument to the problems faced by urban dwellers in adapting to new environments. Although it is interesting to speculate that city dwellers work out where they are, calculate what is likely to happen, and evaluate different possibilities before deciding what to do, the evidence for such a view is slim and rests on a simple and questionable analogy between unsubstantiated evolutionary trends and the practical problems faced by urban dwellers in their day-to-day living. It is not surprising therefore to find that most researchers have ignored this line of inquiry and have preferred to study the current awareness that individuals have of the urban environment. In this connection, Appleyard (1973) has noted that there are three distinct sorts of environmental knowledge.

1. Operational knowledge

This is concerned with understanding the mode of operation of the environment. It therefore necessitates knowledge of both the location and attributes (e.g. size, hours of operation, cost) of those features (e.g. shops, schools, bus routes, parks) that are critical to the functioning of the environment. This type of knowledge also includes the remembering of buildings and other features that provide cues in selecting and following paths through the city.

2. Responsive knowledge

This is the sort of knowledge that comes about as a result of individuals responding to striking features in the physical environment. For example, bright and distinctive buildings sometimes stand out from the general urban fabric and are therefore noticed. Billboards may be in the same category. Responsive knowledge extends, of course, beyond the visual to include sounds and smells (such as those associated with areas of heavy industry).

3. Inferential knowledge

This sort of knowledge does not come about from direct experience but rather from the ability of individuals to extrapolate beyond what is actually known and to make probabilistic inferences about things that have not yet been experienced. At the heart of this sort of knowledge is the way in which individuals develop a generalizable system of environmental categories. For example, prior experience with one central business district may enable an individual, in a strange city, to deduce the position of the central business district by surveying the skyline and noticing the heights of buildings.

Of these three sorts of awareness, operational and inferential knowledge are *human-dominant* in the sense that it is the whims and experience of the individual that determine what information is remembered and used. In contrast responsive knowledge is *environment-dominant* because it is the characteristics of the environmental feature (e.g. its size, colour, placement), rather than attributes of the individual person, that determine whether the feature is noticed and remembered. Of course, all three types of knowledge are complementary. Thus a city comes to be known by an individual in terms of the *actions* undertaken by that individual, the *images* which the urban environment makes in the individual's mind, and the system of *symbols* or categories that the individual uses to classify features of the environment. Together the three sorts of knowledge have two functions: they facilitate location and movement; and they provide a general frame of reference whereby an individual understands and relates to the environment (Hart and Moore 1973). Environmental cognition is therefore a vitally important part of the interaction between people and their physical surroundings. It may even be, as Proshansky *et al.* (1970, 175) have suggested, that an individual's cognitive structuring (and hence mental representation) of the environment is organized in such a way as to maximize freedom of choice in subsequent behaviour.

The representation of the urban environment in the mind of an individual comes about as a result of two information systems. The first is the substance of direct experience and the second involves indirect experience, that is the exchanging of experiences with other individuals in day-to-day social interaction (Appleyard 1973, 112). In other words, individuals become aware of the environment both through their own behaviour and through learning about the views, actions, and experiences of others. Both sorts of knowledge are meshed together to provide an overall mental representation. Of course incoming information is not simply accumulated. Rather it is sorted and structured in such a way as to render it useful. There is no point in an individual trying to remember everything about a city. It is far more efficient to 'schematize' information and to distil general principles that purport to show how the city is structured and functions. Thus, it is commonly asserted that individuals record information about the urban environment in the form of *schemata* (see Gold 1980). These schemata can be thought of as the frameworks in the mind on which information can be hung.

Unfortunately very little is known about how information is stored in the mind. Researchers interested in mental imagery and schemata have tended to talk about 'the mind' in only very vague and general terms. For instance it is commonly assumed that information exists in the form of stimuli outside the mind, that the mind observes, selects, and structures incoming information prior to evaluating such information, that choices about where to go and what to do are made according to decision rules in the mind, and that the mental states of different people are examinable and comparable (Burnett 1976). The precise workings of the mind remain, however, a mystery. In fact there are three competing philosophical viewpoints on how the mind accommodates knowledge. The first, *empiricism*, assumes that knowledge is built up by encountering the world through the senses. In other words, the environment is perceived (in the strict meaning of that term) and perceptions form the basis of knowledge. The second viewpoint, combining *rationalism* and *nativism*, assumes that knowledge is innate and precedes experience. According to this view, incoming information merely serves to awaken latent ideas in the brain. The third viewpoint, *constructivism*, rejects empiricism as too deterministic (in so far as empiricism holds that the nature of an individual's knowledge is determined entirely by the stimuli that happen to impinge on that individual's sense organs, with no allowance being made for the manipulation and structuring of information by the individual). Similarly, rationalism and nativism are rejected as untenable because both deny that there is a world outside the realm of ideas and both therefore overlook the complex nature of the real world urban environment. Instead constructivism argues that what is known is actually *constructed* by an individual while that individual is engaged in interaction with the environment (see Burnett 1976; Walmsley and Lewis 1984, 45–6). According to this perspective it is only possible to study the real world through humans and, even here, the study is not of reality *per se* but of reality as a product of the act of knowing. In short, each individual constructs his or her own reality.

It is very difficult to establish what form individual constructions of reality take. Russell and Ward (1982) have suggested a simple distinction between *locational knowledge* (which they term 'the mental atlas') and *non-locational knowledge* (termed 'the mental encyclopaedia' because it comprises facts and figures about the attributes of phenomena rather than details about the location of phenomena). A similar suggestion has been made by Hanson (1976) who emphasized the importance of travel patterns in influencing what knowledge an individual acquires. According to Hanson, a distinction can be drawn between knowledge of locations and knowledge of the attributes of the phenomena that exist at the locations in question. A more far-reaching examination of the construction of environmental knowledge has been made by Evans (1980) who pointed out that there are two relatively distinct sets of models in cognitive psychology on how information is cognitively structured. The first set of models can be thought of as *propositional models*. These state that information is stored in the mind in lists or other similar frameworks. These lists are, in essence, schemata and Evans contends that individuals might carry around in their minds schematic representations of the urban environment (e.g. lists of possible recreation sites, lists of shopping centres offering certain goods). Such representations help humans to search for and comprehend environmental information that is critical to location and orientation decisions. The second set of models are *analogical models*. These state that information about an object is stored in the brain in a form that is roughly isomorphic to the object's true physical structure. In other words, perception of an object excites a pattern of neural responses such that an image of the object is recorded in the brain. In order to recall a mental representation of an object, an individual re-excites the appropriate neural links. It is sometimes claimed that evidence in support of such analogical models is to be seen in the way in which individuals, when required to remember an array of objects in a circle or on a table, tend to remember them positionally. Such laboratory experiments may not however yield much insight into the mental representation of environments, such as cities, that are too large to be visualized in their entirety. Indeed, there is a good deal of evidence that individuals do use frameworks or schemata to help them comprehend large-scale environments. Nowhere is this better seen than in the tendency for cognitive maps of familiar environments (i.e. frameworks for the assimilation of knowledge) to display systematic distortions such as the omission of minor details and the straightening out of complex geometrical shapes into more manageable patterns of straight lines and right angles (Day 1976).

It may well be then that there are at least two different ways in which individuals learn about, and adapt to, their immediate environment. This is certainly the view of O'Keefe and Nadel (1978). They argue that the mental representation of *absolute* space takes the form of a *locale system*, located mainly in that area of the brain known as the hippocampus. In contrast mental representation of *relative* space involves *taxon systems* which are located in other parts of the brain. A good example of a taxon system would be the sequence in which places appear along a given route (e.g. a journey to a shopping centre, a drive to a friend's home). Such a sequence establishes the *relative* positioning of elements in the urban environment, together with the links between the elements. This sort of taxon learning is incremental in nature (in so far as knowledge of one unit along a route depends on knowledge of the preceding unit); it is also a type of learning that is rapidly accomplished (in that one traverse of a path is often enough to enable an individual to remember that path) but also a type of learning that is relatively rigid (as illustrated by the tendency of individuals to become hopelessly lost once they have made a wrong turn along a route that they thought they knew). In contrast, construction of a locale system is motivated by curiosity rather than by a need to remember routes to certain destinations. In other words, in developing a locale system, individuals build up an overall representation of the urban environment which can be subsequently used to aid understanding of how the city is structured and how it functions (see Russell and Ward 1982, 660).

The distinction between taxon and locale systems of learning may, of course, be more apparent than real because the two types of learning probably complement each other. Learning routes around a city undoubtedly contributes to the development of an overall image of the city just as the existence of some mental representation of absolute space will have a bearing on route selection. As a result, it is not surprising to find that researchers interested in human adaptation to unfamiliar urban environments have found it virtually impossible to differentiate the learning of relative space from the learning of absolute space. Golledge (1978), for example, has combined the two in proposing a three-stage model whereby individuals first learn locations (such as landmarks), then the links (or routes) between locations, and finally the areas that surround groups of locations

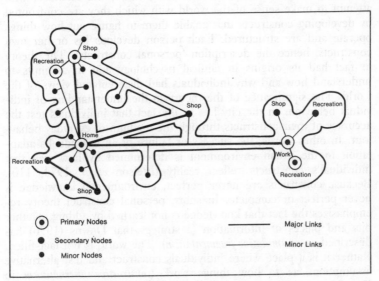

Fig. 2.4 The learned environment. *Source*: Golledge (1978)

(Fig. 2.4). Although this model runs counter to Lynch's (1960) suggestion that people rely on paths for frameworks in early learning and that an awareness of landmarks develops only with familiarity, it is supported by the findings of Hart and Moore (1973) and Siegel and White (1975), all of whom discovered that landmarks are learned first and thereafter serve as mental anchor points. Obviously this model of learning assumes that most knowledge comes about as a result of direct experience. In a very fundamental sense, therefore, learning is idiosyncratic since no two people ever have exactly the same experience. In practice, however, similar people living in the same area tend to have similar knowledge of the urban environment because their travel patterns tend to be constrained to the same area (Hanson 1976) and because they tend to have similar motives for acquiring information (Gold 1980). Of course not all environmental knowledge derives from interaction in the form of travel. Social considerations (like status, prestige, fear) are important in determining what individuals learn of the environment, as are historical factors. Both influence the *meaning* that the environment has for an individual.

It is very difficult to measure the meaning that the environment has for an individual, just as it is very difficult to describe the frameworks or structures that individuals use in their minds for the categorization of environmental information. One methodology which may help in this direction is to be found in *personal construct theory* (Kelly 1955). According to this theory, human beings are proto-scientists who attempt to make sense of the world with which they are confronted by developing constructs that enable them to figure out how things operate and are structured. Each person develops his or her own constructs, hence the description 'personal constructs'. The theory in fact had its origins in clinical psychology and in attempts to understand how and why individuals had disorientated views of the world. The significance of the theory to the understanding of individual behaviour in the city lies in the fact that individuals test the accuracy of their constructs through the medium of everyday behaviour. In other words, the success or failure of an individual's adaptation to the urban environment is determined by how well that individual's constructs reflect reality (Ittelson *et al.* 1974, 110). Because constructs are never perfect, environmental knowledge is never perfect or complete. In short, personal construct theory re-emphasizes the fact that knowledge is not learned by adding together bits and pieces of information (a strategy that Downs (1976) has described as *accumulative fragmentalism*). The world is not fact-filled. Rather it is a place where individuals construct and test alternative assumptions as to how things work (*constructive alternativism* in Downs' words).

Personal construct theory is most usually applied to studies of environmental knowledge by means of the *repertory grid technique* (Fransella and Bannister 1977). One variant of this technique is the *minimum context* approach. According to this, individuals are presented with the names of environmental features (e.g. shopping centres) in triads and requested to say how one of the three features differs from the other two. These differences are then converted to bipolar scales which can be thought of as the constructs that individuals use to interpret the environment. In the case of shopping centres the bipolar scales may include the following: large-small, planned-unplanned, cheap-expensive, and large range of shops-limited range of shops. It is rare for individuals to develop more than thirty constructs for evaluating a given type of environmental feature. Once the constructs are established, the individual is called upon to score the different environmental features under study on each of the constructs or scales (e.g. score different shopping centres on a number of constructs). The result of this exercise comprises a matrix of the repertoire of constructs used to interpret and evaluate a set of environmental features together with the scores for each feature on each scale, hence the term 'repertory grid'. Understandably, each individual has a highly personal grid consisting of the constructs used by that person and the scores that the person gives to the environmental features under consideration. As a result, it is impossible to compare the grid of one person with that of another unless they just happen to have the same set of constructs. In reality, such coincidence is rare. After all, the repertory grid methodology is not a psychological test so much as a technique for uncovering the way in which an individual thinks about the environment. Nevertheless the methodology does provide a first step in identifying the sorts of considerations that individuals take into account when adapting to new and unfamiliar environments. What the methodology does not do is provide clues as to the distance metrics underlying an individual's mental representation of the environment. It cannot therefore be used to throw light on general spatial behaviour such as wayfinding and orientation.

2.3 COGNITIVE DISTANCE, ORIENTATION AND WAYFINDING

Successful adaptation to an unfamiliar urban environment is dependent on an individual developing four sorts of knowledge: knowledge of nodes (i.e. locations such as schools, shops, and workplaces that are visited as part of day-to-day life); knowledge of the closeness of nodes to the individual; knowledge of the location of nodes relative to each other; and knowledge of sets of nodes and their interlinking paths (Briggs 1973a). Each of these forms of knowledge is itself dependent on an appreciation of the distance separating the nodes from each other and from the individual. The idea of distance that people carry around in their heads (usually called *cognitive, estimated,* or *subjective* distance) is however very different from *objective* real world distance. The first researcher to make a thorough examination of the relationship between subjective and objective distance was Thompson (1963). He studied the shopping behaviour of a number of consumers in San Francisco and found that their estimates of the distances between home base and a number of shopping centres were greater than the actual distances. This finding has since been corroborated in a number of experiments, some of which have used estimates of road distance, others estimates of straight line distance, and some even estimates of travel time (Pocock and Hudson 1978, 53). The general pattern seems to be for subjective or cognitive distance to be greatly overestimated, relative to objective distance, for short distances but for the degree of exaggeration of subjective distance to diminish as the real distance in question increases (Fig. 2.5). This tendency for short distances to be massively over-

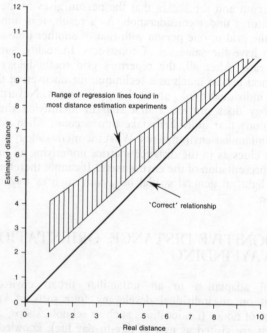

Fig. 2.5 The relationship between estimated and real distance

estimated has been attributed by Lowrey (1973) to the difficulties that individuals encounter in actually getting started on a journey. For example, the effort involved in a journey of one mile (deciding to go, preparing to go, getting the car out or walking to public transport) is almost as great as the effort involved in a journey of two miles (because the extra travelling requires little effort). As a result, according to Lowrey, massive overestimation of short distances can be put down to the problems individuals face in overcoming inertia and actually commencing a journey.

Any attempt to explain the overestimation of subjective distance relative to objective distance must of course face up to two critical questions: Is the overestimation consistently found in all situations? Does the overestimation show up irrespective of the different methods that can be used for measuring cognitive distance? Both these questions have attracted a good deal of attention. Thus, although overestimation is commonly and widely observed, there are situations where subjective distance has been found to be *underestimated* relative to objective distance. For example, Day (1976), in a study of Sydney (Australia), found that distances were overestimated up to 1200 yards, whereafter slight underestimation occurred. Similarly, Pocock and Hudson (1978) noted that subjective distance was underestimated for locations beyond about seven miles from the individual making the estimates when the experiment was conducted in London, and beyond about three-and-a-half miles when the experiment was conducted in Dundee (Scotland). Day interpreted his finding in terms of different modes of transport and argued that 1200 yards was about the upper limit of the range of distances that his respondents were prepared to walk. Beyond that distance individuals invariably used public transport. The time and effort saved by the use of public transport, coupled with the fact that such transport was often underground and therefore largely devoid of environmental stimuli, meant that respondents perceived and experienced these journeys as relatively short. Obviously the same explanation cannot be applied to Pocock and Hudson's finding. In this case it may be that what is important is familiarity. More distant locations may well be less familiar and therefore more prone to error when distances come to be estimated. In other words, distant locations may be thought of as nearer than they really are simply through ignorance. This, of course, is rank speculation. It does however raise the question of the reliability and validity of the techniques that are used to measure subjective distance.

Studies of subjective distance have focussed on different measures of distance: route distance (e.g. Lee 1970), straightline distance (e.g. Lowrey 1970), and shortest travel time (e.g. Briggs 1973b). In all cases it has been found that the range of estimates obtained from the individuals participating in the experiments is enormous. In statistical terms, there is a high level of *variance* in the estimates for the distances between the individuals and the locations under study. Despite this, most researchers have been content to work out average estimates. For example it has been common practice to get a group of students (who are more amenable to this sort of exercise than the population at large) to estimate distances to (say) twenty locations. The variance in these estimates is then ignored. Instead an average estimate for the group is calculated for each of the twenty locations. These average figures for subjective distance are then plotted against real distance to reveal the characteristic pattern of overestimation. In other words, many researchers interested in subjective distance have turned a blind eye to the fact that individuals differ widely in their estimates of distance. The simple relationship of overestimation between subjective and objective distance is, in other words, only apparent when a great deal of 'noise' is filtered from the data. In fact, when regression lines are plotted between subjective and objective distance for individual people, there emerges a great variety of slopes and intercepts with few of the lines exhibiting the 'characteristic' pattern of overestimation (Walmsley and Lewis 1984, 69). Moreover, this issue of variability raises the question of *reliability*, that is the extent to which the same data would be obtained by an independent researcher replicating an experiment. Most studies of subjective distance have asked respondents to give their immediate, intuitive estimate of the distance between themselves and given locations. It is very difficult to assess the reliability of this sort of data. It is not possible to repeat the question with the same set of people at a later date because the very exercise of thinking about the distance to a given location will influence all subsequent estimates of that distance. As a result it is impossible to recapture immediate and intuitive impressions.

An equally serious problem is that of *validity*, that is the extent to which the methodologies that are adopted actually succeed in measuring subjective distance. There have essentially been four strategies used to elicit estimates of cognitive distance. The first and most simple strategy has been to ask people how many miles (or kilometres) it is to a certain location. The second strategy has been to present respondents with a list of locations alongside each of which is a scale graduated in either miles or kilometres. The advantage of this method is that it enables respondents to recall previous estimates when making a new estimate, thereby introducing an element of relativity into their judgements. The third strategy emphasizes relative judgements even more. It adopts the point of view that people think of distances in relative rather than absolute terms. Accordingly, respondents are asked to indicate the distance to a given location (e.g. a suburban shopping centre) by placing a mark on a datum scale involving well known places (e.g. home to central business district). The final strategy involves getting respondents to draw a map of the urban environment. Distances may be deduced from such maps either explicitly (where respondents add a scale) or implicitly (by again measuring distances relative to a datum such as the distance between home and the city centre). Day (1976) used all four of these techniques and found no significant differences between them in terms of the distance estimates that they produced. This finding has since been challenged by Phipps (1979) and Cadwallader (1979) who argue that the choice of methodology does have a bearing on the data obtained but that it is impossible to know which methodology produces the 'true' measure of subjective distance. Cadwallader has also contended that it is unlikely that there will exist a simple relationship between subjective and objective distance because people do not have internalized spatial representations based on Euclidean geometry and hence do not measure distance in terms of conventional metrics such as miles and kilometres. A similar sentiment has been expressed by Robinson (1982) who argued that cognitive distance can be measured in absolute terms (i.e. in miles or kilometres), in ratio terms (i.e. by referring to a well known and familiar route), or in relative terms (i.e. respondents specifying which location is nearer when a large number of locations are presented in all possible pairwise combinations). Absolute judgements have been favoured by many researchers (probably because they are the easiest to verify) despite the fact that most people 'rely largely upon relative judgements, resort to ratio judgements only when finer discrimination becomes a matter of significance, and elect to employ absolute judgement only rarely and, even then, with hesitation, uncertainty and qualification' (Robinson 1982, 284).

The difficulties involved in measuring cognitive distance would only be of academic interest were it not for the fact that subjective distance influences three sorts of trip-making decisions: whether to stay or go; where to go; and what route to take (Cadwallader 1976). In other words an individual's impressions of distance have a major bearing on that individual's orientation and wayfinding within the city. It is however very difficult to generalize about how individuals cognize distance and most researchers have preferred to look only at the regularities that emerge when cognitions are averaged over a group of the people. Nevertheless it is probably true to say that three sorts of factors influence an individual's estimate of distance: factors relating to the individual; factors relating to the locations used as stimuli in distance cognition exercises; and factors relating to the interaction between the individual and the locations in question (Briggs 1976). These can be considered in turn.

There are a number of factors relating to the individual which influence distance cognition. Age is obviously important, particularly in young children where increasing age is reflected in more accurate distance cognition as well as growing awareness of a wider range of locations (Siegel 1977; Matthews 1981). Increasing length of residence in a city is also reflected in increasingly accurate impressions of distance (Golledge, Briggs and Demko 1969), although the evidence for this seemingly logical situation is less than clearcut (Cadwallader 1976), possibly because long term residents can become out of touch with the restructuring and development of the urban environment. Indeed it seems that it is familiarity with the city, rather than length of residence, which is the best predictor of the accuracy of distance estimates (Lee 1970). This is in line with the observation that the relative position of objects in space is accurately comprehended with little experience whereas memory for exact object location, and hence knowledge of distance, improves with experience (Evans 1980). A good deal of research effort has also gone into trying to identify the impact of gender on distance cognition. Unfortunately the results are less than clear cut. For instance most research on sex differences in spatial cognition has found few differences before adolescence. From this point on males begin to develop an ability to judge distance more accurately than females (Evans 1980). Of course this may not be a biological difference so much as a difference that arises from the different socialization processes operating for boys and girls (with society positively reinforcing domicentric activities on the part of females) and from the fact that girls tend to have more restricted a home range than boys (Saegart and Hart 1978). Certainly there is no evidence that the superior spatial orientation skill demonstrated by boys in classroom experiments with geometrical shapes is reflected in real world spatial orientation (see McGee 1979). The final personal variable that seems to have some impact on distance cognition is socio-economic status. Generally speaking, upper status professional people tend to have broader 'mental maps' and a better appreciation of distance than do other groups, possibly because of their more extensive contact networks (Orleans 1973). However, even here, the evidence is mixed. Appleyard (1976), for example, has shown how, in Venezuela, the lower status groups tended to have better city-wide mental maps than the upper status groups because they travelled more than the rich who tended to stay within exclusive suburbs. It may well be, then, that it is not class so much as travel experience that influences distance cognition and the accuracy of mental maps.

The characteristics of the locations used in distance estimation experiments have a major bearing on how individuals construe distance. According to Appleyard (1969a), two considerations determine whether a location, and in particular a building, will be remembered. These are social concerns such as the socio-cultural significance and usage pattern of the building, and physical characteristics such as the height of the building in relation to its surroundings. Of these two, Appleyard suggested that socio-cultural factors were the more important. Although this may be true, research has generally focussed on physical characteristics. For example, it has been shown that subjective distance is less overestimated in cities that have a formal structure or a central river than in cities lacking these features (Pocock and Hudson 1978, 53). Likewise, regularly structured settings, with ordered pathways that meet at right angles, are more readily comprehended, and their distance relations better understood, than irregular settings (Evans 1980). At the same time, downtown distance estimates seem to be exaggerated much more, relative to objective distance, than out-of-town distances (Golledge, Briggs, and Demko 1969). This massive overestimation of downtown distances has been corroborated in a number of areas (see Walmsley and Lewis 1984, 69). It may result from increased travel time per unit of distance in downtown areas, or it may relate to the denser packing of land uses around the city centre and the concomitant increase in stimuli impinging on the individual traveller (Walmsley 1978). Both these factors could make a journey seem longer than it otherwise would be. Such an explanation may however be an oversimplification because Lee (1970) has found evidence in Dundee (Scotland) of downtown distances being less exaggerated than out of town distances. The explanation usually put forward to explain this anomalous finding ignores experiential travel time and the density of environmental stimuli and concentrates instead on the fact that city centres in Britain are generally attractive places whereas many city centres in North America (where Golledge, Briggs, and Demko worked) are places to be avoided on account of their association with such phenomena as ghettos and high crime rates (Canter and Tagg 1975; Rapoport 1976). This sort of explanation suggests that the nature of the relationship between the individual and the locations used in distance estimation experiments is critical. In this connection it is important to note experimental evidence which shows that the 'pleasingness' of landmarks to a group of respondents has an influence on the accuracy of cognitive distance judgements such that the mean error in distance estimates increases as 'pleasingness' decreases (C. Smith 1984).

One of the first aspects of the interaction between individuals and locations to be considered in distance estimation was the attractiveness of the end point of the journey to be estimated. Thompson (1963), in his pioneering paper, suggested that a positive evaluation of the end point tends to foreshorten distance estimates (the foreshortening being relative because distances still tend to be overestimated when compared to reality). Specifically, attractive shopping centres were perceived as closer than unattractive or unknown centres. Since that time several researchers have noticed similar tendencies. For example, estimations of the distance to parks, schools, and high-status areas tend to be relatively foreshortened whereas estimates of distances to motorways and to disagreeable land uses tend to be relatively exaggerated (Eyles 1968; Lowrey 1973). The nature of the connecting path between an individual and a location also seems to have an influence on estimates of the distance to that location. The more turns there are in the journey, the longer the trip will be thought to be (Sadalla and Magel 1980). Similarly, paths with many intersections tend to be thought of as longer than paths with few intersections (Sadalla and Staplin 1980). This may be because more complicated trips present more information to the individual which, in turn, requires a greater storage area in the brain, thereby creating the impression in the individual that the trip is a long one. However it seems unlikely that this is a complete explanation. For example, many cognitive distances are non-commutative, in that they are estimated to be of different lengths when viewed from different directions (Pocock 1978), despite the fact that they have a constant number of bends and intersections. Moreover, distances across the River Thames in London have been found to be overestimated more than distances along the river, thereby suggesting that the 'texture' of the urban environment may have an impact on distance estimation (Canter 1977). Familiarity also seems to play a part to the extent that familiar and preferred routes are underestimated relative to unfamiliar and disliked routes, both at the city scale (Pacione 1975) and at the scale of individual streets (Meyer 1977). This suggests that an individual's emotional involvement with a place may have a bearing on distance estimates to that place. This possibility was first investigated by Ekman and Bratfisch (1965) who confidently predicted an 'inverse square root law' relating emotional involvement (EI) with a place to estimates of the subjective distance (SD) to that place. The 'law' took the form

$$EI = \frac{b}{\sqrt{SD}}$$

where the value of b is determined by the arbitrary units of measurement. This 'law' excited a good deal of interest. It seemed to suggest a constant relationship between two factors (familiarity-involvement and subjective distance) which are at the heart of individual orientation and wayfinding. Unfortunately, however, the 'constancy' of the relationship is more apparent than real in that it only seems to apply when individuals are asked to estimate familiarity and distance for towns up to a distance of about 1500 kilometres in continental Europe. Beyond this range, both at the local level and the global level, the square root relationship ceases to exist (Walmsley 1974a).

There are several reasons why a simple relationship between emotional involvement and subjective distance is unlikely to obtain. One relates to the nature of the urban environment in question. For example Walmsley (1978) has shown how small, densely settled areas with many road intersections can seem to be much larger than they are in reality. In such areas distance can be greatly exaggerated. Another reason has to do with direction. Individuals in cities orientate themselves in relative rather than cardinal (N, S, E, W) terms. Specifically, they tend to orientate themselves in such a way that their mental map of the city is based on their home area and focussed on the central business district. There are good reasons for this sort of orientation. After all, central business districts still dominate the retail, office, and entertainment life of many cities and are generally at the hub of radial transport networks.

The orientation that individuals exhibit towards the central business district has been most in evidence in studies of consumer behaviour (Hanson 1977). Lee (1962) and Potter (1977) have shown, for instance, that consumers orientate themselves towards the central business district to the extent that two shopping centres are visited in that direction for every one centre visited in an out-of-town direction. There is not however a simple relationship between orientation and behaviour. Different sorts of people tend to have different levels of information about the city and hence different types of orientation. This was clearly shown when Potter (1979; 1982) investigated the 'information field' of consumers in Stockport. An *information field*

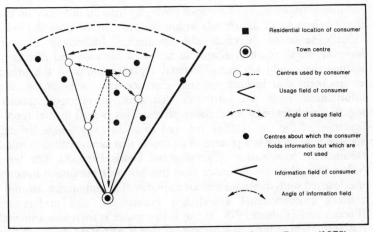

Fig. 2.6 Consumer information and usage fields. *Source*: Potter (1979)

comprises those shopping centres about which the consumer has information. The field usually takes the form of a wedgeshaped sector, centred on the home and focussed on the central business district (Fig. 2.6). Potter showed that the angle of this sector varied, with lower socio-economic individuals having a much narrower 'information field' than higher socio-economic groups. Likewise people over sixty and people with very large families had narrower information fields than the rest of the population.

The observation that information fields vary between different types of people of course raises the question of where individuals gain information about the environment. Private sources, such as direct personal experience and word of mouth communication with friends, are undoubtedly important, as are public sources such as the mass media (Walmsley 1982b). A good deal of information is probably also gathered by simply riding around the city (Clark and Smith 1979). Information collection, in other words, is almost a haphazard activity but one which has a major impact on orientation and therefore on wayfinding. It should be remembered however that the role of the environment in orientation is not entirely passive. Certain design features in the environment can facilitate navigation whereas others can contribute to both a sense of feeling lost (orientation) and a sense of being lost (wayfinding) (Zimring 1983). The relationship between environmental design, information flow, and orientation is of course enormously complex and can only really be understood in the context of overall mental imagery.

2.4 URBAN IMAGES

Subjective impressions of distance obviously have an influence on the travel behaviour of individuals within the city. So too does the individual's sense of direction and orientation. Individuals do not, however, think of cities simply in terms of distance and direction. Rather they build up overall mental representations of the urban environment that include not only distance and direction but also information about the attributes that exist at various locations, together with feelings about those places. This overall mental representation of the city is often referred to as an *urban image*. Strictly speaking, an image is a picture of an object that can be called to mind through the imagination (Walmsley and Lewis 1984, 8). The term 'urban image' means far more than this however because it denotes the learned and stable mental conceptions that summarize an individual's environmental knowledge, evaluations, and preferences (Pocock and Hudson 1978, 3). An urban image is therefore a mental representation of the real environment that is partial (in the sense that it does not cover the whole city), simplified (in the sense that it omits a great deal of information even for the areas that are covered), idiosyncratic (in the sense that every individual's urban image is unique), and distorted (in the sense that it is based on subjective, rather than real, distance and direction) (Pocock and Hudson 1978, 33). The form taken by an individual urban image is influenced by the perceptual ability, cognitive skills, personality, values, and culture of the individual involved (Downs 1970a; Gold 1980). In simple terms, then, an urban image summarizes an individual's overall environmental experience. Moreover it sometimes does this in a symbolic form and often operates below the level of awareness (Ittelson *et al.* 1974).

There is nothing new in the use of the concept of an image to describe the way in which individuals adapt to their surroundings. Three decades ago Boulding (1956) suggested that all behaviour was dependent on an image. In this sense an image is both an individual phenomenon (in that it summarizes the individual's view of the world and of the social system within which the individual operates) and a cultural phenomenon (in that similar people in similar situations tend to develop similar images as a result of being exposed to similar experiences and similar information flows). Boulding's ideas were greeted warmly and cited widely. Despite this Powell (1978) has argued that the full import of Boulding's writings often went unappreciated. In particular, Powell argued that there has been a widespread failure to acknowledge the complex nature of an image and a reluctance to recognize that images comprise at least ten components: a spatial component summarizing an individual's relationship with the environment; a personal component dealing with an individual's ties with other people and organizations; a temporal component (arising from the fact that images change over time); a relational component concerned with the tendency for individuals to picture the world as a system of regularities; conscious, subconscious, and unconscious components that determine the extent to which the image operates at or below the level of awareness; a blend of certainty and uncertainty in the degree to which the world is known; a mixture of reality and unreality (since an image can be based on imaginings just as much as on experience); public and private components dealing with the extent to which an image is shared; a value component concerned with evaluating whether parts of the image are good, bad, or indifferent; and, lastly, an affectional component whereby the image is imbued with feeling.

The concept of an image has probably been adopted most enthusiastically in historical geography where it has been used, with benefit, to interpret the changing perceptions of new lands that lay behind the colonization of the New World (Powell 1978). In contrast it is only relatively recently that the concept of an image has been extended to the study of urban living. Moreover, the emphasis in this field has been on the *spatial* component of the image rather than on the image as a whole. This is understandable in so far as the spatial component is possibly the most important element of an image and is accessible, in mapping exercises, in a way that other components of the image are not (Boulding 1973, viii).

The spatial component of urban images has usually been studied by getting individuals to draw sketch maps of the city as they see it. The end product from such exercises is usually referred to as a 'mental map' or 'cognitive map'. Mental mapping, in other words, refers to the processes which enable people to acquire, code, store, recall and manipulate information about the nature of their spatial environment (Downs and Stea 1973c, xiv). Although mental maps have a long history, dating back at least to Trowbridge in 1913, it was not until the 1960s that interest in mental mapping began in earnest. It was at this time that researchers like Burton (1963) and Brookfield (1969) drew attention to environmental perception as a key element in the interaction between people and their physical surroundings. It was at this time, too, that Gould (1966) explored a number of mathematical techniques for scaling and mapping environmental preferences. Part of the fascination of mental map exercises lies in the intellectual challenge of bringing order to the apparent chaos that results from asking a number of individuals to either draw their image of reality or to evaluate alternative locations as places to live. Moreover, there is a 'lucky dip' element in many mental map exercises in so far as it is never clear in advance what generalities will be observable in a collection of sketch maps (Boyle and Robinson 1979). The term 'mental map' remains however a very vague one.

The summary descriptions of sets of individual sketch maps may be labelled 'cognitive maps' but they are really nothing more than convenient sets of shorthand symbols that can be used to describe the environment (Downs and Stea 1973a, 9). The term 'map' is in fact no more than a metaphor because it is not known whether information is stored in the brain in terms of spatial coordinates (Downs and Meyer 1978). Despite this, Beck and Wood (1976) have attempted to describe the processes involved in cognitive mapping. Specifically, these authors have argued that there are eight key processes: synchronization (the integration of sequentially experienced geographical phenomena into a coherent framework); rotation (the transposing of the world of experience into a two-dimensional system of spatial coordinates); scaling (the representation of the world at a size other than the one at which it is experienced); generalization (the reduction of a great mass of information to a few simple propositions); symbolization (the selection of symbols to represent geographical features in the cognitive map); verbalization (the labelling of cognitive maps with place names); representation (the visualization, or 'holding in the head', by the mapper of an image of what is to be drawn); and externalization (the actual process of drawing a cognitive sketch map).

The categorization of processes suggested by Beck and Wood (1976) has attracted little attention, possibly because it is very difficult to differentiate one process from another in the overall activity of cognitive mapping. Indeed most researchers have preferred to focus on the nature of the end product (the cognitive map) rather than on the underlying process (cognitive mapping) and, generally speaking, cognitive maps have been approached in one of two different ways, depending whether the focus of attention is on the *content* of the map (i.e. what is where) or on the *preference* that individuals have for different parts of the environment. The former are generally known as *designative* images and the latter as *appraisive* images (Pocock and Hudson 1978).

The study of designative images is basically concerned with three questions: What do people need to know for successful functioning in the urban environment? What do they actually know? Where do they get their information? In answering these questions, it has become obvious that people ideally need to know something of the location, distance, direction, and attributes of places within the city, that what they do know tends to be an incomplete, distorted, and schematized version of reality, and that information is obtained from both public and private sources (Downs and Stea 1973a). There are however no simple answers to the basic questions. In fact there is no one methodology or approach for identifying designative images but rather a range of different techniques. One of the simplest techniques is the one used by Ladd (1970) when she asked adolescent black males, aged between twelve and seventeen, to draw a map of their neighbourhood in Boston (USA). The resultant sketch maps were placed in one of four categories by a number of independent judges: *pictorial drawings* that depicted a street scene; *schematic drawings* that mentioned streets and areas but in a disorganized and uncoordinated way; *images that resembled a map* in that they could be used for orientation and basic wayfinding, albeit with little additional information; and identifiable *maps with specific landmarks* which served to make the area recognizable (Fig. 2.7). Interestingly, mapping style was unrelated to age. A similar approach was used by Appleyard (1969b; 1970) who again asked respondents to draw a sketch map. Appleyard's analysis of the resultant drawings differed from Ladd in that he distinguished between two general types of map, each of which could be subdivided according to cartographic style. These two types were *sequential* maps (which focussed on the linkages or routes between places) and *spatial* maps (which concentrated on landmarks

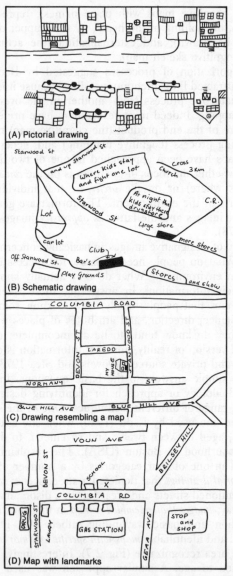

Fig. 2.7 A typology of urban sketch maps. *Source*: Ladd (1970)

and areas rather than routes) (Fig. 2.8). According to Appleyard, higher socio-economic groups drew more complex maps than lower socio-economic groups. He also suggested that, with time, individuals tend to shift from using spatial maps to using sequential maps as their

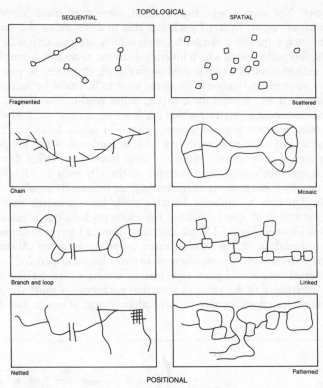

Fig. 2.8 Styles of cognitive mapping. *Source*: Appleyard (1969b)

understanding of the environment shifts from simple topology (e.g. notions of proximity, separatedness) to Euclidean geometry and an ability to comprehend relations of distance and direction. This suggestion has however been challenged by Spencer and Weetman (1981) who pointed out that the type of map that is drawn depends on the subject matter under study in so far as neighbourhoods tend to be depicted as spatial maps and streets as sequential maps irrespective of the length of time that the map-maker has spent in the environment in question. Similarly Matthews (1984b) has shown that children use a mixture of both spatial and sequential maps irrespective of how long they have lived in an area.

Although Appleyard's views are interesting, they have not had the same impact on the study of urban images as has the pioneering work of Lynch (1960). In long and involved interviews, Lynch asked residents of Boston, Jersey City, and Los Angeles to draw sketch maps of the centres of their cities. Specifically, respondents were asked to draw a map as if they were drawing it to help a stranger to the city. Not surprisingly, the resultant maps were much simplified versions of reality. In fact Lynch was able to differentiate the content of the maps into five elements: *paths* which are the channels (e.g. roads, footpaths) along which individuals move; *nodes* which are places that individuals can enter (e.g. shopping mall, churches) or places at which strategic navigational decisions have to be made by individuals finding their way around the city (e.g. major road intersections); *edges* (sometimes called barriers) which are lines separating one part of the city from another (e.g. an abrupt change in urban fabric) or linear obstacles impeding movement (e.g. rivers); *landmarks* which are points of reference used in navigation; and *areas* (sometimes called districts) which are medium-to-large sections of the city with an identifiable and usually homogeneous character (e.g. an historical suburb, a dockland). Attempts to replicate Lynch's study have generally met with success and in all cases the basic five elements have been reasonably easy to identify. Figure 2.9, for instance, shows a Lynchean landscape as portrayed in sketch maps drawn by students of an Australian country town with a population of twenty thousand people. Indeed the pervasiveness of Lynch-type images among urban residents has led researchers to the point of view that such images must serve one or more functions in day-to-day urban living. Thus it has been

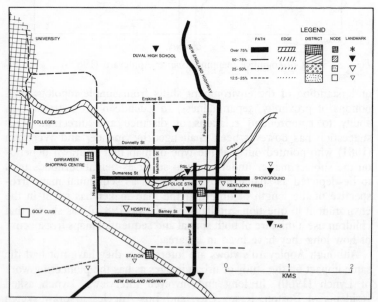

Fig. 2.9 A Lynchean landscape: Armidale, Australia. *Source*: Walmsley and Lewis (1984)

suggested that designative images are used by individuals as a basis for interpreting information, as a guide to action, as a frame of reference for organizing activity, as a basis for individual intellectual growth, and as a provider of emotional security (Downs and Stea 1973b, 80).

An individual's knowledge of a city is, according to Lynch, a function of the *imageability* of the urban environment, that is the extent to which the components of the environment make a strong impression on the individual. Imageability itself is influenced by a city's *legibility*, that is the degree to which the different elements (paths, nodes, etc.) of the city are organized into a ·coherent and recognizable pattern. Neither visual prominence nor architectural detail guarantees imageability to a particular feature because places and spaces only become significant when they are given meaning through a combination of usage and emotional attachment (Pocock and Hudson 1978, 31–2). For example, Rapoport (1977) has shown how residents of some Australian cities distort maps of their neighbourhoods so as to include higher status, physically better-kept areas that have a more significant level of imageability.

One of the good things about the methodology developed by Lynch is that it provides not only information about the overall image that people hold but also information about (1) the sequence in which elements were incorporated into the map, (2) gaps in an individual's knowledge, (3) mapping styles, and (4) scale distortions. Lynch's methodology is not however without problems. To begin with, there is ambiguity over some elements; for instance, a church may be both a landmark and a node depending on the use to which it is put (Walmsley and Lewis 1984, 65). More importantly, it is unclear to what extent the images that result from sketch maps are influenced by artistic prowess. It may be, for example, that more detailed maps are produced by better mappers rather than by individuals with greater degrees of environmental knowledge. Certainly images derived from sketch maps differ markedly from images constructed from verbal descriptions (Lynch 1960, 146). This highlights another weakness of Lynch's methodology, namely the fact that sketch maps tend to emphasize the visual at the expense of urban areas that may be noteworthy for other reasons (e.g. sound, smell). In other words, the focus of attention in Lynch's methodology is on individuals passively encountering the urban environment rather than purposefully interacting with it. Despite these shortcomings, and despite its time-consuming nature, Lynch's methodology does seem to be workable in that people do seem to be able to commit their images to paper and do seem to distort reality in predictable ways. Images are invariably more regular than reality, roads are commonly 'straightened', and intersections are frequently drawn as right angles (Day 1976).

The most fundamental weakness with Lynch's methodology is that, like all work on designative images, it tells the researcher nothing about an individual's feelings for the environment. Such feelings can only be discovered through the study of *appraisive* imagery. According to Pocock and Hudson (1978), there are two sorts of appraisive image: an *evaluative* image where individuals express an opinion about the environment and an *affective* image where respondents specify a preference for different parts of the environment. Research on evaluative images has commonly focussed on environmental quality and respondents to surveys have often been asked to say how attractive or unattractive they think various landscapes are. For logistical reasons, the environments to be evaluated are often presented to respondents in the form of photographs. One of the problems with this type of research is that the dimensions along which an environment is to be evaluated have to be specified by the researcher (e.g. attractive-unattractive, quiet-noisy, beautiful-ugly) and there is no way of knowing whether respondents consider these dimensions to be important. Of course not all work on evaluative images has looked at environmental quality and not all research has blithely assumed that it is possible to specify in advance the environmental characteristics that individuals consider important. Downs (1970b), for example, took great care to discover what characteristics of a shopping centre (Broadmead in Bristol, England) were considered important by a sample of students. He showed that student evaluations of Broadmead comprised an image that related both to characteristics of the retail establishments in the centre (price, visual appearance, quality of service, shopping hours) and to characteristics of the centre as a whole (structure and design, pedestrian circulation, traffic conditions, range of shops). In short, the image that students had of Broadmead involved evaluation of the centre on eight different dimensions. This means that the imageability of a shopping centre can be influenced by any one of a number of characteristics. Interestingly, the significance of the characteristics that Downs identified is to be noted in the work of Potter (1977) who showed that arterial shopping centres have poor imageability on account of their specialized function (i.e. limited range of shops), their linear morphology (i.e. difficult pedestrian circulation), and their 'low qualitative tone' and fabric discontinuity (i.e. poor structure and design).

Despite the work of Downs, studies of evaluative images have not proved very popular, possibly because they tend to deal with specific environmental features and therefore reveal little of general application. As a result, work on appraisive imagery has tended to focus on affective images. Indeed the terms affective and appraisive image are often used synonymously. The methodology that is usually adopted to define affective images was pioneered by Gould (Gould

1966; Gould and White 1974). Essentially, this methodology requires a group of individuals to specify how much they would like to live in a number of different locations. The specification process can involve either rank ordering or the use of scales. In both cases, the end product is the same: a matrix of individuals against places where values in the matrix represent appraisals of places. This matrix is then reduced by factor analysis. Scores for each location on the main factor obtained from this analysis are then scaled in such a way that a value of 100 is given to the most preferred location and a score of 0 to the least preferred location. When these scores are plotted in map form, and 'contours' interpolated, there emerges a residential desirability surface which indicates where the group as a whole would most like to live (Fig. 2.10). Gould's methodology has been adopted widely and with interesting results. For instance, most maps of residential desirability reveal a strong affiliation to the home area, a liking for scenically attractive areas, and 'sinks' around areas (often large cities) that are considered unattractive. It should be remembered, however,

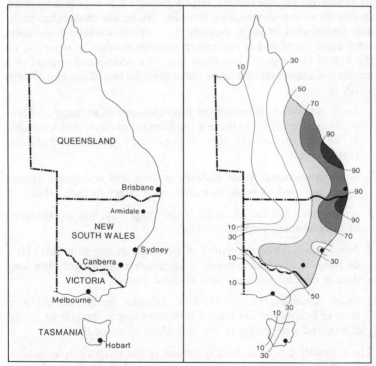

Fig. 2.10 The residential preferences of final year undergraduates in Armidale, Australia. *Source*: Walmsley (1982a)

45

that the methodology asks respondents for unconstrained preferences (i.e. where they would like to live if all other things were equal). In reality, of course, migration is very highly constrained by job opportunities, family ties, cost, and a host of other variables. As a result, affective images are poor predictors of migration flows. In fact, affective images probably provide a better reflection of personality type than of migratory intention. Walmsley (1982a), for example, has shown how, in Australia, introverts and extroverts have different residential preferences, the former liking quiet, inland country towns and the latter preferring both the frontier settlements of northern Australia and the bustle of large cities. A further weakness of most studies of affective images lies in the fact that they have concentrated on very large regions, often nations, rather than cities. This may be interesting, given that the advent of high technology may make industry, and therefore employees, relatively footloose (Pacione 1982a), but it reveals little about how individuals appraise different parts of the city as places to live.

Work on both evaluation and appraisive images undoubtedly holds its attractions for researchers, largely because it is easy to undertake. In fact the ease with which such studies can be undertaken has probably contributed in large measure to a situation where researchers seem more interested in replicating experiments than in reflecting on the nature of images. Thus there has been widespread neglect of a number of important questions concerning images (Stea and Downs 1970, 6).

1. *Image composition.* What are the main elements of an image and how do these interrelate? Is there a common set of elements identifiable in all images or do the elements vary with the particular environment?

2. *Image arrangement.* What distance metrics and orientation frameworks are used to relate elements of an image to each other?

3. *Image extent.* Are the elements of the image linked in a continuous or discontinuous surface?

4. *Image change.* Does the nature of an image change with time? How do images change as a result of environmental change? How long does it take for such changes to come about?

5. *Image variability.* Do people have different images for different sorts of behaviour? Do images vary according to the culture, social status, and personality of the individual concerned?

The assumption behind these questions is that images can be studied successfully in experiments of one sort or another. Not all authorities are so positive and Bunting and Guelke (1979) have openly questioned whether images can be measured and whether there is any congruence at all between image and behaviour. Indeed it seems that many researchers are now beginning to question the usefulness of trying to uncover urban images in mental mapping exercises. The long-standing view that cognitive mapping is 'the most powerful, flexible, and reliable method of spatial problem solving' (Downs and Stea 1977, 36) is now being challenged. Boyle and Robinson (1979), for instance, have argued that cognitive mapping plays only a minor and intermittent role in influencing behaviour. In their view, mental maps are seldom used in genuine 'spatial problem solving' (i.e. deciding where to go and what to do) although they may have some minor role to play in facilitating the completion, without careful deliberation, of some commonplace tasks. In short, many researchers are now of the opinion that mental maps play little part in the co-ordination of spatial activities. The notion of a mental map may even be 'a potentially dangerous nostrum' (Downs 1981).

There have been two responses to the criticisms levelled at mental maps. The first has been to look at new ways of studying imagery. In particular, attention has been directed to a range of techniques, other than sketch mapping, whereby an individual's imagery can be studied. For example, Saarinen (1973) has outlined a number of projective techniques: word association tests (where individuals say what comes into their mind when they hear a given place name, thereby indicating what the place means to them); construction techniques like the Thematic Apperception Test (where individuals are given a picture of a particular environment and required to construct a story about what is happening in the picture); cloze procedures (where individuals fill in the missing parts of a stimulus, for example the missing parts of a map, thereby giving an indication of the completeness of their overall image); and choice techniques (for example, individuals drawing their 'home area' on an existing street plan). The second, and more important, response to the criticisms levelled at mental maps has forsaken attempts to get people to draw their image of the environment and instead has focussed on how individuals handle environmental information. The assumption here is that individuals code incoming environmental information in terms of *schemata*. These schemata can be thought of as frameworks in the mind on which information is hung. The concept of schemata had its origins in gestalt psychology, notably in the idea that perception proceeds in accordance with innate abilities which organize environmental stimuli into coherent, structured forms or patterns (Gold 1980, 11). In perception, in other words, schemata 'impose meaning on the blooming, buzzing confusion around us' (McArthur and Baron 1983, 215). Little is known, however, about the innate organization of environmental stimuli that occurs in perception because psychologists have much preferred to look at *what* is perceived rather than at *how* information is structured. Likewise, in relation to urban images, far more attention has been paid to features of the environment than to structures in the mind (Canter 1977). As a result, the assertion that individuals classify incoming environmental information in terms of schemata is really little more than an article of faith (see Walmsley and Lewis 1984, 68–74). The only researcher to have examined schemata in any detail is Lee (1968; 1976). He asked 219 middle class Cambridge housewives to draw their neighbourhood on a town map. He also asked for details of friendship patterns, club membership, and shopping behaviour. The map, combining both territorial and social considerations, that resulted from each interview was referred to by Lee as that person's *socio-spatial schema* (Fig. 2.11). Obviously each person had a unique socio-spatial schema. However, there was a sufficient element of agreement among the responses for Lee to differentiate three general types of schemata: social acquaintance neighbourhoods based on tightly knit communities where everyone knows everyone else; homogeneous neighbourhoods characterized by a uniform quality of housing; and unit neighbourhoods which approximate the planners' ideal in so far as they contain a balanced range of amenities and a variety of house types. Interestingly, the average size of a schema was 40 hectares (100 acres). The number

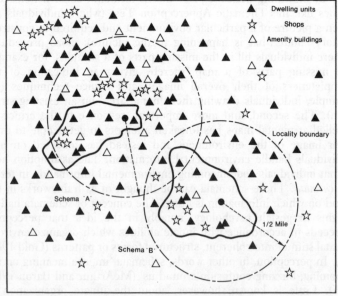

Fig. 2.11 Socio-spatial schemata. *Source*: Lee (1968)

of elements (houses, shops, etc.) within each schema varied such that the largest numbers of elements were found in the schemata of respondents of high social status (Bardo 1984).

Of course Lee's use of the term 'schemata' is a very precise one. He demonstrated that individuals synthesize the territorial and social aspects of neighbourhoods in such a way as to have a clear impression, or structure, in their mind of the neighbourhood to which they belong. Presumably, therefore, individuals may have socio-spatial schemata for other areas of the city (such as the central business district) and may use these for navigation and as a guide to behaviour. In this sense a socio-spatial schema is a dynamic structure that can be added to or altered in various ways. For example, the discovery of a new road or path could transform an individual's whole orientation to the city (Lee 1976, 335). In simple terms, then, a socio-spatial schema is a framework which enables an individual to *remember* a city. Lee in fact acknowledged the importance of Bartlett's (1932) work on memory in stimulating his own ideas. Unfortunately, though, Lee gave little indication as to what form schemata may take. He suggested that some places may be remembered pictorially whereas others may be remembered in terms of verbal constructs such as 'near-far'. He also pointed out that it is impossible to differentiate 'social' from 'geographical' components of the city. Yet his Cambridge experiment was largely concerned with mapping the extent of socio-spatial schemata and therefore gave little consideration to interpreting the *meaning* that the urban environment had for the individuals surveyed. This is undoubtedly because 'meaning' is a complex issue that is, in itself, deserving of detailed examination (see Chapter 3).

Chapter

3

Ascribing meaning to the urban environment

The study of urban images by means of sketch mapping produces interesting results but reveals very little about the manner in which individual human beings interpret the environment. For example, although sketch maps give implicit clues as to which features of the environment are deemed to be important, the maps say next to nothing about the way individuals ascribe meaning to the urban environment. Sketch maps, in other words, are remarkably uninformative when it comes to identifying how individuals experience the environment. In particular, the pioneering work of Lynch (1960), which has been replicated time and time again, concentrates too much on *imageability* and *legibility* and too little on meaning. Admittedly, this weakness has been rectified to some extent by Harrison and Howard (1980) who, after having elicited standard sketch maps from subjects in Denver (USA), interviewed respondents in order to discover why elements in their maps were thought to be significant. The results showed that significance stemmed from three sources: the appearance of the building or feature (notably its size, colour, design, and shape); the location of the element within the general urban structure (especially its location relative to the main paths); and the social, political, ethnic, and historical meaning that attaches to the building or feature. Although these results are interesting, and provide insights into urban imagery, they say nothing about how meaning is attached to place. Nor do they suggest a methodology whereby the development of meaning can be explored. In fact it may well be that environmental meaning is very difficult to study by means of conventional social science techniques. For example, surveys, which are possibly the principal tool of social scientists, tend to be inappropriate because social scientists do not really know what categories of environmental experience to investigate, nor how to define 'meaning'. As a result, individual experience of the city tends not to have been explored properly. Many researchers shun consideration of a person's experience as both private and qualitative, and therefore outside the realm of 'objective' social science, while others dismiss experience as 'epiphenomenal', that is to say it has no causal role in behaviour and action and therefore no explanatory value in accounting for how individuals deal with their environment (Wapner *et al.* 1980, 224).

This neglect of experience is unfortunate because it is through experience that the environment develops meaning for an individual. Thus the urban environment is not simply architectural space; rather places become endowed with significance through the actions that are permitted or enjoined within them (Wapner *et al.* 1980, 226). Experience of course can take many forms. It may well be, for example, that experiences which manifest themselves in the form of factual beliefs about the environment ('discriminanda' that distinguish one place from another) are developed in a different part of the cognitive system, and at a slower rate, than evaluations of the environment ('preferenda' that permit the ordering of parts of the environment according to whether they are liked or disliked) (Zajonc 1980). Irrespective of whether or not this is the case, what seems to be needed is a methodology that enables the researcher to capture the meaning that the environment has for an individual. According to Wood and Beck (1976), this may necessitate the development of a new experimental mapping language. Their suggestion, *Environmental A*, involves drawing symbols (such as a hammer for a factory, a skull and crossbones for danger, a sleeping eye for relaxation) on an overlay superimposed on a sketch map. In other words, the mapping language explores feelings and impressions about places. Moreover it does so in a fashion which suggests that it is sensitive enough to measure consensus feelings about different sub-areas of the city (Spencer and Dixon 1983). Despite this, *Environmental A* has not been widely used. Instead researchers have preferred to contemplate the question of what philosophical basis should be adopted for an inquiry into environmental meaning. Couclelis (1983), for instance, has chided social scientists for mimicking last century's experimental physics and for trying to reduce human behaviour down to a series of deterministic laws instead of focussing on the complex and irreducible interactions that take place between people and their physical surroundings. Likewise, Christensen (1982) has argued that the student of human affairs needs to contend with two orders of meaning: the first is the 'lived world' of interpretations and meanings that individuals develop in order to facilitate interaction with other human beings, and the second is the world of scientific theoretical frameworks developed in order to try to generalize about the 'lived world'. Above all, though, researchers have looked to *humanism* as an alternative to mainstream social science and as a way of coming to terms with the subjective interpretation that each individual has of the urban environment.

Humanism as a philosophy is open to a variety of interpretations. In fact, so varied are the interpretations of humanism used in social science that it is probably more appropriate to talk about a battery of *humanistic approaches* than it is to attempt to isolate a single philosophical position. These humanistic approaches have three things in common. First, they are *anthropocentric* in outlook. That is to say, they make the individual the centre of study and focus on the fact that all human beings have their own world view (Lowenthal 1961). Such world views are often ambivalent or ambiguous and are always difficult to interpret (Tuan 1973). Secondly, humanistic approaches to understanding the interaction between people and their physical surroundings adopt a *holistic* perspective whereby an attempt is made to interpret an individual's world view in its entirety rather than to break it down, for analytical convenience, into discrete components. This means, for example, that researchers of a humanistic persuasion see little point in experiments designed to examine such things as distance cognition because distance, although important, is not something that can be separated out from the totality of an individual's world view. Thirdly, humanistic approaches emphasise *intersubjectivity*. This means that they attempt to identify the common elements to be identified when people interact with their surroundings. In short, humanistic approaches break away from the objective, scientific view of human beings and place their emphasis squarely on the realm of human experience (Ley and Samuels 1978a, 50–1). The central issue is the way in which individuals experience and interpret their surroundings (Buttimer and Seamon 1980). The methodology by which such studies are conducted varies somewhat but usually encompasses both participant observation (especially living with a group in order to take part in, and thereby observe, day-to-day behaviour) (Jackson 1983) and in-depth interviewing (usually involving several hours of tape recording). In addition various forms of encounter may be used as when a researcher deliberately intrudes into everyday behaviour so as to provoke a response that makes explicit how the individual under study thinks about his or her environment. Above all, though, humanistic approaches attempt *verstehen*, that is researchers attempt to understand an individual's world view by imagining themselves into the individual's situation so as to see the world through the individual's eyes. In this way the researcher can understand the *intentions* that lay behind a given course of action and the *values* that lead an individual to act in a given manner (Buttimer 1974). This type of understanding is of course very difficult to achieve because a researcher can only understand a subject's behaviour to the extent that they share common cognitive categories and conceptualizations of the environment (Ley and Samuels 1978b). Despite this, humanistic approaches have attracted considerable support in recent years.

The attraction of humanistic approaches seems to lie in the fact that they are against the fragmentation, for analytical convenience, of the totality of human behaviour, they are against attempts to reduce human beings to the status of responses awaiting stimuli, they are against the abstraction of behaviour from the context in which it occurs, and they are in favour of more emphasis on subjectivity, intentions, values, meanings, and the affective bond that develops between people and their surroundings (Walmsley and Lewis 1984). Within humanistic approaches generally, there are three philosophical positions that have attracted particular attention. *Phenomenology* is perhaps the best known (see Relph 1981a). Although there are many different approaches to phenomenology, most social scientists derive their inspiration from Schutz (1967) who transformed phenomenology from a pure philosophy into an academic method. In simple terms, phenomenology is a radical method of enquiry that proceeds from pure consciousness without presupposing an existent world (Walmsley 1974b). It therefore focusses on the contents of the mind and it adopts the view that the researcher needs to know as much about the eye that sees as about the object that is seen if the researcher is ever to understand behaviour. One of the central arguments of phenomenology is that social scientists should study consciousness since it is through consciousness that human beings come to know the world. In particular, phenomenologists focus on the pre-intellectual world of immediate, everyday experience (termed the *Lebenswelt*) and attempt to understand this world through a process of *verstehen* and empathizing with the individuals whose behaviour is under study. *Existentialism* is, in many ways, similar to phenomenology in that it seeks to define the relationship between *being* (existence, reality, material conditions) and *consciousness* (mind, idea, image) (Samuels 1978, 23). However, existentialism pays particular attention to the tendency for all individuals to display an attachment to, and an alienation from, space. The central argument is that individuals define the environment as opposite to, and separate from, themselves. In other words, individuals *alienate* themselves from the environment and then set about overcoming this alienation by developing relationships with the environment that give meaning to human existence (Samuels 1978). Unfortunately the central thesis of existentialism is that reality and existence can only be experienced through living and cannot be made the object of thought. This is really an anti-intellectual stance and it is not surprising therefore that the impact of existentialism on the study of urban living is slight. *Idealism* is different again. According to this philosophy, the activity of the mind is the foundation of human knowledge and the world can therefore only be known indirectly through ideas (Guelke 1981). There is, in other words, no 'real' world that can be known independently of the mind. According to this point of view, an individual's action can only be understood by rethinking or reconstructing the thought contained in the action.

Humanistic philosophies have so far made relatively little impact on those social sciences most concerned with the study of urban living. There are many reasons for this. To begin with, such philosophies are often difficult to understand, especially when they are based, as is often the case, on an arcane vocabulary (see Billinge 1983). Moreover, humanistic approaches generally tend to be overly concerned with the activities of the human mind and insufficiently concerned with material conditions (i.e. where people live, how well-off they are) (Ley 1981). Even the methodology of *verstehen* is alluded to more as a panacea for the methodological problems encountered when mainstream social science tries to define and measure 'meaning' than as a strict method of enquiry (Smith 1981). There is, for example, no way of validating *verstehen* and no way of knowing therefore whether two independent researchers, attempting *verstehen*, would reach the same conclusion. In fact there is a very real danger in humanistic approaches that researchers will either see order where none exists (Tuan 1976) or will become preoccupied with the unique and esoteric to the point where description becomes an end in itself. Of course these weaknesses should not be overemphasized, partly because humanistic approaches can sometimes be used to advantage to complement more 'scientific' empirical approaches (Eyles 1985) and partly because qualitative social science can make significant contributions to the understanding of human behaviour, and therefore be judged to be 'valid', on account of the cogency of its theoretical reasoning even when researchers can have little statistical confidence in the representivity of their data (Mitchell 1983). Pocock (1983), for instance, has pointed out that much of quantitative social science has been concerned with samples that are every bit as small as those studied from a humanistic perspective and that there may be some virtue in exploring an issue in depth rather than aiming for statistical representativeness. Certainly humanistic approaches, although appearing strange and unfamiliar to researchers schooled in mainstream social science, have made limited but significant contributions to the study of urban living, as will be demonstrated at various points throughout the remainder of this chapter.

3.1 FEELINGS ABOUT THE CITY

The meaning that individuals ascribe to the different parts of the city has a lot to do with how they feel about those places. As was noted already, it is extremely difficult to study such feeling by requiring individuals to draw a sketch map of their image of the city, even if they then comment on why they drew the map as they did. Part of the reason for this lies in the fact that all such sketch maps are idiosyncratic. For example, when Bonnes–Dobrowolny and Secchiaroli (1983) asked respondents to define the centre of Milan (Italy), they found that most definitions comprised two distinct elements: a 'stereotypic' central area (based on Piazza Duomo) that most people felt was part of the city centre, and a 'private' central area that varied from individual to individual.

The idiosyncratic component of sketch maps is not to be wondered at. After all, whether or not a place has meaning for an individual is likely to be influenced by at least three factors: (1) the extent of the individual's knowledge of the objective attributes of the place; (2) the emotional attachment that the individual has with the place; and (3) the individual's feelings about the behaviours that are associated with that place (Genereux *et al.* 1983). Each of these factors is likely to vary from individual to individual and over time for any given individual. As a result, it is not surprising that 'meaning' is difficult to pin down. Additionally, of course, meaning is hard to define and measure because it is often *taken-for-granted*. Much urban living is unselfconscious in the sense that it is undertaken without a great deal of prior thought. We all expect neighbours to be neighbourly (even if this extends to no more than a 'nodding' acquaintance); we expect to be able to relax in a park; we expect city centres to be busier and more impersonal than suburbs; and we expect people to be quiet in a church and noisy at a football match. In other words, we associate certain behaviours with certain venues. We therefore take much of everyday life for granted. Precisely which behaviours are taken-for-granted in which places varies of course from culture to culture. Culture, in this sense, provides a frame of reference for helping people to cope with the world. Culture therefore influences the meaning that individuals attach to things. This is not to say, however, that culture is a 'thing' that is immutable and which has a clear and distinct influence on behaviour. Such cannot be the case because, ultimately, what we call 'culture' is the very *process* by which people attach meaning to the world.

The argument that culture influences the meaning of things is not a new one. After all, artefacts lend stability and value to human lives by engendering a sense of self and by salvaging past experiences (Tuan 1980a). Additionally there is a well-established tradition of naming time periods in terms of the 'things' (i. e. artefacts) associated with them. Thus we talk of the 'Bronze Age' and the 'Iron Age'. From this perspective, the evolution of humankind is measured, not by gains in morality, intellect, or wisdom, but rather by human ability to fashion things of ever greater complexity in increasing numbers (Csikszent-mihalyi and Rochberg-Halton 1981, ix). In very simple terms, then, material objects help people to define who they are and who they wish to become. It is easy to illustrate this by means of a grand overview of human evolution. It is much more difficult to identify the objects that give clues as to the nature of contemporary society, largely because it is difficult for observers of society to disengage themselves from the taken-for-granted world in order to study it. Nevertheless some conclusions can be reached. For example, status symbols (e.g. type of car, residential address, leisure time activities) symbolize to the rest of society, in the individual's judgement, the type of person that the individual aspires to be. Such examples are of course obvious.

Table 3.1 Generational differences in objects that have special meaning, Chicago 1977

Object	% respondents mentioning object		
	Children (n = 79)	Parents (n = 150)	Grandparents (n = 86)
1. Furniture	32.9	38.7	33.7
2. Beds	29.1	8.0	9.3
3. Visual art	8.9	36.7	22.1
4. Sculpture	6.3	26.7	17.4
5. Collectibles	17.7	12.0	11.6
6. Musical instruments	31.6	11.3	23.3
7. TV	36.7	11.3	23.3
8. Stereos	45.6	18.0	5.8
9. Radios	11.4	6.0	7.0
10. Books	15.2	24.0	25.6
11. Photos	10.1	22.0	37.2
12. Plants	8.9	19.3	12.8
13. Plates	6.3	14.7	22.1
14. Silverware	1.3	4.0	10.5
15. Glass	3.8	11.3	7.0
16. Pets	24.1	4.0	1.2
17. Aquariums	8.9	2.0	1.2
18. Appliances	5.1	17.3	15.1
19. Refrigerators	11.4	1.3	5.8
20. Lamps	7.6	9.3	9.3

Source: Csikszentmihalyi and Rochberg-Halton (1981)

More subtle linkages between objects and culture are less easily identified, possibly because social scientists tend to look for the understanding of human life in the internal psychological processes of the individual, or in the patterns of relations between people, rather than in the role of material objects (Csikszentmihalyi and Rochberg–Halton 1981, ix). Material objects are nonetheless important. This was clearly shown in Csikszentmihalyi and Rochberg–Halton's (1981) survey of what a sample of people in Chicago (USA) households thought were special objects to them (Table 3.1). Stark differences emerged in the meaning that objects had for children, parents, and grandparents, with beds and television being most important for children and memorabilia such as photographs most important for the aged.

The meaning that attaches to material objects extends, of course, to the home in which people live. To most people 'home' means security. It also gives identity and can be used to communicate that identify to the rest of society. It is not uncommon in Australia, for example, to find Greek migrants painting their houses in the Greek national colours of blue and white, thereby informing the community at large of their background, values, and identity. The fact that a great many people derive security and identity from their home suggests that *place*, as well as material objects, may make a fundamental contribution to the meaning of a person's life. This, in turn, suggests that an attachment to place is one of several needs that are experienced by all human beings.

3.2 HUMAN NEEDS IN THE CITY

City dwellers have many needs. These range from the need for basic facilities like housing through to less basic needs such as the need for recreational opportunities. Many of these needs are met by services or facilities that are provided by governments of one sort or another. It is not surprising, therefore, to find that public sector policy analysts have spent a good deal of time trying to define and measure 'need'. The task is not an easy one. Bradshaw (1972), for instance, has identified no fewer than four types of need. The first is *normative need*. This refers to the situation where a 'desirable' standard is laid down by an 'expert' and judgements made about the provision of facilities relative to that standard. In such cases the standard is not absolute but rather may vary between so-called 'experts' and over time. *Felt need* is somewhat different. It refers to the wants that are expressed by individuals when they are asked, usually in a survey, if they feel a need for certain services or facilities. As such it is a poor indicator of 'real' need because the answers that individuals give to such questions tend to depend on both their aspirations and their perceptions of what they think is available or even possible. *Expressed need* is best thought of as felt need turned into action. The actual usage made of a facility can be taken as a measure of expressed need. For example, the number of people actually using a civic park could be taken as a crude index of the expressed need for the park. Of course there may be occasions when there is an unmet expressed need for a service or facility. Thus the length of the waiting list for public housing can be taken as a rough measure of the expressed but unmet need for such housing. Finally, *comparative need* refers to the situation where service provision for one group is contrasted with service provision for another group with similar characteristics. In its crudest form it involves comparison of the per capita provision of a facility in one area with the per capita provision in other similar areas. Need expressed by this method is the gap between what services exist in one area and what services exist in another, weighted to take stock of differences between the areas (e.g. the need for maternity services could be weighted relative to the number of women of child-bearing age) (Bradshaw 1972, 641).

Bradshaw's taxonomy of need may appear thorough-going but it does have drawbacks. For one thing, the four types of need are less easily measured than might at first appear, as has been noted by Clayton (1983). The definition of normative need, for example, begs the question of how reliable the experts are and how influenced they are by considerations of political feasibility and by economic and personnel constraints in setting the normative 'standards'. Likewise, the measurement of felt need raises methodological questions (e.g. how representative can a survey be, given constraints on time and money?) as well as questions of validity (e.g. is a need genuinely felt or is it only brought to mind as a result of being interviewed?). Expressed need, too, is a concept of debatable value because its apparent level can be easily manipulated by pressure groups which see a political advantage in inflating apparent levels of need. For example, senior citizens may be encouraged to put their name down for sheltered accommodation so as to embarrass a government which, in the eyes of the pressure group, is taking few initiatives to provide such accommodation. And the concept of comparative need is of limited use unless it can be demonstrated that the level of service provision in the datum area is in some way correct (Clayton 1983). Above all, the taxonomy says nothing about needs that lie outside those catered for by public sector services. In other words, the taxonomy says nothing about the need that many humans have for a sense of belonging and nothing about the need for self-fulfillment. For guidance in the definition of these sorts of needs it is necessary to look outside the policy arena.

The pioneering work in defining the totality of human needs was undertaken by Maslow (1954) who suggested a six-stage hierarchy of needs: (1) physiological needs (e.g. food, shelter); (2) the need for safety and security (e.g. protection from danger; privacy); (3) the need for affiliation (e.g. the need to belong to a community); (4) the need for esteem (e.g. the need for an individual to be recognized as worthy by those with whom he or she interacts); (5) the need for self actualization (e.g. fulfilment of potential); and (6) cognitive and aesthetic needs (e.g. the need to learn and to appreciate beauty). The implication in this hierarchy is that higher order needs cannot be realized until lower order needs have been met. Of course Maslow's work referred to needs in general. It has been extended to a discussion of the needs experienced in urban living by Faulkner (1978) and Table 3.2 gives examples of those attributes of the urban environment associated with the satisfaction of each of Maslow's needs. Thus, at one extreme, basic physiological needs are met by the provision of dwellings, clinics, and retailing outlets while, at the other extreme, high order cognitive and aesthetic needs are met by providing an aesthetically attractive built environment and by providing educational and cultural facilities.

Careful study of Table 3.2 reveals that each level of Maslow's hierarchy of needs is met, for an individual, by the attributes of the neighbourhood or community in which the individual lives. This, in turn, suggests that the nature of the local area may have a major influence on the quality of urban living. According to Lee (1982) this influence of the local area is particularly important in relation to the development of personal identity, social life, and political life. However, a good deal of debate surrounds the impact of urban living on personal identity. Some writers argue that the modern city has grown so large and is changing so fast that individuals lose their sense of identity or flee to the suburbs to retrieve it; others argue that the full potential of the individual can only be realized in the rich diversity of modern city life (Lee 1982; Mumford 1961). Part of the reason for the existence of these contradictory viewpoints lies in the almost complete neglect by social scientists of the role of place in human psychological development (Proshansky *et al.* 1983). This neglect is lamentable because the built environment undoubtedly has an influence on how city dwellers define themselves within society. Place identity is, after all, a part of self-identity. Place identity grows out of direct experience with the physical environment. It therefore reflects the social, cultural, and ethnic aspects of place. At the same time it is central to a person's well-being in that it helps maintain self-identity and facilitates adaptation to changing circumstances (Proshansky *et al.* 1983).

The influence of the local area on social life is no more clear cut

Table 3.2 A typology of urban needs

Need category	Description	Attributes of the urban environment associated with the satisfaction of needs (examples)
1. Physiological	Provision of food, shelter and health care	Retailing/wholesaling systems distributing food, clothing and health supplies. Health care clinics and hospitals. Essential services (water, sewerage, power). Dwellings.
2. Safety–security	Protection from physical harm and intruders. Privacy and absence of overcrowding. Protection of property.	Fire and police protection services. Road safety. Absence of noxious environmental elements (pollutants). Residential areas that ensure privacy.
3. Affection–belonging	Harmonious relationships with other members of the community. Identification with and acceptance of groups within the community.	Facilities for community organisations (meeting places). Physical layout of neighbourhood such that cooperative and harmonious inter-family relationships are fostered. Physical identity of the neighbourhood.
4. Esteem	Status and recognition by others in the community.	Opportunities of home ownership. Prestige of neighbourhood.

| 5. Self actualization | Role relationship *vis à vis* others. Realization of one's potential. Creativity/self expression. | Built environment that facilities creativity and self expression. Employment opportunities and community organizations that enable the use and development of skills. |
| 6. Cognitive/Aesthetic | Provision of educational experience, intellectual stimulation and experiences. Aesthetically appealing events and phenomena. | Educational and cultural facilities. Recreational facilities. Aesthetically appealing built and natural environment. |

Source: Faulkner (1978)

than its influence on personal identity. Again different opinions are to be found in the literature. Webber (1963), for instance, has argued that advanced western societies are becoming increasingly character- ized by the existence of 'communities without propinquity'. By this he implied that the nature of society is changing: instead of individ- uals having their greatest involvement (i.e. greatest sense of community) with those among whom they live (i.e. neighbours, as defined on the basis of propinquity), a situation is arising where, at least for professional and managerial groups, 'communities' might be spatially far-flung but nevertheless close-knit, intimate, and held together by shared interests and values (i.e. communities based on common interest rather than propinquity) (Walmsley and Lewis 1984, 34). This view has come in for considerable criticism, partly because it has become obvious that many communities are still firmly based on propinquity. Certainly post-war neighbourhood and community plan- ning in Britain underestimated the complexity of the interrelationships that existed between physical setting and social life, largely because policy makers knew surprisingly little about the informal social lives of urban residents and even less about how they build up social networks over time in a particular place (Lee 1982, 165). It is not surprising, therefore, that policy makers failed to appreciate the genuine feelings and predictable stages of 'grief' that followed forced residential relocation and the upsetting of stable social networks (Fried 1963).

It is something of a paradox that, despite uncertainty about, and neglect of, the influence of the local area on personal identity and social life, there seems to be occurring a resurgence of interest in local areas as political units. Certainly, area-based programmes have been widely adopted in many countries. This is despite the misgivings that many commentators have expressed about the efficacy of such programmes, notably the fact that many apparently 'areal' problems (e.g. high unemployment in the inner city) are caused by the structure of society (e.g. inequalities in workforce training and job opportun- ities) rather than by the nature of the local environment and hence are unlikely to be solved other than by society-wide (cf. areal) pol- icies. Perhaps the popularity of area-based programmes represents simply a political desire to be seen to be doing at least *something* about pressing social problems. This, in turn, suggests that people often have a strong sense of belonging to their local area and wish that sense of belonging to be recognized in the political sphere. The need for a sense of belonging may in fact be one of the keenest felt of all the needs that confront the urban dweller.

3.3 A SENSE OF PLACE

The thesis that advanced western society is becoming increasingly characterized by 'community without propinquity' rests on the contention that it is interaction, not place, that is the essence of city life (Webber 1964). Lenz-Romeiss (1973) has supported this proposition in a wide ranging discussion of both the 'mental mobility' of our age (the fact that the mass media bring to our attention events and places that are beyond the tiny realm of our direct experience) and increasing geographical mobility (both on a daily and life-time basis). However, although questioning whether cities in the future will be needed to the extent that they have been needed in the past, even Lenz-Romeiss is forced to acknowledge that mobility may be resisted by individuals because of the detrimental effects it can have on their lives. In the words of the French proverb, 'partir, c'est mourir un peu' (Lenz-Romeiss 1973, 15). As a result, city dwellers who move their place of residence lose a little of their sense of belonging as their sense of place becomes ruptured. This can have dire consequences for the individuals concerned in that it can damage personal identity, as was noted in Section 3.2. In fact the alienation and homelessness that is apparent in some sectors of the community may have partial roots in the growing rupture between people and place. The so-called 'conquest' of terrestrial space may have been accomplished technologically and economically but it has not yet been accomplished at a human level because it seems, at least experientially, that people become bound to their locality and have their quality of life reduced when this 'binding' is broken (Seamon 1979, 9). In other words, for most aspects of daily living, individuals do not experience the world as an object but rather are fused with the world through a web of feelings (Seamon 1979, 161). Thus, even for the most active sections of society, mobility will never destroy the importance of locality (Pahl 1968, 48). For most people, the pleasures of mobility will never provide a sensation that can satisfy the basic human need for a sense of belonging to a particular place. And, of course, for those sections of the community that have limited mobility anyway – notably the young, the old, the sick, and the poor – a sense of place will continue to play a paramount role in everyday life. In short, and despite trends towards increasing mobility, experience and consciousness of the world will continue to be centred on place (Walmsley and Lewis 1984, 160). Place and locality are still, and will continue to be, crucial variables for all urban experience (Blowers 1973). It may even be that increasing spatial mobility creates a reciprocal need for a firm home base, thereby strengthening place attachment (Norberg–Schultz 1971). It is certainly imperative that planners take stock of such 'place-bonding' rather than focus their attention simply on the manipulation of the physical environment (Gans 1968).

When an individual is asked if that individual knows a stranger, the reply is often 'I can't place her'. This suggests that, in common parlance, people and places are compounded in identity. The term 'place' therefore implies both a location and an integration of nature and culture. Thus, the meaning of a place comes neither from location, nor from the trivial function that places serve, nor from the community that occupies it, nor from superficial and mundane experiences (Relph 1976, 43). Rather a sense of belonging to a place is really an affective bond that develops between people and locations over a period of time. Tuan (1974) has labelled this sort of affective bond *topophilia*. Although topophilic sentiments can range in variety and in intensity, and can cover aesthetic and tactile as well as emotional responses, a sense of belonging is one of the most prominent (Walmsley and Lewis 1984, 161). Of course, it would be wrong to romanticize about a sense of place and to assume that it is a sentiment held by all human beings. Whether or not individuals feel a sense of place depends very much on the social and physical environment in which they live. For instance, no fewer than two-thirds of the respondents in Ley's (1974) study of the black inner suburb of 'Monroe' in north Philadelphia (USA) said that they would not mind the area being razed and redeveloped.

It is very difficult to measure a sense of place. Quite obviously a study of the importance of a sense of place in urban living requires an anthropocentric view of the city whereby places can be seen through the eyes of residents. Nothing can be gained in the study of a sense of place by restricting attention to census data with their emphasis on *homo dormiens* (Ley 1983, 95). What seems to be required is a humanistic perspective that focusses on the meaningfulness of phenomena in everyday life and on the inseparable relationship between human values and creativity on the one hand and objects in the environment on the other hand. Herein lies a problem: the relationships between people and the environment are reciprocal for, whereas it is human intent and action which ascribe meaning and transform empty space into experienced place, so too can place act back on people with a result that its meaning can constrain their values and actions (Ley 1983, 132-3). It is, in other words, impossible to differentiate the effect of people on place from the effect of place on people and people–place interaction must therefore be studied in its totality. Some researchers have suggested that the key to understanding the significance of place lies in participant and other simple observation techniques. A case in point is Cooper's (1978) attempt, upon returning to Minneapolis (USA) after a long absence, to appreciate the sense of place that attached to two newly designed public spaces by sitting in those spaces and observing the behaviour that occurred there. More usually, however, a phenomenological approach has been adopted whereby researchers have tried, through a process of *verstehen*, to understand how individuals view places and to comprehend the intentions that lie behind the behaviour deemed appropriate to such places. Unfortunately such an approach all too often places too much reliance on anecdotes with a result that description becomes an end in itself and research takes on a non-cumulative flavour (Ley 1978, 45). This non-cumulativity may, of course, be more apparent than real. After all, a great deal of social science is non-cumulative in a simple additive sense but yet it provides important insights into the causes and character of human behaviour (Jackson 1985). The fact remains, nevertheless, that it is very often difficult to relate one phenomenological study of place to another.

An additional problem compounding attempts to measure a sense of place is the fact that a sense of place can apply at a variety of scales, often reflecting a proprietorial interest that an individual has in a place. For example an individual can feel a sense of belonging to a favourite chair, to a building, to a neighbourhood, to a city, or to a nation. Indeed a good deal of work has gone into studying the sense of place that attaches to a home (see Sanchez-Robles 1980) and to community facilities such as dance halls (see Cressey 1971). For the most part, however, attention has focussed on *urban neighbourhoods*. In this regard, a fillip to research was provided by those who evaluated post-war reconstruction in Europe. In the rebuilding of cities, especially in Britain, planners tended to assume that a sense of community could be created simply by providing neighbourhood centres. Young and Willmott (1957) showed that this was not true and that the provision of buildings was not a sufficient condition for the development of communities. In particular they showed that, in the East End of London, very few people wanted to be relocated to new housing for fear that relocation would upset the attachment they felt to family, to local pubs, to the local market, and to a wide range of neighbourhood facilities. Space and society, in other words, are far from being independent of one another; rather they interpenetrate to such a degree that societies can be thought of as drawing their own self-portraits on the ground on which they live (Lenz-Romeiss 1973, 33). Space, then, is irrevocably humanized and is both a mirror and a moulder of human purposes (Ley 1983, 143). As a result places tend to take on the character of the people who live there. Nowhere is this better seen than in so-called 'urban villages'. These villages are typically located in medium to high density inner city areas and characterized by intense local social networks, a high degree of neighbouring and use of local facilities, and the presence nearby of extended family members (Ley 1983, 147). They therefore offer a contrast to suburbia which is often designed in terms of physical villages but rarely works in the societal sense as villages.

In urban villages, repeated interaction with others in the routines of daily life leads invariably to a shared set of expectations and to a degree of consensus in attitudes and behaviour that may eventually lead to the emergence of a distinctive subculture (Ley 1983, 201). In this way the places at the centre of the urban village provide a summary of the people who live there, not least because they prescribe the ongoing transactions that characterize the lifestyle of the village (Ley 1983, 165). In other words there is an element of intersubjectivity to life in an urban village to the extent that the inhabitants are not solitary beings but rather share in a collective set of attitudes and meanings, notably in relation to the interpretation of the environment. The social reality of urban living is not therefore something that is given; instead it is something that is constructed and maintained through continuous interaction and communication. The words of Ley (1983, 203) express this clearly: 'The routines of daily life create a particular view of the world and a mandate for action. It is the unselfconscious, taken-for-granted character of the life–world that makes it so binding on its members, that ensures its realities will remain secure'.

The taken-for-granted world of the urban village is centred, like much of the rest of city life, on a *symbolic* world. The intersubjective world view that is characteristic of life in urban villages leads to the widespread adoption of a set of shared symbols. This is very clearly seen in the way in which place names can become symbols. Where an individual is from is very often a label in social life which can be used to define who that individual is or even who that individual is allowed to become (Ley 1983, 158). In fact Lenz-Romeiss (1973) has argued that it is attachment to local social groups, via identification with a place name which stands as a symbol for the group, that is at the heart of adaptation to city life. In this context place names stand for social relationships; to feel allegiance with a place name is to be acquainted with the people who live at that place. The role of symbols is, of course, not limited to providing a sense of identity. In addition they can also have social-normative meaning that binds a group together by giving clues as to what are considered proper forms of behaviour. Thus symbols serve to make life easier for urban residents, not just by fostering a sense of social integration, but also by providing a store of acquired knowledge that enables individuals to deal with new situations (e.g. being in a new town) without having to begin their learning processes completely afresh (Lenz–Romeiss 1973). Symbols, in other words, are an integral part of an individual's learned image of the city (though they seldom show up in conventional mental mapping exercises). In this sense the whole urban fabric may be a symbol. Certainly architecture can be symbolic, as when big office blocks typify the pillars on which society is built (see Section 3.5).

The symbolism of architecture involves non-verbal communication. Its significance has been realized for a long time. Porteous (1974), for example, has shown how the spatial form of Latin American mining company towns may be manipulated, by systematic segregation, to reinforce the social hierarchy. The same congruence between spatial structure and social structure can be seen in many North of England mill towns, with the mill owner in an elevated position looking down on the terraced housing of the workers. The symbolic use of place names is very different from this type of architectural symbolism in that it relies on verbal communication. The significance of this lies in the fact that it brings into focus the question of just how people use language. At a simple level it has been shown that the popular use of place names may be at odds with what might have been expected from 'objective' use of street directories. Walmsley (1976) has demonstrated, for instance, that the majority of a sample of Sydney (Australia) women, when asked to name the suburb in which they lived, gave a name which was at odds with that derived from a street directory. Guest and Lee (1983) have gone even further and shown that residents of Seattle (USA) identify with several different place names that often denote overlapping or hierarchical communities. Although the degree of consensus in the use of place names for local areas varied throughout Seattle, and was influenced markedly by the nature of the physical environment, Guest and Lee found a distinct tendency for consensus to be highest in high status areas. This raises the interesting possibility that status and the use of language may be related. This possibility was first looked at by Bernstein (1959) who drew a distinction between *formal language* (that is language composed of sentences which are accurately formalized grammatically and syntactically) and *public language*. The latter is characterized by short, grammatically simple sentences of poor syntactical construction, the repetitive use of conjunctions (e.g. so, then, because), the limited use of adjectives and adverbs, the infrequent use of impersonal pronouns (e.g. one, it), and a high level of usage of idiomatic phrases. This distinction was taken up by Goodchild (1974) in a study of urban environmental perception. Goodchild noted that formal language is very much the preserve of managerial and professional groups while public language is used by much of the rest of the population. This research went on to suggest that the difference between the two is a function of conceptual ability: those using public language are less likely to conceptualize aesthetic aspects of the environment and instead are preoccupied with the basic needs of day-to-day life. As a result, Goodchild suggested that one would expect higher socio-economic groups to more readily reveal community area attachment because they can more readily understand and articulate the concepts involved. A similar view was expressed by Sanchez-Robles (1980) who suggested that public language is used by the working class and formal language by the middle class with a result that the middle class have a better ability to conceptualize about the built environment. Sanchez-Robles' study showed, for example, that middle class housewives have a higher degree of conceptual structure than do working class housewives as regards their evaluation of their homes.

Language undoubtedly plays an important role in influencing the bond that develops between individuals and places. Discussion so far in this Section has focussed on the affiliation that people feel to a place. In essence, then, the object of study has been the 'rootedness' of individuals, that is to say their sense of being 'at home' in an unselfconscious way (Tuan 1980b). The nature of such 'rootedness' was very clearly demonstrated in Godkin's (1980) study of a group of alcoholics and, particularly, in his examination of the way in which places become reservoirs of significant life experiences and thereby lie at the centre of a person's identity and sense of psychological well-being. It should be remembered, however, that individuals can have a sense of place without feeling 'at home' in that place. In short, places can develop a 'spirit', termed *genius loci* by Norberg-Schulz (1980). According to this view, places are permanent 'environmental-human wholes' which maintain themselves temporally while actual events and generations come and go, thereby ensuring that the character of a place transcends the behaviour of the particular people living there at a particular historical moment (Seamon 1984, 175). Thus some regions of a city can be almost universally interpreted as places of *status* irrespective of whether or not individuals identify *with* such places (e.g. high status suburbs). Other regions, notably ghettos or possibly even large public housing estates, are places of *stigma* in the eyes of many. Some parts of cities are places of *stimulus* (e.g. leisure oriented suburbs like Kings Cross in Sydney and St Kilda in Melbourne, Australia) while others are places of *ennui* and *boredom* (e.g. metropolitan fringe suburbs as viewed by teenagers) (see Ley 1983, 145–64). Above all, some parts of the city may be seen as places of *stress*. Figure 3.1, for example, shows the perceived stress associated with certain streets in Ley's study of 'Monroe', Philadelphia (USA). Interestingly and predictably, pedestrian paths avoided the areas of highest stress.

The central point of Norberg-Schulz's argument is that places are essentially what they are, and that human intervention, through planning and environmental design, will be successful in creating livable places only when it recognizes that essence and creates human environments that are in tune with the *genius loci* rather than at odds

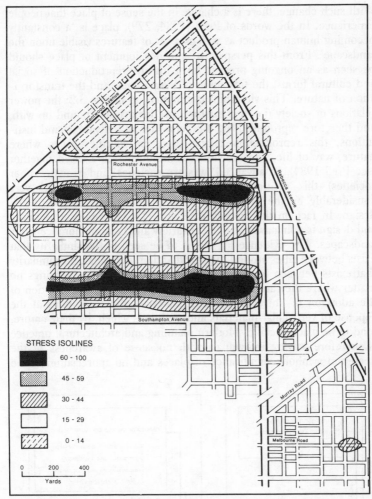

Fig. 3.1. Stress levels in 'Monroe', Philadelphia, USA. *Source*: Ley (1974)

with it (Seamon 1984, 176). This is not to say that the character of a place is absolutely fixed. This cannot be because, quite obviously, places change over time. To take an extreme example, the character of Botany Bay (Australia) changed dramatically with European settlement in the late eighteenth century. Similarly, the character of many European cities was changed as a result of war-time bombing. On a more subtle level, the process of gentrification is transforming many inner city areas around the world from working-class communities to havens for 'yuppies' (young, upwardly mobile, professional people).

With such change, there is a change in the sense of place that people experience. In the words of Pred (1984, 279), place is 'a constantly becoming human product as well as a set of features visible upon the landscape'. From this perspective, the development of place should be seen as an ongoing process involving the reproduction of social and cultural forms, the formation of biographies, and the transformation of nature. This viewpoint is summed up in Fig. 3.2: the power relations of society (i.e. its structure) are inextricably bound up with, and therefore reproduced by, the behaviour of individuals and institutions, this reproduction taking place in specific places where nature, way of life, and individual consciousness are fused together (see Pred 1984). In advanced, western societies (and in many other societies) this continuous creation of place is influenced very considerably by the practice of town planning and environmental design. In fact, in the opinion of Relph (1981b), uniform planning and design is doing away with local variety and creating homogeneous landscapes. The evidence for this is to be seen in the similarity that exists between cities around the world and, in particular, the similarity that exists between buildings such as hotels and office buildings no matter where they are located. This similarity is largely a function of the adoption of universal building materials and techniques at the expense of vernacular materials and traditions which, by their nature, tend to be place specific. Modern planning and architectural practice is therefore leaving individuals with no sense of awareness of the deep and symbolic significance of places and no appreciation of the

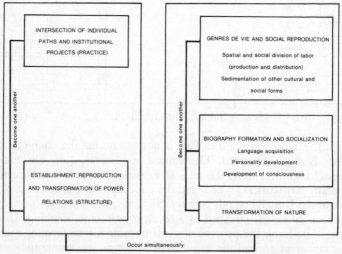

Fig. 3.2 The development of a sense of place. *Source*: Pred (1984)

role of places in personal identity. In other words, modern planning, coupled with 'modernist' trends in architecture and engineering, is fostering 'placelessness' (Relph 1981b) and homogeneous landscapes which, in turn, are engendering a feeling of alienation and home-lessness. Just how humans will react in the longer term to such land-scapes is difficult to predict.

3.4 THE APPRECIATION OF LANDSCAPE

'Landscape' is a concept that is used a good deal in everyday life. Landscape is something that is all around, something that is being continuously created and altered (often unconsciously as much as through conscious design), and something that is imbued with symbolic and cultural meaning (Meinig 1979a). As a result, changes in the landscape give clues as to changing evaluations of the environment. Landscape, in this sense, need not be spectacular; it may in fact be very ordinary and taken-for-granted by most people (Meinig 1979b). It is nevertheless an artefact of human use of the environment and its character results from the totality of human influences (Walmsley and Lewis 1984). This is not to say that all human beings interpret the environment in the same way. This is far from true because landscape interpretation and appreciation is very much an idiosyncratic process: thus a capitalist may interpret a landscape in monetary terms, an artist in aesthetic terms, a scientist in ecological terms, and a social activist in terms of injustice (Meinig 1979c). Nevertheless, landscapes do provide clues as to the type of people that occupy them and almost all objects in the landscape convey some sort of message (Lewis 1979).

Given the variety of interpretations that may be placed on a land-scape, it is extremely difficult to generalize about landscape appreci-ation. Appleton (1975b) has in fact bemoaned the lack of any theoretical foundation for the study of landscape evaluation. In his view, empirical studies of landscape evaluation could be strengthened if they were underpinned by a convincing theoretical base. Unfor-tunately such is not the case and the vast majority of studies on land-scape interpretation are concerned with problems (e.g. the conservation of a threatened landscape) rather than with theory. As a result it is probably inevitable that the study of landscape appreci-ation in the immediate future will proceed empirically. It is also almost inevitable that future work on landscape interpretation will focus, as in the past, on the visual component of landscape, largely because this is the characteristic of landscape that impinges most directly on everyday urban living. This research is likely to be concerned with identifying which landscape elements are perceived as pleasing and which combinations of elements are attractive. The rationale behind such research is simple: if we can discover what people find pleasing and attractive, then we can design landscapes to accommodate those tastes. However, in collecting value judgements – no matter how objectively – and in converting them into scientific conclusions, we should not deceive ourselves into believing that we are able to proceed without making many assumptions about the fundamental nature of *aesthetic* experience and its relationship to the enjoyment of landscape (Appleton 1975b, 21).

Questions of landscape aesthetics have rarely been given the attention they deserve. Instead researchers have preferred to discuss questions of preference, taste, perception, and management (Punter 1982, 100). As a result, it is not surprising that a considerable gap has developed between the philosophy of aesthetics in general and the philosophy of landscape aesthetics in particular. In essence, landscape aesthetics is concerned with identifying what it is that people find pleasing in the landscape – particularly the visual landscape – with a view to arriving at some definition of what it is that constitutes 'beauty'. Of course, in any discussion of landscape aesthetics there is a clear distinction to be made between aesthetic evaluation and aesthetic preference; commentators may, for example, agree on the *value* of a particular landscape but differ in their personal *preferences* for that landscape *vis-à-vis* other (possibly inferior) landscapes (Craik 1972a). Even the distinction between evaluation and preference may be too simple a view of landscape aesthetics. According to Punter (1982) there are at least three general foci to work on landscape aesthetics: *perception* studies concerned with both how individuals perceive landscape and with the links that exist between vision, perception, comprehension, preference, and action; *interpretation* studies concerned more or less exclusively with the meanings imputed to landscape; and studies of *landscape quality*. Each of these merits attention.

The 'perception approach' to landscape aesthetics has tended to assume that human brains seek to integrate separate visual stimuli into a meaningful whole, maximizing redundancy and simplicity of form (Punter 1982, 103). In this regard, it seems that there are three criteria against which landscapes may be assessed (Litton 1972). The first is *unity* which refers to the quality of wholeness whereby all parts of the landscape cohere, not merely as an assembly but as a single harmonious unit. The second criterion is that of *vividness*, that is the quality which gives landscape distinction and makes it striking. Vividness is, then, the quality that makes some items in the landscape appear larger than life when the landscape is recalled to mind. For example, when Pocock (1982) asked subjects who had left Durham (England) to recall the view from Prebends' Bridge, many drew the

Cathedral as very large, at least relative to the bank of the River Wear, thereby suggesting that the Cathedral is a vivid component of that particular landscape. The third criterion involved in landscape perception is that of *variety*. Landscapes, for instance, can be thought of in terms of visual complexity versus simplicity, chaos versus order, ambiguity versus clarity, arousal versus habituation, and common-placeness versus uniqueness (Punter 1982).

The topics of complexity and ambiguity have been the most studied of these dimensions of variety. McHarg (1969), for example, argued that human aesthetic responses are prompted by a long history of interaction with a natural world that is ecologically rich, complex, and ambiguous. Human beings, as a result, tend to look for, and appreciate, these features in the urban landscape. Rapoport and Kantor (1967), likewise, adduced evidence from psychology to argue that human beings prefer an environment rich in complexity and ambiguity. Their argument was that repeated exposure to complexity and ambiguity tends to improve perceptual performance whereas deprivation in this sphere has a detrimental effect on the mind. The implication is that there exists, for human beings, an optimal rate of perceptual input. Individuals, in other words, dislike both very simple and chaotically complex perceptual fields. Although this is an interesting argument, and one that might have important implications for environmental design (see Lynch 1971), it draws mainly on experimental psychology, notably on studies which have shown that rats in stimulating environments can both increase their brain weight and improve their learning relative to control rats (Krech *et al.* 1962). Whether these sorts of results can be extrapolated to human behaviour is very much an open question. Certainly the results throw little light on the question of whether scenic beauty is an objective property that lies within the landscape or a subjective impression based on personal predispositions and the mental processing of information. Nor do they throw any light on the question of whether aesthetic value is a constant over time and among different groups of people (Zube *et al.* 1982, 21). This is because Rapoport and Kantor's argument, like most work on landscape perception, is lacking a firm theoretical foundation.

One of the few writers to propose a theoretical perspective on landscape perception is Appleton (1975a). In seeking to identify what it is that people find attractive about certain landscapes, Appleton turned to *habitat theory* according to which 'aesthetic satisfaction, experienced in the contemplation of landscape, stems from the immediate perception of landscape features which, in their shapes, colours, spatial arrangements and other visible attributes, act as sign-stimuli indicative of environmental conditions favourable to survival' (Appleton 1975a, 2). In other words, human responses to landscape are conditioned by survival mechanisms developed by primitive ancestors. This point of view has been taken even further in *prospect-refuge theory* which proposes that the landscapes which appear most satisfying to human beings are those which provide an ability to see (prospect) without being seen (refuge). In other words, what Appleton is suggesting is that human perception of landscape is constrained by innate mechanisms. At first flush, the relevance to contemporary urban living of a theory concerned with environmental perceptions that were refined thousands of years ago may appear slight. Appleton argues, however, that prospect-refuge theory finds expression mainly through symbolism; panoramas, vistas, vantages, and falling ground can all symbolize prospects while hides, shelters, woods and buildings (providing they are penetrable) can all symbolize refuges. As a result, it becomes possible to design cities to provide effective symbolic substitutes for those environmental features which, in their natural forms, suggest an opportunity for seeing without being seen. A combination of narrow streets and wide open squares can, for example, afford an individual with the security of lateral cover until the moment when the individual is ready to concede the refuge as the price of achieving a wider prospect (Appleton 1975a, 196). Just how important prospect and refuge are in urban living is of course very difficult to ascertain.

The second of Punter's (1982) approaches to landscape aesthetics focusses on *landscape interpretation*. In so far as this is a topic that is very much concerned with the meanings that individuals ascribe to the environment, it has been touched upon earlier in this chapter. Indeed, with the growth of humanistic approaches in social science, the term 'landscape' has largely been supplanted as a focus of attention by the concept of 'place' which emphasizes physical setting, people and patterns of behaviour, and meanings given to and derived from those settings, all as an indissoluble tripartite complex (Punter 1982, 106). Despite this, the topic of landscape interpretation has not been overlooked by researchers. In particular, considerable attention has been paid to the question of what makes certain environments, and therefore landscapes, *valued* (see Gold and Burgess 1982). Individuals seem to have a need to identify with place (see Section 3.3). Very often this manifests itself in the form of association with particular landscapes. Nevertheless researchers are far from being able to say what constitutes a good view or a beautiful landscape, nor have they found a satisfactory means by which to articulate the nature and significance of the intimate attachments that people develop for landscape (Burgess and Gold 1982, 3). Part of the reason for this lies in the fact that landscapes are very complex and can be interpreted in a wide variety of ways. There is often, for example, a wide gulf between what might be thought of as *elite* tastes for landscape (e.g. those of painters and writers) and *public* tastes. In addition, the character of a landscape can be manifested in many ways. For example, attitudes of locals towards the Fenland landscape of eastern England are partly influenced by (1) the humanly constructed landscape where inhabitants are acutely conscious of their continuous struggle against the elements, notably floods, (2) a deep-seated peasant mentality which is related to an intense desire to own land and to exploit natural resources, and (3) strong feelings of isolation where drainage channels separate families and entire communities from their neighbours (Burgess 1982).

Prominent among the landscapes that are interpreted as valuable are the landscapes that 'capture' bygone times. In one sense, of course, any valued landscape is memorable; after all, we revisit it in our minds, if not in reality, and recall its real or imagined lineaments so as to preserve and heighten previous experience (Lowenthal 1982, 74). Landscapes from the past are however even more memorable and valuable. They are appealing because they help us to distance ourselves from the present, to get away from the here and now, and to turn back to a time for which we have no responsibilities (Lowenthal 1982, 77). The past also appeals because it provides a sense of continuity, durability and identity. Individuals who are deprived of their own past landscapes (e.g. prisoners or forced migrants) often have their sense of purpose and personal worth destroyed with a result that, without the past, they cannot 'prevision' a future worth having (Lowenthal 1975, 15). In short, past landscapes can serve as a bulwark against massive and distressing change and, in this sense, they act as a potent force in human affairs even though what usually constitutes 'the past' is not an objective record of events and places so much as a human creation moulded by selective perception, memory, and invention (Lowenthal 1985).

Studies of *landscape quality* differ from studies of landscape perception and landscape interpretation in that they rely less on humanistic approaches. Instead they very often adopt a quantitative approach to measuring landscape. Early work in this field was very much concentrated in Britain where the Town and Country Planning Act 1947 and the National Parks and Access to the Countryside Act 1949 required governments to evaluate the aesthetic quality of different landscapes for the purposes of protection and enhancement (Blacksell and Gilg 1975, 135). For the most part research has striven for a relatively objective inventory of landscape elements and a classification of landscape types on the basis of scores or rankings (Unwin 1975). Generally, two types of method have been employed: *field* methods where observers have estimated the quality of the landscape available at a given location; and *surrogate* methods whereby observers have been confronted with a series of photographs to assess (Dearden

1980). Fines' (1968) pioneering work combined both methods. He set out to assess the landscape of East Sussex (England) in its totality. In order to reduce the subjectivity of observers, he used a small panel of specialist observers who, prior to fieldwork, viewed and assessed a carefully chosen set of colour photographs of selected landscapes. The responses to those test views enabled the definition of six descriptive categories (unsightly, undistinguished, pleasant, distinguished, superb, spectacular) which subsequently served as a quantitative basis for field assessments (on average two viewing points being used for each square kilometre of landscape). About the same time Linton (1968) was preparing an alternative quantitative method for assessing landscape quality that differentiated landform (i.e. terrain type) from land cover (i.e. land use and vegetation). In this approach landforms were classified into six types, each being allocated a number of points: (1) lowlands (1 point); (2) hill country (5 points); (3) bold hills (6 points); (4) mountains (8 points); (5) plateau uplands (3 points); and (6) low uplands (2 points). Additionally, a points system was used for land use: urban (−5); continuous forest (−2); treeless farmland (+1); moorland (+3); varied forest and moorland (+4); richly varied farmland (+5); and wild areas (+6). From this basis composite scores could be calculated for any given landscape by adding the landform score to the landuse score.

There are immense problems with the methodology of both Fines and Linton, most notably the fact that both are extremely subjective and both focus exclusively on the visual landscape (Punter 1982). In addition Fines' work raises the question of how representative photographs can be. Moreover, it may well be elitist to use a panel of specialists, especially given that it has been shown that the perception of environmental quality differs between experts and non-experts (Zube 1974; Harrison and Howard 1980). Above all, neither methodology is suited to the assessment of the quality of urban landscapes where changes in landuse are often very subtle. Indeed, Linton seems to dismiss the possibility of any quality attaching to urban landscapes, given their high negative score on his scale. And, of course, neither Fines nor Linton really takes stock of the precise position of the observer in landscape assessment. To some extent this has been rectified by Craik (1972b) who emphasized the position of the observer relative to the scene (i.e. up, down, etc.), the extent of view (both panoramic and focal), lighting, and the presence of specific landscape features and shapes. However, even this modification does little to make the assessment schemes applicable to the urban environment. This is unfortunate because townscape does have a very important influence on the well-being of city dwellers and therefore merits attention. The buildings, trees, water, traffic, advertisements and so on that make up townscape all evoke a response in people.

'Smellscape' may also be important (Porteous 1985). In other words, people react to what they sense as they walk along the street and they therefore encounter the urban landscape in a series of sequential revelations. Likewise, they react to being above or below the rest of the townscape and to being either hemmed in or exposed. Above all, they react to the very fabric of cities: the colour, texture, scale, style, character and personality that gives each city its uniqueness (Cullen 1971). Unfortunately, however, the speed of change in cities has led to a breakdown in communications between environmental designers and urban residents. The pressures to house more people and to provide more amenities, involving architects and engineers almost inevitably in mass production techniques, have led to feelings of unfamiliarity and confusion on the part of city dwellers trying to cope with changing surroundings. This suggests that city dwellers, if they are to become less confused, might need to be educated in how to interpret the environment (see Tilden 1967). In this respect it is interesting to note the increasing popularity of town trails.

Goodey has been a pioneer of the 'town trail movement' and has spent a lot of effort in trying to educate the public to understand the environment in which they live (see Goodey 1978). The rationale for urban trails is a simple one: 'through interpretation, understanding; through understanding, appreciation; through appreciation, protection' (Percival 1979, 9). For the most part, however, urban trails have concentrated on history and architecture rather than on experience of place (Goodey 1982). Thus the goal of many trails has been to make the public notice features (especially buildings and street patterns) that would otherwise go unnoticed or be taken-for-granted. It is often left to the follower of the town trail to impute social, economic, and cultural meaning to buildings. This sort of strategy is distressing because it fails to realize that it is not in architecture *per se* that many people find beauty but rather in the associations that architecture brings to mind (Oliver 1982). In other words, the ideal urban trail would be one that extends beyond a listing of points of architectural interest and attempts to capture the total experience of urban living (Goodey 1982). In so doing it would explore the ways in which the design of an environment is an exercise in symbolism.

3.5 SYMBOLISM IN ENVIRONMENTAL DESIGN

Individuals seek meaning in the landscape. According to Tuan (1971), meaning implies two things. First it implies order and harmony. Thus individuals find meaning when they can discern order and harmony in the chaotic world of facts and thereby remove the irritation and insecurity that chaos generates. Meaning also implies significance. In this sense a phenomenon can be said to have meaning if it is a sign to something beyond itself. In other words, much of the meaning of the environment is contained in its *symbolism*. This is an important point, particularly in this day and age when much of the urban environment is, to a significant extent, planned and therefore has its *symbolism contrived* to at least some degree. However, it raises the question of what it is that turns an environmental feature into a symbol. Unfortunately there is no easy answer to this question because meanings in the environment may be as varied and complex as people themselves. Ideally, of course, an environment should communicate to its users information about the type of activity that is appropriate to various places, information about the intensity with which that activity is conducted (e.g. crowding), and information about the comparative significance of places (Steinitz 1968). In practice, this sort of communication is not easily achieved. Symbolism in the environment is, after all, very closely linked to culture and, in these pluralistic days, there is probably less agreement over the meaning of symbols than there was in the past. As a result, different people are likely to interpret the environment in different ways. However, this is not to say that generalizations are impossible. Some interpretations of the environment certainly do seem to be very widely held. For example, waves breaking on a beach may often have the same decibel count as heavy traffic but they are invariably perceived as being less noisy because the ocean is a symbol of all things natural (Appleyard 1979). Similarly, in western cities, the freestanding house, no matter how close to another, enhances feelings of ownership, territory, privacy and self esteem. Likewise totalitarian regimes, notably Nazi Germany and Eastern bloc countries, used (and continue to use) architecture as a form of 'monumental propaganda' to symbolize power and authority (Rapoport 1977, 320–1). In a similar vein, of course, advanced western economies of today tend to use high rise office blocks as symbols of corporate power and more generally indulge in what Goodman (1972) has called 'the architecture of repression'.

In the past the very shape of cities was symbolic in that it very often projected images of cosmic order on to the plane of human experience (Wheatley 1971). The mandala, for instance, dominated town design from prehistoric times to the Rennaissance and in so doing symbolized harmony between humans and the cosmos (especially at the centre which was often a sacred site), unity between individuals (the shape providing social cohesion and unity of purpose thereby harnessing thought and effort to the common good), and reconciliation of opposites (the fact that the unity conferred by citizenship transcended diversity within the population) (Smith 1974) (Fig. 3.3). The *shape* of modern cities is no longer significant because urban sprawl mili-

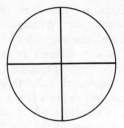

Fig. 3.3 The mandala. *Source*: Gold (1980)

tates against symbolism. Nevertheless, the *structure* of modern cities can be highly symbolic. Residential addresses, for example, are often a symbol of status and position. Moreover, differentiation within the structure of the built environment influences communication between people by either separating or linking various individuals and groups (Rapoport 1977). In this sense, the built environment serves as a form of non-verbal communication (Rapoport 1982). The messages it conveys, if read, understood and obeyed, give clues as to what is deemed appropriate behaviour for different locations within the city (Rapoport 1977, 326). In other words, the physical environment provides a set of cues which people interpret so as to provide a basis for making inferences as to what is deemed to be acceptable behaviour (Becker 1977). A simple example of this is to be seen in the way in which, in middle class American and Australian suburbs, well main-tained lawns are used as symbols of status and good behaviour (Rapoport 1977, 327). In short, the built environment can serve (like fashion and facial expressions) as a form of non-verbal communication that instructs city dwellers as to what is acceptable where. In the medieval village, where everyone knew everyone else, this sort of communication was probably unnecessary but in large and often anonymous urban communities (where social hierarchies may be unclear), environmental cues as to appropriate behaviour are undoubtedly important (Rapoport 1982). This means that urban dwellers operate to a very significant degree in a symbolic environ-ment. Most humanistic social scientists would accept the view that symbolism, in this sense, exists in the mind and is therefore an element of consciousness that can be investigated by trying to empathize with the conscious world view of city dwellers (e.g. Tuan 1978). Others have challenged this view and have argued that symbolism in the urban environment goes beyond the realm of ideas and deep into the subconscious.

Cooper (1974), in a significant study of the house as a symbol of self, turned to Jung's writings on the human psyche, notably his views on the collective unconscious, archetypes, and symbols. Jung postulated that human beings are linked to their primitive past by a universal or *collective unconscious*. Within this collective unconscious there are certain basic and timeless nodes of psychic energy that Jung labelled *archetypes*. It is very difficult to explain what is meant by 'archetype' because an archetype precedes conscious experience and therefore cannot be expressed fully through conscious thought processes. Nevertheless, in Cooper's (1974, 131) view, an archetype can be thought of as 'a structure which somehow has shaped and organized the myriad contents of the psyche into potential images, emotions, ideas, and patterns of behaviour'. The significant point, then, is that the archetype provides a *potential* for representation in the conscious mind; it can do no more than create this potential because, as soon as an archetype is encountered through dreams or rational thought, it 'becomes clothed in the images of the concrete world' (Cooper 1974, 131). In other words, archetypes manifest themselves through what Jung called *symbols*. Thus a symbol, although it possesses objective, visible reality, always has behind it a hidden, profound, and only partly intelligible meaning which represents its roots in the archetype (Cooper 1974, 131).

In Cooper's view, human beings were symbol-making animals long before they were toolmakers in that they reached high levels of specialization in dance, ritual, and religion *before* they specialized in material aspects of culture. Moreover, this symbol-making continues today. Cooper, for example, believes that *self* is one of the most basic of all archetypes and that, as such, self is symbolized through the home. In this context Cooper (1974, 133) asserts that, 'when asked to describe their ideal house, people of all incomes and backgrounds will tend to describe a free-standing, square, detached, single-family house and yard'. This is a bold claim. Even if it were true, it is unclear why such tastes should result from an archetype rather than from a general socializing process (perhaps with roots in the advertising industry) and from present policies in respect of housing market incentives and land use (Shlay 1985). There is undoubtedly evidence that, over the centuries, humans have used cosmic symbols in the design of temples and cities but it is not clear just how individual homes, with their enormous variety is scale, structure, and layout, symbolize an archetype.

Jungian archetypes were taken up again in a slightly wider examination of symbolism by Smith (1974). He began with the proposition that experiencing the environment is a creative act that involves a response to the environment as perceived. Social scientists interested in environmental experience therefore need to know how perception occurs and how memory influences perception. Although acknowledging, much to the chagrin of planners and architects, that up to 90% of the familiar built environment remains unperceived by the conscious mind of the average urban dweller, Smith argued that perception is undeniably important. 'Perception' in this sense involves not merely the impinging of stimuli on the human sense organs but also the interpretation of symbols within the environment. According to Smith (1974), there are four sorts of symbolism that have a bearing on this interpretation process. One is obviously the *archetypal symbolism* discussed by Cooper (1974). Because these symbols materialized at a very early stage in the evolution of the human species, they are collective and possibly even universal. Archetypal symbolism therefore contrasts markedly with *associational symbolism* whereby a particular environment becomes symbolic through associations based on direct personal experience (as when a particular beach can symbolize family holidays experienced during childhood). This sort of symbolism is a very private affair that is beyond the control of environmental designers. A more public form of symbolism is *acculturated symbolism*. This sort of symbolism again relies on association. However, the association in question is cultural rather than personal in origin. Thus Big Ben can symbolize 'Britishness' just as 'monumental neo-gothic structures like Manchester Town Hall inform all citizens that their councillors are always motivated by pure Christian principles' (Smith 1974, 53). The final type of symbolism identified by Smith is *symbolism of the familiar*. Its importance is clearly demonstrated in cases where the familiar everyday environment comes to symbolize security and continuity.

Smith (1974) agrees with Cooper (1974) that symbolism was the vehicle for human development and that use of symbolism is one of the main features that distinguishes humans from lower primates. According to this view, an elaborate repertoire of symbolism was developed at the predatory and nomadic stages of cultural development and subsequently extended into urban symbolism. Thus humans, over the centuries, delighted in contrasting the purity and sophistication of their artefacts and buildings against the arbitrariness and chaos of nature. As a result, according to this view, certain historic cities make a deep impact on the contemporary mind in that they satisfy needs in a way in which industrial and post-industrial cities do not, namely they offer a permanently valid symbol of the complete human situation, with its tensions, darkness, and light (Smith 1974, 69–72). It is difficult to say whether this contention is valid or not, or whether historic cities just seem simpler than contemporary cities. However, what is particularly appealing about Smith's work is not this contention about the historical form of cities, but rather his argument, admittedly speculative, that the growth, development, and structure of the human brain has a major influence on the manner in which individuals interpret symbolism in the environment.

In terms of neuroanatomy, the human brain comprises three parts (see Sagan 1977). The most primitive part is the *reptilian complex*. In evolutionary terms this is the oldest part of the brain. It controls the neural chassis of the body. It is, moreover, a part that plays an important role in aggressive behaviour, territoriality, ritual, and the establishment of social hierarchies. Next comes the *limbic system*, the part of the brain that controls, as its names suggests, the limbs. This is also the part of the brain that generates strong and vivid emotions, notably fear and timidity. Finally, there is the *neocortex* (Fig. 3.4). In evolutionary terms, this is the most recently developed part of the brain. Its function is to control 'advanced' behaviour, especially abstract reasoning and sophisticated memory. Smith (1974, 187) has argued that this reasoning potential of the neocortex has only been actualized to a really significant degree in the last 5000 years of human development. Archetypal symbolic themes were obviously developed well before this period and hence were established in the collective memory at a time when the limbic system was the dominant part of the brain. In Smith's (1974, 187–8) view, the fact that symbolism was passed on culturally for several thousand years meant that the chances of it becoming a permanent part of the circuitry of the brain were quite high. Thus, just as there are 'deep structures' in the brain that control language (see the work of Chomsky as reviewed by Greene (1972)), so too, in Smith's view, are there 'deep structures' that control environmental symbolism. According to this view, then, the limbic brain not only exists to control movement but seems also to contain circuitry which generates a psychological appetite for symbolic references going right back to archetypal origins (Smith 1974, 188).

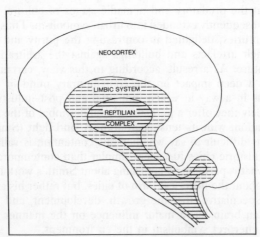

Fig. 3.4 A stylized representation of the human brain. *Source*: Sagan (1977)

To consider such views about the limbic system is not, of course, to belittle the importance of the neocortex. After all, the neocortex is the seat of all rational activity, verbal activity, and logical thought (Smith 1977). It is therefore the part of the brain concerned with the development of socio-spatial schemata (see Chapter 2). Smith has in fact suggested that there are two neuronal pathways involved in all perception: one is connected to the neocortex and the other to the limbic system. Thus there is, on the one hand, a hunger for excitation and exploration (stemming from the neocortex), counterbalanced by a need for security and harmony between the subject and the environment (stemming from the homeostatic tendency of the emotionally intensive limbic system) (Smith 1977, 34). According to this view, the limbic system will perceive the environment according to biological criteria like the matter of escape. It may be, then, that the mode of operation of the limbic system provides support for the prospect-refuge theory of landscape appreciation (see Section 3.4).

It would be wrong to view the brain as being structured only along the simple lines depicted in Fig. 3.4. In addition to being differentiated into three parts, the brain is also divided into two hemispheres. In terms of environmental perception, the left hemisphere handles verbal information (e.g. advertising, signposts) and sorts information into concepts which are semantically organized (e.g. it organizes cognitive maps in terms of landmarks with verbal identification). In contrast, the right hemisphere takes stock of such things as shape, location, colour, texture, tone and rhythm. Compared to the left hemisphere, it is almost 'inarticulate' because it mediates experience to consciousness in a way that is often too deep for words (Smith 1977, 40). Of course, even this differentiation may be a gross over-simplification for it may well be that some aspects of language and writing (e.g. the deeper meaning of poetry) are strongly influenced by the right hemisphere whereas some aspects of shape and location may be handled in the left hemisphere. Nevertheless, in Smith's (1974) view, advanced western society is becoming biassed in favour of the serial processes (e.g. language and writing) associated with the left hemisphere. This is another bold assertion. It rests on very little evidence. Despite this, it is interesting in the sense that it comes at a time when many social scientists concerned with environmental interpretation are expressing an interest in the way in which the study of symbolism in language can throw light on the study of environmental symbolism.

One of the first social scientists to interest himself in the signs and symbols of language was Saussure. He noted the existence of many forms of non-verbal communication and, in his *Course in General Linguistics* (first published in 1916), he postulated the existence of a general science of signs, or *semiology*, of which linguistics would form only one part. Strictly speaking, of course, semiology has two meanings: first, it refers to the scientific study of all human communications; and, secondly, it refers to the study of all human phenomena to the extent that they have anthropological meaning (e.g. architecture). According to the former meaning, semiology focusses mainly on *explicitly* designed communication systems and the way in which these are 'decoded' by their users. According to the second view, messages are *implicit* in phenomena and therefore have to be interpreted rather than decoded (Mounin 1980). Saussure's ideas were more in line with this second view. What he proposed, in other words, was that social behaviour rests on shared meanings and that meanings are communicated by systems of signs. Language, from this point of view, is only one specific system of signs. Semiology rests on the assumption that, in so far as human actions convey meaning, and in so far as they function as signs, then there must be an underlying system of conventions which makes meaning possible (Culler 1976, 97). The goal of semiology, according to Saussure, is therefore to explore the conventions on which systems of signs are based in order to make explicit the implicit knowledge that enables people in a given society to communicate with each other and to understand each other's behaviour. This is not an easy task. Non-linguistic signs may often seem natural to those who use them but it may require some very considerable effort on the part of the researcher to see, for example, that the politeness or impoliteness of an action is not a necessary and intrinsic property of that action but rather a conventional meaning (Culler 1976, 98). Ritual, etiquette, and status symbols all serve as systems of signs but none of them is easy to interpret. Some writers have even doubted whether, in the social life of today, there exist any extensive systems of signs outside human language (Barthes 1964, 9).

Saussure's views made little impact on social science for many years. Nor did the writings of Peirce fare much better (see Hartshorne and Weiss 1974). Like Saussure, Peirce was interested in the process of thought and the way in which meaning is expressed in language. Also like Saussure, Peirce suggested that language, meaning, and thought are all connected in a general theory of signs. The word Peirce coined for the study of the interrelationships between language, meaning, and thought was '*semiotics*'. In other words, semiotics and semiology both seek to study the structure of systems of signs. They therefore differ from *semantics* which is concerned with the conveyance of meaning by the grammatical and lexical devices of a language (Weinreich 1968, 165). Unfortunately writings on both semiology and semiotics suffer from obtuse terminology. Moreover the differences between the two are not always clear and the terminology used seems to vary according to whether the researcher is based in North America (where Peirce worked) or in Europe (where Saussure worked).

In the 1960s and 1970s, semiotics (and semiology) began to have some impact on architecture, notably in non-English speaking countries. In attempting to apply the semiotic approach to architecture, the general aim was to see the built environment as a system of signs and as a systematic and specific organization of forms and meanings (Agrest and Gandelsonas 1977, 97). The basic question asked was: 'What kind of meaning is connected to the city by what kind of mechanisms?' (Krampen 1979, 1). Much of the impetus for this sort of semiotic approach stemmed from the lack of meaning that characterized the uniform architectural design of the postwar building boom. In metaphorical terms, architects (and planners) adopted the view that 'if architecture is a language then the city must be a text' (Krampen 1979, 32). In other words, a building, from this perspective, was seen as embedded in the urban environment in the same way that a word is embedded in a sentence.

Generally speaking, semiotics has made a bigger impact on urban design than has semiology. Until semiotics began to be considered in the late 1960s, architecture was dominated by a type of 'functionalism' in which buildings were 'designed with machine-like precision around a particular brief, and realized three-dimensionally according to the latest available technology' (Broadbent 1976, 474). Paradoxically, many of these so-called 'functional' buildings were decidedly non-functional in that they were noisy, cold, and dark. With the advent of the semiotic approach, the tendency arose for buildings to be designed with deliberate meaning. This is not to imply that the semiotic approach is easily applied in architecture. Nor is it to suggest that the semiotic approach is a simple body of knowledge. It is in fact possible to look at the way in which buildings serve as signs on at least three levels (see Broadbent 1976). First, the *pragmatic* level deals with the origins, uses (by those who make them), and effects of signs (on those who interpret them). This is a complicated field of study, especially given that architecture can act on many senses simultaneously. Next comes the *semantic* level which deals with the way in which signs actually carry meaning. In this context a distinction can be drawn between the *signifier* (e.g. a building) and the *signified* (e.g. the concept to which the sign refers). For example, in some senses an office block can be interpreted as a signifier passing on the message of corporate power. The third level at which the semiotic approach can be used is the *syntactic* level. This deals with the combination of signs (e.g. buildings), irrespective of their specific meanings and the effects those meanings have on those who interpret them. In architecture, syntax is usually reduced to considerations of geometry (Broadbent 1976).

Buildings obviously convey meaning as signs on a pragmatic, a semantic, and a syntactic level. Buildings can therefore become symbols by virtue of association with general ideas. For example, the European modernist school of architecture, with its emphasis on 'lucid forms and hygienic spaces', saw skyscrapers rising out of a park as the embodiment of progress (Bruegmann 1982). Likewise, the fact that the tallest buildings in western cities are invariably office blocks rather than cathedrals (as was the case in medieval cities) can be taken to symbolize the secular life on which advanced western cities are based. In short, architecture can signify a way of life, traditional ideas and beliefs, socio-anthropological values (notably in respect of crowding), and information about economic power (Jencks 1980). The semiotic approach provides an interesting framework for considering the way in which these signified meanings are generated and perpetrated, even if it does not, as yet, throw much light on precise processes involved.

Spatial behaviour in the city

The study of urban images and of the meaning ascribed to the environment helps in fostering understanding of where people go and what they do. Investigation of people's so-called 'spatial behaviour' is however no easy matter. In principle, it may seem that all researchers need to do is describe what happens and then generalize in order to arrive at the principles governing people-environment interaction. From this perspective environments can be thought of as 'opportunity fields' which, depending on their design, facilitate a wide range of behaviours (although some behaviours may be more difficult to pursue than other) (Michelson 1977). In reality things are very different. Environments, instead of being neutral 'containers' within which behaviour is acted out, may actually cause or even force a certain form of action (Herz 1982). Psychologists have been aware of this for a long time. Barker (1968), for example, coined the term 'behaviour setting' to refer to small environments (such as classrooms) that elicit very specific responses (e.g. patterns of classroom participation) from individuals in ways that supersede the influence of personality and interpersonal relations. At a larger geographical scale, the widely observed tendency for an individual's social interaction to take place predominantly within the local environment may result from constraints (e.g. on time and travel for social interaction) as much as from the purposeful choice of friends (Huckfeldt 1983). In short, in observing spatial behaviour, researchers need to bear in mind that what they record may not be preferred behaviour; in many cases a desire to undertake a certain form of behaviour has to be suppressed and alternative behaviour substituted (e.g. consumer behaviour may be determined by the mode of available transport rather than by the perceived desirability of visits to competing shopping centres). It would be wrong, of course, to view the environment as always frustrating human desires because clever environmental design can actually facilitate behaviour by providing settings that accommodate human needs, goals, and patterns of behaviour without undue limitations (Michelson 1976). Take a simple example: the construction of a pedestrian mall in Townsville (Australia) resulted in an increase in eye contact, conversation, and social interaction between users of the street (Amato 1981). Shopping malls are, of course, a part of the city with which individuals interact relatively infrequently, if at all. A more logical starting point in any consideration of spatial behaviour in the city is the individual's place of residence and the fact that individuals identify with such places immediately raises the question of whether humans are territorial animals.

4.1 HUMAN TERRITORIALITY

If a territory is thought of as the space around an individual or group which that individual or group thinks of as in some way its own, and which therefore distinguishes it from other individuals or groups, then the concept of territory has at least intuitive appeal in the study of human behaviour (Gold 1982). Certainly it is relatively easy to make a *prima facie* case for humans as territorial animals: for example, one does not have to be immensely perceptive to note that most individuals are deeply attached to private (cf. communal) dwellings and many also feel a strong affinity with a home town or even a nation state. The fact that humans are occasionally aggressive in protecting such 'territories' has led some writers to suggest that humans are territorial animals in much the same way that lower primates are (see Ardrey 1967; Morris 1977). This argument, despite its popular appeal, rests on a false analogy, as careful consideration of animal territoriality shows. In the animal world much behaviour is regulated by territory (Eibl-Eibesfeldt 1970) which serves at least four functions: it ensures the propagation of the species by regulating population density; it keeps animals within communication distance of each other so that both food and danger can be signalled; it facilitates coordination of group activity, thereby holding the group together; and it provides the individual with a known terrain containing places to learn, play, escape, and hide (Hediger 1961). Human territoriality is by no means similar (Levy–Leboyer 1982). In a fundamental sense, humans differ from lower primates in that humans require a homesite to which they can return each evening, a place that will be there every night. Nonhuman primates, in contrast, commonly move around in a troop and do not return to the same place at night (Washburn 1972). Moreover human 'territories', given the geographical range of individual daily mobility, are very much more extensive than those of lower primates. They may even extend to conceptual spaces, such as nation states, which are so large that they cannot be experienced in their entirety; in such cases territorial affiliation is something with its roots in history and its reinforcement in the system of government. Above all, though, in human territoriality there is no clear link between territory and aggression, as exists for other animals. In short, human territoriality is a sociocultural rather than a biological phenomenon (Baldassare 1978). It is not directly related to the propagation of the species or to the provision of food. Instead human territoriality is best thought of as a *learned* response to small scale environments that satisfies basic human needs for security and identity (Walmsley and Lewis 1984, 41). In particular, territoriality provides a culturally derived means of either enhancing or impeding social interaction (Sack 1983). To argue otherwise, and to claim a biological basis for human territoriality, is to adopt an ideological standpoint that in effect acts as a prop to the status quo by devaluing human capacity to design societal patterns other than the ones we presently have (Suttles 1972).

The fact that human territoriality is a socio-cultural phenomenon means that territorial behaviour in humans is far more varied, less consistent, and less predictable than it is in animals. Indeed, in its fundamental form, human territoriality involves little more than a relationship between an individual or group and a particular physical setting, such a relationship being characterized by a feeling of possessiveness and by attempts to control the appearance and use of the setting in question (Brower 1980, 180). In simple terms, then, territoriality for humans serves the purpose of regulating social interaction. According to Brower (1980), individuals want to control social interaction for reasons of personal security (e.g. avoid conflict), self-esteem (e.g. avoid loss of face or status), or self-identity (e.g. avoid challenge to life-style) and this control is facilitated very largely by the *appropriation of space*. In other words, individuals may, for example, delineate boundaries (e.g. erect fences) or adopt territorial signs (e.g. layout a garden) to signal to the rest of the population that they consider they have proprietorial rights over a given area.

Altman (1975) has suggested that this sort of appropriation of space involves three distinct types of territory, based on both the degree of control exercised over a territory by its occupants and the duration of possession. First come *primary* territories where occupancy is permanent and invasion is resented (e.g. the staff room in a school is out-of-bounds to students). Next are *secondary* territories where the individuals concerned have some control despite the fact that there is ostensibly open access (e.g. bars where regulars meet). Finally there are *public* territories where appropriation of space is respected only for the duration of short-term occupancy (e.g. sitting on a park bench). Another, perhaps better, way of looking at human territoriality is to see it as existing at three distinct social levels: the community; the small group; and the individual (Edney 1976). In each case, the main benefit of territoriality is diminished randomness, added order, and hence predictability in the environment.

At the community level, territoriality operates to encourage group identity and bonding, as when urban residents feel a loyalty to their neighbourhood. In British cities this type of territoriality has been found to be particularly strong in four sorts of area: middle-class urban 'villages' where physical distinctiveness lends character to a sought-after area; low status Victorian terraces where time and social similarity have stimulated social interaction; in municipal estates comprised of uniform housing and similar social groups; and in medium density areas with well defined physical boundaries and a high degree of internal cohesion (e.g. interaction based on a shopping centre or a church) (Hall 1982). At the small group level territoriality is most in evidence in the way in which teenage gangs stake out and protect their 'turf' (Porteous 1973). Finally, and perhaps most importantly, individual territoriality is clearly to be seen in an individual's attachment to a 'home' which provides not only physical security, psychic security, and a sense of well-being but also a threat-free environment in which the territory holder can control and manipulate sensory stimulation in such a way as to foster the growth of a sense of identity and the means by which that identity can be communicated to the outside world (Porteous 1976).

Human territoriality is very often taken-for-granted. In fact its function would be drastically reduced if it could not be taken-for-granted. This means that the study of territoriality is often very difficult. In some instances individuals have been required to draw a freehand sketch of what they consider to be their territory. In other cases they have been asked to draw a line on an existing map (Everitt and Cadwallader 1972). Both these techniques have shortcomings: the former demands a certain artistic prowess whereas the latter assumes a map-reading capability that may be lacking in some people. An alternative methodology asks individuals at what point they feel they are on 'home territory' when returning from north, south, east, and west, after a day-outing. The resultant points can be plotted on a map and the size and the shape of the territory interpolated (Walmsley 1976). Also compounding the problem of studying human territoriality is the fact that territorial rights are often communicated through symbols (Rapoport 1977). Such symbols are unlikely to be universal; rather they are likely to be class-specific. Rainwater (1966), for instance, has shown that the most disadvantaged groups in American society are concerned with shelter per se ('the house-as-haven') whereas prosperous working-class households tend to opt for the 'standard all-American package' of materialistic gadgetry. This suggests that the home reflects the dialectic interplay of individuality and society. In other words, there are forces for people to be linked with, and influenced by, the larger community and, at the same time, forces separating them from societal influence (Altman and Gauvain, 1981). Planners need to take stock of these forces, and of the way in which they are resolved differently in different situations, so as to understand more fully the varied nature of human territoriality. For example, there is a good deal of evidence that redevelopment and resettlement can lead to a genuine feeling of grief as the march of progress ruptures territorial attachment to place (Fried 1963; Greenbie 1974).

In addition to fixed territories, humans also ascribe meaning to the space around them irrespective of where they are. In this sense space can be viewed as a non-verbal communication system, often termed 'the silent language' (Hall 1959). Although this communication system encompasses 'fixed feature space' (e.g. architectural design), and 'semi-fixed feature space' (e.g. interior design), most attention has focussed on 'informal space' (the distances maintained by an individual in encounters with others). Sommer (1974, 204) coined the expression 'personal space' to refer to 'the emotionally charged space bubble around each individual which is regarded as private and personal'. Invasion of personal space produces tension and sometimes withdrawal, either actual withdrawal or psychological withdrawal (e.g. averting the eyes). A rather more refined differentiation of the same phenomenon has been proposed by Hall (1966) who identified intimate, personal, social and public distances within the general realm of personal space (Fig. 4.1). The distances quoted in Fig. 4.1 are, of course, culture-specific in that they relate to white, middle-class

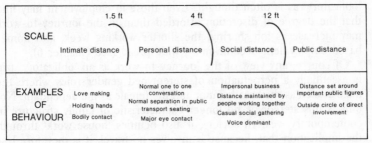

Fig. 4.1 Intimate, personal, social, and public space

American males. Different ranges would certainly apply if attention were switched from a 'non-contact' culture (like the United States) to a 'contact' culture (e. g. Arabs, Latins) where individuals are more tolerant of high densities and engage in frequent touching during social interaction.

4.2 MOBILITY IN THE URBAN ENVIRONMENT

The significance of human territoriality to the understanding of spatial behaviour in the city lies in the fact that it provides individuals with a base, usually the home, from which forays are made. Almost all individuals return to a home each day (although the timing of such a return may vary as, for example, in the case of shift workers). As a result the home base is the starting point for much daily routine. What individuals actually do in their daily routine is 'the result of a complex and variable mix of incentives and constraints serving to mediate choice, often functioning in differentially lagged combinations, with some activities directly traceable to positive choices, and some attributable to negative choices in the sense that constraints overshadow opportunities for choice' (Chapin 1974, 9). In addition to being a blend of choice and constraint, human spatial behaviour within the city can be thought of as a mixture of 'obligatory' and 'discretionary' activity. Although this is a distinction that is often made, the difference between the two categories is rather blurred (Parkes and Thrift 1980, 212). Thus, there can be little doubt that the journey-to-school is an obligatory trip because the law in most countries requires compulsory attendance at school for children in a certain age range. The journey-to-work has similarly been thought of as an obligatory trip on the grounds that most people need to earn money from employment in order to sustain life at an acceptable level. Sadly, however, the idea of the journey-to-work as an obligatory trip has become a cruel joke for increasing numbers of unemployed in the 1970s and 1980s. Obligatory travel, in other words, may not be as 'obligatory' as is often thought. Even those in employment may find that the degree of discretion afforded them in the journey-to-work may increase as job sharing, the shorter working week, and home-based employment become more widespread (see Chapter 6).

Of course, any view of the journey-to-work as an 'obligatory' trip is essentially a perpetuation of stereotyped gender roles where the male is seen as the breadwinner and the female as the dependant. Not only is this stereotype no longer characteristic of family structure in contemporary western society, it also belittles 'house work' through the implication that, because it involves no travel, it is therefore less important (see Section 4.4). In short, great care must be exercised in designating some activities as obligatory and others as discretionary. Take shopping as a final example: shopping is obligatory in the sense that few people in present-day society can provide for all their requirements and most therefore need to buy goods and services from retail outlets. However, consumer behaviour usually involves far more than the mere satisfaction of basic needs; rather individual shoppers tend to vary their behaviour over time, to divide their purchases of particular commodities between competing shopping centres, to buy non-essential items, and to build up images of the retail environment, in such a way as to reflect their income, sex, age, occupation, ethnic affiliation, culture, personality and motivation (Shepherd and Thomas 1980; Walmsley and Lewis 1984, 81–8). Given this degree of variability it is obviously better to think of 'obligatory' and 'discretionary' as relative concepts or as end points on a continuum. Thus, an activity may be deemed discretionary for an individual if, for that individual, the activity involves a greater degree of choice than constraint (Chapin 1974, 38).

The fact that what is discretionary for one person may not be discretionary for another has led many researchers to eschew such distinctions and to concentrate instead on measuring what people actually do, that is, their *overt spatial behaviour*. There are a number of important methodological problems to be overcome in any such investigation, not the least of which involves a decision as to whether to study a very large cross-section of the population interviewed on each day of the week about their activities on the previous day (thereby providing a sample that is representative of each day) or whether to study a much smaller sample of individuals who are required to keep a diary of their activities over a given period (i.e. a longitudinal study). The first strategy, which has been widely adopted, generally produces accurate data (in that few people forget what they did the previous day) but it necessitates a very large sample size (and hence a virtual army of interviewers). The second strategy involves a much more manageable sample size but encounters problems in maintaining interest, and therefore diary entries, the longer the study persists (Nachmias and Nachmias 1976). To a certain extent, this problem can be minimized by paying respondents although this does have the effect of putting up survey costs. Of course both strategies suffer from the weakness that respondents select what they report with a result that there is, for example, an under-reporting of socially unacceptable behaviours (e.g. slothfulness) (Moser and Kalton 1983, 327–30).

Such is the variability of behaviour from individual to individual that researchers can seldom afford the luxury of focussing on individual 'actors'. Instead the tendency is for researchers to seek out differences in behaviour between aggregates of individuals. To this end it has been customary to categorize respondents according to socio-economic and demographic data and then compare and contrast the behaviour patterns of each subgroup. The alternative method of using survey data to derive measures of the individual's complex travel patterns, and then to examine the extent to which socio-economic variables are related to these measures, has proved cumbersome largely because it is difficult to devise descriptive statistics that take stock of the length, timing, and purpose of trips as well as the mode of travel and the question of whether or not the respondent was accompanied (Hanson and Hanson 1981). The population units of most interest in the study of travel behaviour are those 'subsocietal segments which reflect a relatively homogeneous life situation in terms of economic circumstances, ethnicity, stage in the life cycle, and other lifestyle criteria' and, predictably, those that have been studied most are those with possible political importance (Chapin 1974, 11).

According to Chapin (1974) the term 'human activity pattern' can be used to refer to the patterned ways in which aggregates of residents in cities go about their daily activities. For instance, in Chapin's view, it is meaningful to talk about how archetypal persons (e. g. unemployed, male, inner city youth; widowed senior citizen; etc.) pursue their rounds of daily activity. Each human activity pattern is determined by the *propensity* and *opportunity* for the individuals in that particular aggregate to engage in certain activities. Propensity itself depends on 'predisposing' factors (e.g. motivation) and 'preconditioning' factors (e.g. role obligations); opportunity depends on the perception of accessibility to necessary facilities (Dangschat *et al.* 1982) (Fig. 4.2). Chapin had in mind to build up a systems model of environment and behaviour that could be used in planning. To this end he introduced the notion of 'urban activity systems' as 'an

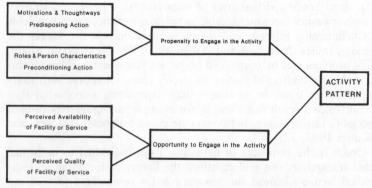

Fig. 4.2 Determinants of activity patterns. *Source*: Chapin (1974)

umbrella kind of term for the patterned way in which individuals, households, institutions, and firms pursue their day-in and day-out affairs in a metropolitan community and interact with one another in time and space' (Chapin 1974, 23). Although the overall systems model proved elusive, Chapin's work was nonetheless useful in providing a mass of information on the range of activities in which people indulge. Specifically Chapin argued that all activities could be classified into one of twelve categories:

1. Main job
2. Eating
3. Shopping
4. Homemaking
5. Family activities
6. Socializing
7. Participation (e.g. church & other organizations)
8. Recreation
9. Watching television
10. Rest and relaxation
11. Miscellaneous
12. Sleep

Moreover, in his major survey of Washington in 1968, Chapin showed that activities varied according to gender, stage in life cycle, and ethnic status with, predictably, the aged having more 'discretionary' activity than the young (Table 4.1).

From the point of view of understanding individual behaviour within cities, it is important to know not only what activities people indulge in but also how far they go away from home base for each activity. Information on the extent of mobility is now available from a variety of travel surveys in a number of countries. A case in point is the British National Travel Survey of 1972/3. Predictably, this showed a distance decay effect with few people travelling long distances. Furthermore, the friction of distance appears to be greater for relatively obligatory travel such as the journey-to-work than for relatively discretionary activities such as entertainment (Department of the Environment 1976) (Fig. 4.3). Unfortunately such major travel surveys are rarely comparable because of their different bases (i.e. some ignore walkers, taxis, trains; some ignore children) (Daniels and Warnes 1980). Moreover, the surveys are usually cross-sectional in the sense that a population is studied in order to ascertain what percentage of total trips are in different categories. This strategy produces data which are situation-specific. Thus, the percentage of total trips that are of an educational nature in a given area is a reflection, above all else, of the number of children in the area. Likewise the tendency, noted in North America, for blacks to have longer

Table 4.1 Time allocation for weekday activities, Washington 1968

| Activity category | Mean duration (hours) | | | | | |
| | White population | | | Black population | | |
	Male (n= 260)	Female (n= 329)	Household head 65+ (n= 109)	Male (n= 123)	Female (n= 259)	Household head 65+ (n= 41)
Main job	5.87	2.66	0.87	4.07	2.35	0.47
Eating	1.38	1.41	1.42	1.01	0.93	1.29
Shopping	0.44	0.74	0.83	0.20	0.46	0.32
Homemaking	1.20	3.82	2.93	1.11	3.84	2.17
Family activities	0.26	0.47	0.26	0.23	0.27	0.09
Socializing	1.09	1.57	1.16	0.95	0.63	0.80
Participation in organizations	0.12	0.23	0.31	0.00	0.13	0.19
Recreation	1.47	1.14	1.85	0.95	0.46	1.42
Watching TV	1.71	1.95	2.98	2.93	2.74	3.35
Rest and relaxation	1.02	0.79	1.55	2.13	1.50	2.50
Miscellaneous	1.66	1.43	1.42	2.77	2.06	1.88
All forms of discretionary activity	5.71	6.19	8.11	7.22	5.75	8.36

Source: Chapin (1974)

journeys-to-work than whites reflects residential segregation of blacks *vis-à-vis* job opportunities rather than differences in travel preferences (Wheeler 1968). In short, it is very difficult to extract anything more than very broad generalizations from a comparison of travel surveys, the principal generalizations being (1) that travel is constrained by the friction of distance and (2) that the movements in progress at any one moment will depend on the time of day, the day of the week, and the season of the year (Daniels and Warnes 1980, 32).

Probably the most studied of all temporal variations in travel behaviour is that relating to the time of day. For example, it has been widely established that work trips peak in the morning and evening, with a lesser peak at midday, shopping trips peak in the morning, drop away during lunchtime, and peak again in the afternoon, and social trips peak in the evening. A detailed attempt to take stock of the way in which behaviour varies with time of day was made in a study of over 1500 randomly selected respondents in Halifax (Canada) (Janelle and Goodchild 1983). This study divided the day into six activity

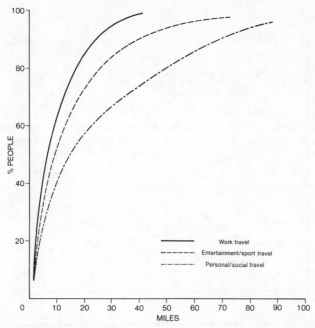

Fig. 4.3 The friction of distance in different sorts of travel in Britain, 1972–3. *Source*: Calculated from data in Department of the Environment (1976)

phases and specified a time at which it was thought that participation in each activity phase would be at a maximum:

Activity	Time of maximum participation
Sleeping	0200 hours
Morning phase of worktime	0910 hours
Lunchtime	1215 hours
Afternoon phase of worktime	1500 hours
Early evening discretionary time	1900 hours
Late evening activities	2230 hours

Respondents then stated their location at each of the specified times. This enabled Janelle and Goodchild to calculate indices of dissimilarity and location quotients to describe the 'spread' of different population subgroups at different times: the former measures segregation between subgroups (a score of 0.0 indicating that the proportional representation of each subgroup in each geographical zone is the same) and the latter measures relative concentration and thus

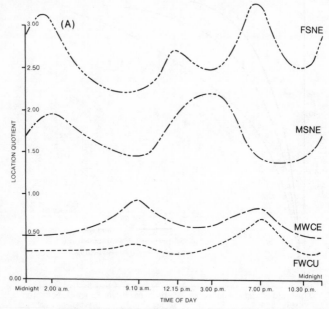

LEGEND: F - Female, M - Male, W - Married S - Single C - Children N - No children E - Employed U - Unemployed

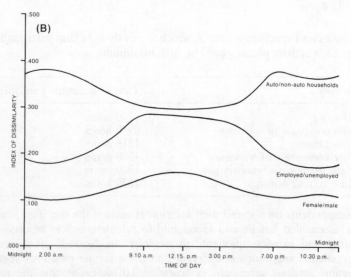

Fig. 4.4 Temporal variations in activity patterns in Halifax, Canada. *Source*: Janelle and Goodchild (1983)

describes how subgroups alter their locational pattern throughout the day (a score of 1.0 indicating that a subgroup has the same level of concentration as the population at large). Figure 4.4a shows very considerable differences in concentration for the area around Dalhousie University according to gender, employment, and the presence or absence of children. Clearly, single unencumbered members of the workforce are at all times much more concentrated. Moreover the single have very much more variability in their location at different times of the day than do the married. In terms of dissimilarity, Figure 4.4b indicates that the dissimilarity in location between all males and all females is limited in extent and does not vary greatly during the day. Conversely, there is marked dissimilarity between the location of the employed and the unemployed during the working day, and very pronounced dissimilarity between car owners and non-car owners, particularly in the evening.

Table 4.2 A classification of urban travel

Category		Examples
I ECONOMIC	a. earning a living	1. To and from work
		2. In the course of work
	b. acquiring goods and services	3. To and from shops and outlets for personal services
		4. In the course of shopping and personal business
II SOCIAL		5. To and from homes of friends and relatives
		6. To and from non-home rendezvous
III EDUCATIONAL		7. To and from schools, colleges, and evening institutes
IV RECREATIONAL AND LEISURE		8. To and from places of recreation and entertainment
		9. In the course of recreation: walks, rides
V CULTURAL		10. To and from places of worship
		11. To and from places of non-leisure group activity (e.g. political meetings)

Source: Daniels and Warnes (1980)

The alternative to looking at where people are at a given time is to divide activity trips according to purpose. Innumerable classifications of trips have been devised. One of the best is that suggested by Daniels and Warnes (1980) (Table 4.2). Unfortunately, however, all such classifications have trouble in coping with the fact that a great many trips are *multipurpose* trips. In other words, there are immense problems, other than those of sampling, in describing the travel behaviour of aggregates of individuals. As a result, it may be more fruitful to look at what leads individual actors to behave as they do. This raises a fundamental problem that has to be faced by any researcher interested in the interaction between people and their physical surroundings, namely the question of whether it is more efficient to study the generalized patterns that emerge in aggregated accounts of behaviour or more efficient to look at individual decision-making processes (Walmsley and Lewis 1984, 37–40).

There is no easy solution to this problem. Advocates of the study of aggregate behaviour see individual spatial behaviour as so complex as to be indeterminate and therefore impossible to study. In their view, it is better to study the generalized patterns that emerge in aggregate behaviour than it is to look at individual thought processes. Studies of individual behaviour are deemed to be impossible and misleading because what is important to society can be seen in aggregate patterns (Watson 1978). The opposite view holds that the study of behaviour in the aggregate is inadequate. The fact that such studies ignore individual activity means that they cannot hope to establish causal relationships between environment and behaviour and hence are of limited explanatory and predictive power. The fact of the matter is, of course, that the two types of inquiry serve different purposes: aggregate analyses are justified when human behaviour is indeterminate, or highly repetitious, or highly constrained by space, time, or environment whereas studies of individual motivations are justified when the goal is to understand what causes behaviour to take a certain form (Watson 1978, 44).

Unfortunately, there have been relatively few studies of mobility within the city from the point of view of understanding individual thought processes. One exception is to be found in the work of Garling *et al.* (1984) who proposed that individuals build up 'plans' which determine how they will behave in the social and physical environment. Such plans are really part and parcel of general cognitive maps (see Chapter 2). Indeed, according to Garling *et al.*, a cognitive map comprises three interrelated elements: (1) places (which are recorded by name, characteristics, and function); (2) relations between places (assessed in terms of metrics and proximity); and (3) travel plans (which contain information about ordered subsets of places together with details of how to get from place to place).

Travel plans, in other words, serve to enable people to reach desired destinations without having to invest too much effort and, as such, they are of great importance in routine travel behaviour. Such travel plans are not, however, executed automatically. Rather they require monitoring and this is achieved by individuals recognizing places, keeping track of their location when moving about, and anticipating features in the environment.

The ideas put forward by Garling *et al.* are, of course, very speculative. Fundamentally, they amount to little more than a series of assumptions, the validity of which has not yet been empirically tested. Their central argument is that cognitive maps (and therefore environmental awareness) influence travel behaviour (which in turn provides feedback information that enables the cognitive map to be modified). This is not a new idea. Indeed, over twenty years ago Wolpert (1965) suggested that individual travel patterns, in his case migration, could only be understood by taking account of the 'action spaces' of the individuals involved. In this sense the term 'action space' refers to the set of places of which an individual is aware. Later, a distinction was drawn by, among others, Horton and Reynolds (1971) between 'action space' and 'activity space', with the latter delimiting the places with which an individual interacts on an everyday basis. The terms 'action space' and 'activity space' have been used widely, and sometimes loosely, ever since. On occasions the terminology has been changed slightly. In all cases, however, it seems that both the action space and activity space of city dwellers take the form of a *wedge*, centred on the home and focussed on the central business district. This was most clearly shown in Potter's (1979) study of consumer spatial behaviour in Stockport (England). In this case, both the 'information field' (roughly equivalent to action space) and the 'usage field' (roughly equivalent to activity space) formed wedges, the latter being nested within the former (Fig. 2.6). Generally speaking, the angle subtended by both the information field and the usage field increased with an increase in socio-economic status to the extent where high status groups had information fields with angles of over 180° at the central business district (indicating that the individuals concerned knew well over half of the city in question).

It would not be possible to delimit activity spaces and action spaces were it not for the fact that much spatial behaviour in cities is routine and repetitive. Indeed, the average urban dweller is very much a creature of routine who finds it difficult, or perhaps simply unnecessary, to change both attitudes and habits. For most people, urban reality is an unspectacular procession of little things which together define the fuzzy outline of a friendship network, an attitudinal set, a lifestyle, and a familiar place (Ley 1983, 99). In other words, an activity space is more than just a physical territory; it is also very much a 'social space'. The term 'social space' is however a troublesome one because of the wide variety of meanings ascribed to it in social science. For example, it can signify 'social areas' defined on the basis of population characteristics, the sense of belonging that sometimes emerges between a group and an area, the conceptual 'sociological space' in which individuals can be arranged on the basis of friendship ties, and a 'behavioural space' defined on the basis of activity and circulation patterns (Buttimer 1972). It is this last definition which is of most relevance here and it is the routine of everyday behaviour that generates such social space. Short distance, everyday, intra-urban journeys may be mundane but in total they have a great impact on the structure and development of urban areas (Daniels and Warnes 1980, xvi).

4.3 TIME-BUDGET STUDIES

The routine which characterizes mobility within the city involves the use of *time* as well as the use of *space*. This was clearly shown in Janelle and Goodchild's (1983) study of how different subgroups of the population occupied different locations at different times during the day (Fig. 4.4). Interesting as this work was, it said nothing about how individuals allocated time to different activities. Indeed individual time allocation tends to have been a relatively neglected field of study in spite of the fact that the pattern of time allocation adopted by the people in a given area is vitally important to transport and energy demand, to urban design, and to family organization. One ambitious attempt to formulate a general theory of individual time allocation has come from Tonn (1984). Basically Tonn was interested in the psychological motivations that underlie behaviour, how individuals choose between different activities, and how different activities are co-ordinated to form a lifestyle. In Tonn's view, the vast range of motivations that underlie behaviour can be classified as belonging to one of three irreducible categories. These are motivations relating to *physiological health* (which find expression in activities such as sleeping, eating, resting, exercising, and attending to personal hygiene requirements), motivations relating to *sexual and sensual desires* (and these find expression in activities such as sex, work, hobbies, athletics, and watching television), and motivations that lead individuals to seek to satisfy a *desire for group belonging* (which manifests itself in work-based activities, in shopping, in general socializing, and in the joining of organizations of one sort or another). Tonn's assumption is that an individual's basic motivations in life determine how that individual uses time. Clearly, an activity can serve to satisfy more than one motivation, as for instance when social activities (such as joining a theatre party) can satisfy both an urge for group belonging and a desire for sensual arousal. Similarly, recreation, which is often dismissed as a discretionary activity, can be thought of as fulfilling a basic need for exercise, stimulation, and belonging. In this sense, then, recreation may not be a self-indulgent activity so much as an attempt to satisfy basic motivations and thereby maintain a sense of well-being. Indeed, from Tonn's perspective, many activities can be seen as being motivated by sensual desires, particularly those activities that satisfy basic human curiosity and the need for mental stimulation.

Given these insights into motivation, Tonn turned his attention to the question of how individuals choose between different activities. Here he introduced the concept of 'nurturement' to denote the value which a behaviour yields towards satisfying one or more of the three basic motivations. This concept is very similar to the economist's notion of 'utility' and to the notion of 'place utility' introduced by Wolpert (1965) as a measure of the attractiveness of alternative locations to potential migrants. As such, it suffers from some of the same weaknesses, notably the fact that it is extremely difficult to measure. Moreover, it is not entirely clear whether individuals strive to maximize 'nurturement' (and thereby optimize their use of time), whether they have a hierarchy of needs which are filled sequentially, or whether they merely seek to strike a balance between competing activities. Indeed, Tonn (1984, 205) himself made some rather contentious suggestions in this regard as, for example, when he remarked that unskilled workers, in comparison to skilled workers and professionals, may allocate more time to leisure activities which yield high internal satisfaction so as to make up for the low satisfaction derived from their jobs.

One of the main reasons why it is difficult to study the way in which individuals choose between activities relates to the fact that what individuals actually end up doing does not simply reflect their preferences. Rather it reflects, to a considerable degree, the *constraints* under which they are operating. These constraints take many forms. Some can be thought of as *pure constraints* in that they relate to the lack of time, lack of money, lack of energy, or lack of opportunity to engage in a certain activity. Other constraints relate to an individual's *personal situation* (e.g. family commitments) and *personality* (notably the ability to accept or adapt to the conditions necessary for participation in a given activity). *Social conditions* can also constrain an individual, as when society dictates the rules (e.g. age of entry) for certain activities or when general socialization influences what is deemed an acceptable hobby. Finally, much activity is constrained by *uncertainty* surrounding the success or otherwise of the activity (e.g. inability to predict with certainty such things as weather and economic costs) (Tonn 1984).

Individuals synthesize motivations, behavioural strategy, and constraints into what can be thought of as a *behavioural schedule* (Tonn 1984). Certain parts of this schedule can be relatively fixed. For example, about one-third of housework activities, especially those related to meals, occur in a fixed time sequence (Berk and Berk 1980). Of course the key problem for individuals in deciding on a schedule is that of calculating how long they can do an activity before satisfaction starts to fall to unacceptable levels. Unfortunately Tonn's theoretical paper gives no clues in this direction. Instead recourse must be made to empirical surveys of actual time allocation. The most thorough-going study of time allocation yet undertaken was the Multinational Comparative Time-Budget Research Project (Szalai

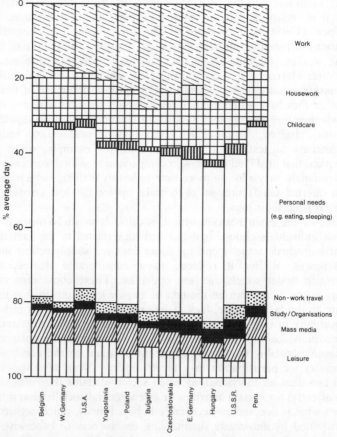

Fig. 4.5 International time-budget comparisons. *Source*: Calculated from data in Robinson *et al.* (1972)

1972). This involved almost 30,000 interviews in twelve countries (Belgium, Bulgaria, Czechoslovakia, West Germany, East Germany, France, Hungary, Peru, Poland, USA, USSR, and Yugoslavia). The project focussed on cities with a population of between 30,000 and 280,000 and it sought to answer the question 'who does what (and what else simultaneously) during the day, for how long, how often, at what time, in what order, where, and with whom?' Predictably, the survey resulted in a mountain of information. Figure 4.5 summarizes the time spent on various activities in the different countries. Clearly, the amount of time spent at work is greater in eastern-bloc countries than in western countries. The converse is true for 'free time' activities. For some activities there is very considerable variability from country to country with no clear overall pattern. The amount of time devoted to household care is a case in point. In some instances the differences between countries are substantial. For example, in regard to the total time devoted to the mass media (principally television), the country with the highest indulgence (USA) had a time allocation that was' 73% greater than that of the country with the lowest figure (Bulgaria). Even for something as basic as catering for personal needs (primarily eating and sleeping), the time allocation in West Germany was 14% greater than the time allocation in the USSR. Given these international differences, it is perhaps unwise to calculate average figures. Nevertheless, such an exercise does produce interesting results. For example, Robinson *et al.* (1972), have shown that, on average and on workdays, employed men have 21% of their waking hours available to them as 'free time'. The figure for working women is only 15%, no doubt because working women more often than not carry the major burden of housework. Housewives had 25% of their waking hours available as 'free time' on workdays. On non-workdays the comparable figures were 56% for employed men, 40% for employed women, and 30% for housewives (for whom Sundays were counted as non-workdays). Clearly, housewives have a more continuous burden of committed time than the rest of the population whereas men are most favoured in terms of free time. Interestingly, there are very few differences between men and women in the way in which free time is spent; overall, about 40% of free time is devoted to the mass media, about 10% to education, religion or other organisational membership, and about 50% to socializing, sport, recreation and rest.

Of particular interest to the study of spatial behaviour is the question of how much free time is actually spent *away* from home. According to Robinson *et al.* (1972), the amount varies considerably: on a working day the average single, employed male spends 32% of his free time away from home, in contrast to only 16% for a married housewife with children. Married males with children fare only a little

better with 18% of their free time away from home on a typical
working day. In other words, the notion of 'leisure' time may be
singularly inappropriate for some sections of the population, notably
women (Anderson 1975). It should be remembered, of course, that
free time activities away from home do not take up as much time as
work activities away from home. A detailed study of activity patterns
in Osnabruck (West Germany), for example, revealed that, on average,
34% of the day was spent sleeping, 37% was spent on activities
within the home, and 29% was spent on activities away from the home
(Von Rosenbladt 1972). Of this time away from home, work accounted
for no less that 52%. Approximately 30% was spent on what were
labelled 'discretionary' activities (6% shopping, 2% personal services
(e.g. health care), 7% leisure, 6% walking, 9% social visiting) and
a further 18% on 'other activities'. Precisely what activity people do
is of course influenced by accessibility. Von Rosenbladt investigated
the effect of increased distance (and therefore increased travel costs)
on mobility and his results are shown in Table 4.3. Some activities
(e.g. shopping) are such that the volume can be reduced if travel costs
increase. The net effect in such cases is that there is no increase in
the time or money devoted to that activity. Conversely some activities
(e.g. health care) cannot be decreased in volume as the costs of travel
increase. Maintenance of these activities in the face of increased
distance therefore imposes additional costs on an individual.

Distance is not the only constraint that influences how people use
their time. This was recognized by Hägerstrand and his co-workers
in what has become known as the *Lund School of Time–Geography*.

Table 4.3 The impact of increased distance on activity participation

Activity	Total population	Youth	Employed men	Employed women	Housewives
Shopping	−	−	+	?	?
Services	+	−	−	+	+
Leisure	−	+	−	−	−
Walking	−	+	−	−	−
Visits	+	+	+	?	+

A minus sign (−) indicates a Type 1 impact, a plus sign (+) a Type 2
impact, and a question mark (?) an uncertain impact.

Type 1 impact: The volume of activities is reduced so that total distance
costs do not rise, or do so only slightly
Type 2 impact: The volume of activities is at least maintained with a result
that increased costs occur

Source: Von Rosenbladt (1972)

According to Hägerstrand, any study of mobility will be inadequate unless it considers time as well as space. This is an important point because all too often social science has approached time from the point of view of comparative statics, that is to say, behaviour has been compared at various points in time without due emphasis being given to consideration of what time means for the individuals involved (Walmsley and Lewis 1984, 76). The appropriate way to take stock of the manner in which time is inextricably involved in human behaviour is, according to Hägerstrand, to view the individual as describing a *life-path* in *time-space*. This conceptualization can operate at a variety of scales (e.g. day-path, week-path, year-path etc.). For example, Fig. 4.6a shows the day-path of a hypothetical individual. Places (work, home) that are essentially points (in that movement within them is inconsequential) are displayed as vertical lines. Because it consumes both time and space, travel is displayed as a

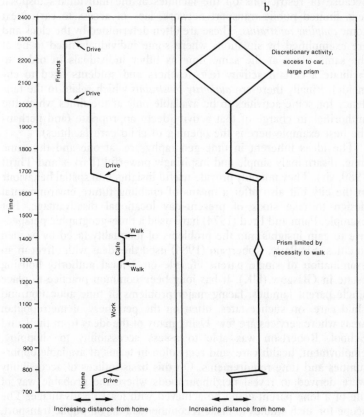

Fig. 4.6 A one-day life-path in time-space

diagonal line. This type of representation of a life-path can be used to investigate *possible* as well as *actual* behaviours. This is done by introducing the idea of a *time-space prism*. This is illustrated in Fig. 4.6b. If it is assumed that the individual in question cannot leave home before 0745 hours and must return by 1700 hours and that work commitments demand attention between 0800 and 1630 hours (except for a lunch break), then some indication of possible activities can be gained by drawing prisms to reveal how far and how long the individual in question can go between prearranged commitments. Obviously, the range of potential activity locations is influenced by the amount of available time and by the mode of travel. In short, the size of the prism is influenced by a variety of constraints which, according to Hägerstrand (1970), fall into three categories. The first are *capability constraints* which limit an individual's activities, either because of biological make-up (e.g. the need for sleep, food) or because of restrictions on the facilities at the individual's disposal (e.g. limited public transport network, lack of access to car). Next come *coupling constraints*. These are often determined by the clock and are exemplified by situations where some individuals need to be at the same place at the same time as other individuals in order to facilitate a certain activity (e.g. teachers and students need to co-incide). Finally there are *authority constraints* which relate to the tendency for some activities to be available only at the times which the authorities in charge of that activity deem appropriate (and perhaps the best example here is the opening of child care facilities).

The ideas inherent in time-geography are, at one and the same time, disarmingly simple and inspiringly powerful (Parkes and Thrift 1980, xiv). They not only provide useful insights into spatial behaviour in the city but also offer a means of enabling future environmental design to take stock of present-day locational disadvantage. For example, Palm and Pred (1974) have used a time-geographic perspective to gain insights into the problems of inequality faced by women in cities. Similarly, Robertson (1984) used the ideas with effect in an examination of single parent lifestyle on a local authority housing estate in Glasgow (UK). It has long been common practice to place single parent families, facing major problems of time allocation and child care, on such estates, often on the periphery of metropolitan areas where services are few. Using many of the ideas from the Lund School, Robertson was able to assess accessibility to shopping, employment, health care, and recreation in terms of available opportunities and time requirements. On this basis indices of accessibility were derived to reveal neighbourhoods where the probable way of life of a lone parent could be achieved with least disadvantage. The scope for such studies to make recommendations on public transport, opening hours of facilities, and public housing policies is enormous.

However, any consideration of time-geography must of course take stock of the fact that what is at issue is an evolving field of social scientific inquiry. In particular, there have been recent attempts to set the basic ideas of time-geography within the broader general field of social theory, thereby linking the study of individual behaviour to writings on 'social reproduction' and 'structuration' (Pred 1981). Further development of this field may cast a good deal of light on the interplay between opportunity and constraint in the day-to-day life of the city dweller.

4.4 CONSTRAINTS ON SPATIAL BEHAVIOUR

Early studies of interaction between people and their physical surroundings soon revealed that behaviour could not be explained simply by looking at the objective environment. It was therefore proposed that it was the 'environment as perceived' rather than the real world which influenced behaviour. Unfortunately studies of 'environmental perception' quickly showed this to be a rather naive proposition; the 'world-in-the-head' proved extremely difficult to define and measure and hence its supposed influence on spatial behaviour amounted to little more than an article of faith that could be neither proved or disproved. In place of an emphasis on 'environmental perception', researchers adopting a behavioural approach to the study of people-environment relations began to talk of attitudes, images, preferences, and of decision-making strategies such as satisficing and bounded rationality (Walmsley and Lewis 1984, 3–15). In other words, it was argued, sometimes only implicitly, that spatial behaviour could be explained by reference to antecedent psychological conditions. When even these models failed to find consistent relationships between spatial behaviour and its psychological antecedents, there arose a tendency for social scientists to attribute the lack of clear cut findings to the operation of constraints which frustrated individuals in the pursuit of their most preferred behaviour. In short, constraints were seen as something which muddies the water, thereby preventing researchers from getting a clear view of desired behaviour. This situation has now changed somewhat but only recently have constraints been examined in their own right. The Lund School certainly helped with this but perhaps the most important contribution was made by Desbarats (1983).

Desbarats began with the observation that the effectiveness of behavioural approaches to the study of people–environment interaction ultimately hinges upon the demonstration of a substantial and consistent causal link between human subjectivity and behaviour and yet this link, to date, remains elusive. The implication that Desbarats draws from this is that there may well be something wrong with both the models that have been used to analyse interaction between people and the environment, and with the way in which spatial behaviour has been measured. In particular she is critical of models based on utility maximization and volitional control because they have encouraged an undue emphasis on the attitudinal determinants of behaviour to the detriment of non-attitudinal components. Thus the traditional approach to the study of movement within the city has been to view spatial behaviour as a dependent variable and to treat information, place, utility, attitudes and preferences as independent variables. Supposedly independent variables influence dependent variables. In reality, of course, the links are very seldom clear cut, largely because individual decision-makers take stock not only of their own attitudes but also of the perceived feasibility of a course of action as assessed both in terms of what society expects of them (i.e. what is deemed appropriate) and in terms of what the environment permits. 'The point here is that spatial choice may bear little relation to movement behaviour and that movement behaviour, in turn, may say more about social structure than about individual preference and choice' (Desbarats 1983, 347). People reliant on public housing, for example, often have a very limited residential choice (viz. the houses available when the individuals reach the top of the waiting list).

Generally speaking, recursive behaviour (e.g. shopping) tends to be slightly better explained by psychological antecedents than does infrequent behaviour (e.g. intra-urban migration) but in neither case is the level of explanation very high. As a result Desbarats (1983, 343) argued that researchers should change the specification of behavioural models of movement 'so that they more adequately account for the mechanisms by which human subjectivity mediates the objective constraints placed on movement behaviour by the social and physical environments'. In other words, models of spatial behaviour should account for inconsistencies between thought and action, not ignore them. Desbarats therefore proposed an integrated conceptual framework to incorporate the mediating and determining role of structural, social, and institutional constraints on spatial behaviour. In this sense, a constraint is anything that produces behaviour that is discrepant with attitudes and preferences. Desbarats' inspiration came from the psychological theory of *reasoned action*. According to this theory, *behaviour* is influenced by *intentions*. Intentions themselves are influenced by *attitudes* and *social norms* which, in turn, are influenced by *beliefs* (Fishbein and Ajzen 1975). In other words, the theory proposes that individuals have beliefs about the environment (e.g. a belief that suburb X is pleasant). Evaluation of such beliefs leads to the formation of attitudes (e.g. favourably disposed to living in X). Such attitudes form the basis for intentions (e.g. intention to buy a

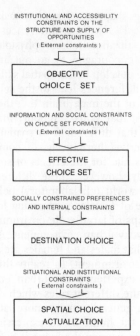

INSTITUTIONAL AND ACCESSIBILITY
CONSTRAINTS ON THE
STRUCTURE AND SUPPLY OF
OPPORTUNITIES
(External constraints)

OBJECTIVE
CHOICE   SET

INFORMATION AND SOCIAL CONSTRAINTS
ON CHOICE SET FORMATION
(External constraints)

EFFECTIVE
CHOICE SET

SOCIALLY CONSTRAINED PREFERENCES
AND INTERNAL CONSTRAINTS

DESTINATION CHOICE

SITUATIONAL AND INSTITUTIONAL
CONSTRAINTS
(External constraints)

SPATIAL CHOICE
ACTUALIZATION

Fig. 4.7 Constraints on spatial behaviour. *Source*: Desbarats (1983)

house in X), but only after stock has been taken of both society's notions of what is proper behaviour (e.g. would the prospective migrant be acceptable in X?) and of the extent of the individual's desire to comply into society's norms. Thus constraints influence behaviour in four ways: they constrict the opportunity set; they mould the formation of attitudes and preferences; they induce the expression of choices that do not conform to preference; and they prevent choice actualization (Desbarats 1983, 350) (Fig. 4.7).

The constraints discussed by Desbarats apply, in principle, to all individuals. In practice, however, certain people are more constrained in their spatial behaviour than others. The number of groups affected in this way is considerable; for example, racial prejudice, religious bigotry, and physical handicap can all inhibit spatial behaviour. There are two groups, however, for whom constraints are particularly note-worthy: women and the aged. The former are significant because, although comprising half the population, their spatial behaviour has been ignored to an astonishing degree. The aged are significant because they are the most rapidly growing section of the population in most countries.

There is ample evidence that males differ from females in spatial skills. For instance, males generally outperform females at rotating drawings, recognizing shapes, orientation tasks, and wayfinding in printed mazes (Harris 1981). Such differences are usually explained in terms of either socialization or neurophysiology. That is, one view holds that males are encouraged to go out and explore more than females and therefore develop better spatial skills while the other view holds that hormonal differences lead to the selective development of the right hemisphere of the male brain (i.e. the hemisphere with the greatest bearing on spatial skills). Support for the latter view is to be found in the fact that differences in spatial ability rarely become apparent before puberty (alternatively, of course, this could simply mean that it takes a while for the effects of socialization to manifest themselves). Strangely, however, these different spatial abilities are not reflected in real world (cf. laboratory) behaviour. There is, for example, no evidence of females performing less well than males in drawing cognitive maps of large-scale environments, or in navigation tasks within the everyday urban environment. As a result, it has been commonly assumed that males and females are alike when it comes to interaction with the environment. In reality this is far from the case.

Men and women experience the urban environment differently mainly as a result of the different roles which they play (Boles 1983). For example, women generally invest more labour in the home and place more value on the home as an expression of personality than do men. Thus, to many women the home is both a physical space and a value-laden symbol (Saegert and Winkel 1981). Of course such differences are not biological so much as social in origin. This needs a little explanation. Metropolitan areas are essentially man-made phenomena in the sense that they are the product of male-dominated planning professions (interpreting the term 'planning' to encompass not only the design process but also the political, administrative, and market forces that do much to shape cities). In other words, the built environment is created in accordance with a set of ideas about how society works, about who does what, and about who goes where (Matrix 1984). Space therefore reflects social organization but, of course, once it becomes bounded and shaped, it is no longer a neutral background but rather exerts its own influence on behaviour (Ardener 1981). The built environment therefore tends to incorporate sexist assumptions about family life and the role of women. The growth of suburbia, for instance, rested largely on the notion that the woman's place is in the home. Women, therefore, as a user group, have tended to bear most heavily the penalties of suburban development (Wright 1981).

It would, of course, be wrong to see the growth of suburbia in conspiratorial terms because a move to the suburbs was widely welcomed by many women happy to accept the benefits of privacy, safety and space (especially in the child-rearing stage of the life cycle) and the promise of active involvement in local affairs. Nevertheless, the drawbacks of suburban living must be acknowledged, particularly as these affect women (Michelson 1977). There is of course nothing new in the argument that suburbia sometimes fails to live up to the ideal expected of it (see Berger, 1960; Gans 1967). What is new, perhaps, is the mounting evidence of the extent of loneliness among suburban women, especially those 'trapped' at home by the need to care for young children (Popenoe 1981). This loneliness is most intense for women outside the paid workforce and living on vast estates characterized by a high proportion of public or low income housing, single car households, and poor public transport (and hence reliance on private motor vehicles). For example, a survey of women in a peripheral public housing estate in Sydney (Australia) revealed that 47% admitted to being 'lonely' and 30% had no friends within walking distance (Sarkissian and Doherty 1984). Likewise, there is Canadian evidence that non-working women get out of the house during the week only half as often as working men and hence have fewer opportunities to make friends (Cichocki 1981). In some instances, the differences may be even more striking; a survey of Melbourne (Australia) showed that, other than for child care and shopping, 18% of women left the home in daylight once a week or less (Anderson 1975). Admittedly women have been very inventive in overcoming these problems of isolation in some places (Genovese 1980; Stimpson *et al.* 1981) but the fact remains that the suburban environment confines women in ways it does not confine men (Wekerle 1980) (although there are obvious dangers in extrapolating from individual case studies to suburbia in general, given the very varied form that suburban development can take). Thus women pay a higher cost than any other family member for single family suburban dwelling (Wekerle *et al.* 1981).

Historically women formed an integral part of communal work spaces. However with urbanization they tended to become removed from such situations and relegated to the private space of the individual home (Wekerle 1980). This presents problems, even for those women who accept the role of housewife and mother. Low density urban sprawl means that the distance between facilities like shops and doctors is considerable. This might not matter if women were mobile. In fact they are not. The 1978/9 British National Travel Survey showed that only 30% of women held a driver's licence (cf. 68% of men) (Pickup 1984). Moreover where women have a licence, the first call on the car is not infrequently for male work. These problems of accessibility are now becoming more acute as the structure and organization of society alters. Changes in retailing, notably the decline of the corner store, have for instance exacerbated travel problems for the immobile suburban woman (and this is a critical issue given that, in some areas, up to 85% of shoppers are women (Bowlby 1978)). More important, though, is the fact that the stereotyped suburban family is changing. Today, in Britain, only one in nine households consists of a man with a paid job, a woman without one, and children under sixteen (Matrix 1984). More and more married women are returning to the paid workforce, to the point where about 40% of American women work outside the home. Unfortunately, the typical land-use patterns of the modern city, with separation of home, work and services, accommodate only minimally to women's changing roles (Wekerle 1981; Roistacher and Young 1980). The suburbanization of jobs has benefited the motorist rather than the public transport user; it has therefore worked to the disadvantage of women who are disproportionately represented among the latter group (Wekerle 1980). It is not surprising, therefore, that many women with child care commitments are effectively barred from much of the full-time labour market on the grounds of time-space constraints (Pickup 1984; Pred and Palm 1978). It is simply not possible for individuals with commitments before and after school to travel to and from job locations that are dispersed away from the main lines of public transport. As a result, women tend to be forced into part-time employment (to overcome time constraints) and have to face a range of job locations that is often restricted to the immediate environment or the central business district (to overcome constraints on geographical accessibility). Such problems of accessibility are, of course, multiplied manifold for single mothers who, because of lack of access to mortgage finance and other reasons, are frequently effectively debarred from much of the privately owned housing market and thus are often forced to restrict their residential choice to limited parts of the city (i.e. those parts in which the rental market is prominent).

It would be wrong to view all women as equally constrained in their spatial behaviour. There are nevertheless useful generalizations to be made. The same is true of older people. The term 'aged' is of course a vague one. To be precise one should really speak of biological age (i.e. the degree to which physiological functioning has declined), psychological age (i.e. the adaptive capacity and self awareness of the individual), and social age (i.e. the roles played by the individual in the community) (Golant 1972). There are two conflicting theories on what happens to individuals as they grow old and retire from the workforce. The first, *disengagement theory*, argues that, in the later stages of life, an individual withdraws or disengages, both behaviourally and emotionally, from the pre-existing social system, thereby bringing about a constriction in his or her activity space (Cumming and Henry 1961). The alternative view is contained in *activity theory* which holds that 'normal' ageing involves the maintenance, for as long as possible, of the activities and attitudes of middle age (substitutes being found for things, such as work, that have to be given up) (Cavan *et al.* 1949). Yet another view holds that there are at least four sorts of old people: *relaxers* who on retirement loosen social ties, minimize social constraints, and simply enjoy their free time; *do-gooders* who are the heirs to the work ethic insofar as they substitute the job of organizing aged society for their pre-existing work role; *joiners* who think that success in old age will be a function of the extent to which they join organizations and keep busy; and *waiters* who lead rather empty lives devoid of much meaning (Fontana 1977).

Despite disagreement among researchers as to the extent of participation by aged individuals in a range of activities, there is general consensus that one of the most salient characteristics of advancing years is decreasing geographical mobility. Golant (1972), for example, in a survey of Toronto (Canada), showed that 58% of respondents aged 55–64 had made a trip out of the home in the previous 24 hours in contrast to a figure of only 31% for those aged 65 and over. Likewise the average number of vehicular trips per day was 1.49 for the 55–64 age group and 0.84 for the 65 and over. This fall-off in mobility with age can be exacerbated by either poor health or low morale, and applies not only to the number of trips but also to the distance travelled with community facilities generally being used in inverse proportion to the distance separating them from the individuals concerned (Herbert and Peace 1980). The corollary to this is that the aged spend a very high proportion of their time within the local environment. It is important to ask, therefore, what effect the local environment has on their behaviour and morale. Rowles (1978) investigated this question carefully in an in-depth study of a small group of old people living in one street of a working class inner city neighbourhood of Lanchester (USA). His work suggests that the aged experience the environment in four modalities. The first is *action* which involves physical movement in space. A distinction can be drawn here between the immediate environment (where basic locomotion is the critical concern), the everyday environment (notably the home and neighbourhood), and the occasional environment (places visited on holidays). The second modality is usually labelled *orientation* and involves the frame of reference that individuals build up in their minds for differentiating the environment into paths and landmarks that can be used in way-finding. The third modality is *feeling*. This encompasses the sentimental attachment (or dislike) that individuals feel towards certain places. The final modality of environmental experience is, according to Rowles, *fantasy*. This is a vicarious form of geographical experience where individuals enrich their life by imagining themselves in locales that are displaced in either time or space (e.g. reminiscing about the past or dreaming about distant relatives). As an individual ages, changes occur within and among these modalities. Thus action is reduced with age leading to a constriction of the environment experienced through that modality (i.e. a reduced activity space). Conversely, feelings for certain parts of the environment may be intensified, as when a sense of sentimental attachment grows for a place that is no longer able to be visited. Likewise, the importance of fantasy as a mode of environmental experience increases with age, often as a compensation for increasing immobility. Changes in orientation are less obvious and there is little evidence to suggest that the aged have other than normal cognitive schemata for differentiating the environments with which they come into contact (Ohta and Kirasic 1983). Other evidence suggests that old people tend to be friendly with old people and so the more aged there are in an area, the more friends they will have (Rosow 1967). This suggests that housing policies which group the aged together (and therefore separate them from the rest of the community) might not be the disaster that is sometimes expected because they might encourage local interaction at a time when travel over greater distances is inhibited. The whole question of housing is, however, an institutional one that is outside the scope of this book. The point to be noted here is simply that older people, like suburban women, are constrained in terms of their mobility and therefore live out their lives in a much more restricted environment than is the case for the working population.

The influence of place on behaviour

The net effect of the many constraints that inhibit the spatial behaviour of the city dweller is to restrict the activity of urban residents very much to the local environment. It is not uncommon, for example, for individuals to spend between two-thirds and three-quarters of their total time, and a majority of their waking hours, in and around the home and its immediate environs. For some groups, such as young children, women outside the paid workforce, and the elderly, the proportions may be much higher. It is important to explore, therefore, the impact of the local environment on the behaviour and attitudes of the city dweller. This can be achieved by looking at the general effect of the local neighbourhood and at the extent to which certain types of places contribute to stress, mental illness, alienation and crime.

5.1 THE INFLUENCE OF NEIGHBOURHOOD ON WELL-BEING

Perhaps the starting point for any discussion of the influence of the local environment on well-being should be an examination of why city dwellers choose, or are forced, to live in certain environments. The literature on residential choice is enormous (see Ley 1983, 237–79; Knox 1982, 112–66) but in very simple terms it appears that the 85% of households who move from one residence to another for voluntary as opposed to involuntary reasons (e.g. eviction), do so because they perceive that the opportunities offered by a new residence outweigh the satisfaction to be derived from the present residence. Principal among the characteristics considered by potential migrants are attributes of the neighbourhood (e.g. social status, friendliness, physical environment, schools) and attributes of the dwelling (e.g. size, cost, accessibility). Precisely how households weigh up the performance of alternative dwellings on these criteria is not yet fully understood. It may be, for instance, that households engage in compensatory choice whereby a good performance on one attribute (e.g. attractive garden) can make up for a poor performance on another attribute (e.g. small size); alternatively households may engage in non-compensatory combinational strategies that involve the differential weighting of the criteria concerned (Young 1984). What is known is that the propensity to move house, and the salience of different characteristics of both the dwelling and the local environment, vary, predictably, with the stage that the household has reached in the life cycle, moves being more common when an independent household is first established (i.e. when an individual leaves the parental home), at marriage, during child rearing, and at retirement (Morgan 1976). It would be wrong, however, to view households as sovereign decision-makers, able to pursue their individual preferences. In reality, most households are very highly constrained by finance and by limited information as to the vacancies that occur in the housing stock of a particular town (MacLennan and Wood 1982). Even the real estate industry may be highly segmented, as was shown in Palm's (1985) study of differences in the 'information set' of Anglo, Black, and Hispanic real estate agents in Denver (USA). As a result residential mobility can only be understood if due regard is paid to the choice processes of the households concerned, the nature of the society under study (notably income inequalities and social segregation), and the activity of 'gatekeepers' who play a major role in controlling access to housing in both the owner-occupied market (e.g. bank and building society managers) and the rental market (e.g. estate agents in the private sector, bureaucrats in the public sector) (Timms 1976). Residential relocation, in other words, entails a balancing of needs, aspirations, and constraints. It also involves expectations to the extent that a household may tolerate inadequacies in the 'now' environment given the probability of likely future changes to that environment (e.g. renovation) or to the household's needs (e.g. reduction in family size) (Michelson 1980).

One of the most thorough-going investigations ever undertaken of residential relocation was that conducted by Michelson (1977) over five years with a sample of 751 households in Toronto (Canada). He assumed, and showed, that people are relatively rational in their actions, when economic circumstances permit, with the result that they match themselves to housing on the basis of their own assessment of what kind of people they are and what they want to do with their lives. What this means is that, in any city, 'the complex of individual preferences, housing needs and financial capabilities, existing housing supply, information flows and market manipulations leads to a sifting and sorting of the population into distinct residential clusters' (Timms 1976, 36). The net outcome of residential relocation within a city is, in other words, a process whereby households are *differentiated* into neighbourhoods. These differ from each other in many ways (physical structure, housing quality, ownership patterns, age, location, status and lifestyle) but yet all are important because of their impact on behaviour and attitudes. As Timms (1976, 24–7) has shown, the behaviour of most individuals is set within a neighbourhood context and, even if life involves association with actors from outside the immediate locale, neighbours remain a constraint to be reckoned with. Even if they are not seen and not known, neighbours may still be a powerful source of social influence. Thus, although the effect of the local residential area may be overlain by a great variety of other influences (e.g. family, church, work, class), it remains of potential importance throughout the life cycle. In short, although neither the neighbourhood nor the neighbours may be the object of much regard, their influence is virtually inescapable (Haggerty 1982).

Although neighbourhoods are accepted as part of urban life by both the casual observer and the city dweller, they are notoriously difficult to define and delimit. Admittedly, Lee (1968) found that 75% of housewives in an area of Cambridge (England) could describe their neighbourhood on a map and that the form of a neighbourhood reflected local activities (such as shopping, social visiting, and organizational membership). Such surveys of subjective perceptions are, however, time-consuming, costly, and not always representative of society at large. They are therefore difficult to apply in any large-scale study of neighbourhoods. Unfortunately 'objective' definitions of neighbourhood are no less troublesome. This is largely because the term 'neighbourhood' is used in a wide variety of ways. Blowers (1973), in fact, has identified five types of neighbourhood depending on the presence or absence of a clear territorial name, a distinctive physical environment, an identifiable social group, functional interaction (e.g. shops, schools), and social interaction (Fig. 5.1). An alternative approach has been suggested by Warren and Warren (1977). They devised a typology of neighbourhoods based on three considerations: the extent to which individual residents identified with the neighbourhood; the level of social interaction within the neighbourhood; and the degree of linkage that exists between neighbourhood residents and the larger community. Thus, an 'integral'

TYPE	Common characteristics and dimensions				
	Territory	Environment	Social group	Functional interaction	Social interaction
Arbitrary					
Physical					
Homogeneous					
Functional					
Community					

Fig. 5.1 Types of neighbourhoods

neighbourhood is one which has a clearly demarcated centre and a set of residents who interact strongly and share common concerns, while being linked to the wider community; a 'parochial' neighbourhood is similar save that the ties with the broader community are weak. A 'diffuse' neighbourhood is one where there are no ties with the wider community and very little social interaction and where the sole distinguishing characteristic is a tendency for residents to identify with the area. Where this local identification is absent, but where there is social interaction and linkage with the larger community, Warren and Warren identified 'stepping-stone' neighbourhoods, so-called because they are often characterized by high residential turnover, often of upwardly mobile individuals. When there is no local identification and no social interaction but only strong linkages with the rest of society, the neighbourhood may be labelled 'transitory'. The fact that it is possible to identify these types of neighbourhood as arising from a process of residential differentiation within the city indicates that residential mobility, and hence neighbourhood change, tends to be incremental, with most moves covering a short distance into districts of similar status. Such limited geographical mobility reflects inertia, in the short term, in the spatial structure of cities and the stability of the social structure (Ley 1983, 279).

No matter what bases are used for defining neighbourhoods, it seems commonly agreed that such neighbourhoods fulfil some or all of a number of roles (Walmsley and Lewis 1984; Popenoe 1973): to begin with, neighbourhoods may provide a means of translating social distance into geographical distance, thereby keeping like with like; they may provide a convenient unit for the provision of goods and services (e.g. shops and schools) (Hallman 1984); they may give identity to different parts of the urban landscape, providing, in particular, a sense of security (especially around the home) and a sense of belonging that can contribute significantly to self-identity and well-being; they may distinguish a territorial group within which spontaneous and organized social contact can take place; they may constitute political communities that can work for the amelioration of living conditions by pressing for modifications to the local environment; and, finally, they may serve as arenas for personal development and for the socialization of children to the point where they accept existing norms of behaviour.

Residential differentiation into neighbourhoods may be a more or less universal and inevitable trait of urban development but it is not accepted as necessarily a good thing in all quarters. Many town planners, for instance, have been very critical of such things as one class housing developments, arguing that they cause neuroses and foster political isolation (Doob 1940). Indeed, in town planning there have been a great many attempts to create mixed rather than segregated neighbourhoods (Gans 1968). Such moves date back at least to the activities of philanthropists like Cadbury at Bourneville (UK) (Sarkissian 1976) and they seem geared to the creation of genuine 'communities' rather than purely residential neighbourhoods. Unfortunately the term 'community' is used in an even wider variety of ways than the term 'neighbourhood'. In fact it has been observed that the expression 'community' has a high level of use but a low level of meaning (Dalton and Dalton 1975), a claim borne out by the fact that the term has been defined in no fewer than 94 ways! (Hillery 1955). To the purist, the term 'community' should only be used when it refers to 'a relatively homogeneous human group, within a defined area, experiencing little mobility, interacting and participating in a wide range of local affairs, and sharing an awareness of common life and personal bonds' (Dalton and Dalton 1975, 2). In practice, of course, such strict usage is seldom observed. Instead the term is also applied to finite and bounded physical territories, to localized social systems (often based on churches or educational institutions), and to the sense of belonging that sometimes people feel one to another, irrespective of proximity, as a result of tradition (e.g. Greek migrants in Australia) (Wild 1981).

Compounding these varied definitions is the fact that the term 'community' is often used as ideology, that is as an expression of what *should be* rather than what *is* (Bell and Newby 1971). Such usage dates back to the early Christian era (with the ideal of brothers and sisters in Christ), cropped up from time to time in notions of Utopia, and came to prominence during the Industrial Revolution when notions of community were contrasted with individualism and with the atomization and the alienation that accompanied an emphasis on private property and profit (Kamenka 1982). It is not uncommon therefore to see modernization and urbanization discussed from the point of view of a shift between *gemeinschaft* and *gesellschaft* society (see Chapter 1). To view all western societies as moving irrevocably along a single continuum towards a state of diminished community affiliation is, of course, a gross oversimplification. Society is certainly changing but it may not be that communities are *breaking up* so much as *breaking down* into an ever increasing number of subcultures (Wellman 1978). After all, it is still possible to identify urban communities (Everitt 1976; Herbert and Raine 1976). Nowhere are such communities more clearly seen than in so-called 'urban villages' (Gans 1962). These are generally cohesive working class neighbourhoods, in moderate to high density areas, characterized by intense social interaction. They are exemplified by Bethnal Green (London) and Greenwich Village (New York). It would be wrong, of course, to romanticize urban villages for two reasons: first, some low class inner city areas are pretty horrible, even in the eyes of the residents, as evidenced in Ley's (1974) discovery of a willingness on the part of residents to leave 'Monroe' (Philadelphia); and secondly, traditional working class inner city areas have been undergoing considerable change in the last couple of decades often fundamentally altering their character as well as their appearance (Jacobs 1961).

One of the most notable changes in working class inner city areas in the last two decades has been the process of *gentrification* whereby middle class people move into, and renovate, traditional working class areas. Gentrification first came to public attention in the 1960s. It became very widespread in the 1970s. In simple terms it involves both an upgrading of the socio-economic status of residents and a transfer of housing stock from private landlords to owner-occupiers (Williams 1984). For instance, Grier and Grier's (1977) study of gentrification in Washington, D.C., (USA) showed that, among in-migrants, the majority of household heads were unmarried and under 35 years of age and had high incomes, tertiary education, and high status white collar employment. Moreover they tended to renovate terraced housing, moving out a block at a time from an established core. The popular image of gentrifiers has therefore become one of 'trendies' displacing 'workers' (Day and Walmsley 1978). That is to say, individuals, attracted by the cosmopolitan lifestyle of the inner city and accessibility to the cultural and recreational facilities of the central business district, buy out traditional owners. In some instances, as in the United States, this process is actively encouraged by governments which see gentrification as a way of privatizing inner city renewal (Williams 1984). Of course gentrification cannot be explained completely by focussing on the changing housing demands of the middle classes. It may be, for example, that the process involves a 'sorting' of existing inner city residents rather than the return of erstwhile suburbanites to the central city (Harrison 1983). Certainly gentrification reflects, as much as anything, the availability of depreciated nineteenth-century housing stock and the simultaneous rise in potential groundrent levels to the point where profitable redevelopment is possible (Smith 1979). Nevertheless, it remains true that gentrifiers, once established, do lay great store by inner city lifestyles (Day and Walmsley 1981). The importance of different lifestyles in the city was first stressed by Bell (1958) who identified 'family-oriented', 'careerist', and 'consumerist' lifestyles. Moore (1972) has suggested that there now exists a fourth category, 'community seekers'. Gentrifiers do not however fit neatly into any one of these classes but rather are to be found among 'careerists', 'consumerists', and 'community seekers'.

In all this discussion of city dwellers opting for a preferred lifestyle, it should be remembered that many individuals are forced to live in areas where they may have little choice over their lifestyle. Nowhere is this clearer than in the case of ghettos. Traditionally, ghettos have been viewed as the temporary location of individuals, often migrants, awaiting assimilation into a host culture. According to this view, ghettos will either dissolve in time or persist as home base for successive communities of immigrants (Blaut 1983). It now seems that such optimism is unwarranted; ghettos are here to stay. In other words, a point may be reached where neighbourhood deterioration becomes so pronounced as to discourage private renewal (Nourse and Phares 1975). Ultimately this may lead to abandoned dead centres in metropolitan areas (Ley 1983).

It is probably generally accepted that ghetto dwellers have a low quality of life. However, great problems are encountered whenever an attempt is made to measure quality of life. After all, 'quality of life' is a term that encompasses both the conditions of the environment in which people live (e.g. pollution, neighbourhood facilities) and some attributes of the people themselves (e.g. health, educational achievement) (Pacione 1982b). The earliest major attempt to measure quality of life in a quantitative manner probably occurred in the United States in 1929 when President Hoover established the Committee on Social Trends. This Committee sought to devise and use what became known as *social indicators* to monitor the transition of the USA to the status of a 'Great Society' (Smith 1973). Basically, a social indicator, in this sense, is simply a statistic that measures the condition of society; for instance, the unemployment rate is often used as a social indicator on the grounds that an increase in the unemployment rate in a country is indicative of a lowering of the quality of life in that country. In practice, of course, national statistics mask enormous variations and it quickly became obvious that researchers investigating quality of life require what have become known as *territorial social indicators*, in other words social indicators disaggregated into small-scale geographical units so as to reveal place-to-place variations in the quality of life. Unfortunately, early American initiatives to monitor the condition of society came to little and it was not until the 1960s that social indicators again came into fashion. At that time the National Aeronautical and Space Administration (NASA) commissioned the American Academy of Arts and Sciences to look at the impact of rapid technological change on society (Bauer 1966). Thus the idea of 'social reporting' was re-born and officially produced social indicators began to be published in a variety of advanced countries.

There are two critical problems in using social indicators to measure quality of life: deciding what to assess and deciding whose views to record. The former problem is usually resolved by arriving at some sort of consensus as to what are considered to be the basic components of human existence. For example, Smith (1973), after a content analysis of books on American society, suggested the collection of indicators for seven components of what he termed 'well-being': (1) income, wealth, and employment; (2) housing and the neighbourhood; (3) health; (4) education; (5) social pathology, crime, and delinquency; (6) social belonging; and (7) the provision of recreation and leisure facilities. The problem of deciding whose views to record was initially resolved in favour of using census and other official data. The supposed advantage of these sources was that they recorded living conditions as objectively as possible (and they were, of course, published for regions, thereby facilitating analyses of place-to-place variations in quality of life). As a result, it seemed for a short time in the 1970s that social scientists might be getting close to answering the question 'who gets what where?' Unfortunately, however, it soon became apparent that census data left a lot to be desired when it came to measuring quality of life. Although such sources often provide ample information on material well-being (e.g. income, home ownership), they say next to nothing about social and psychological well-being (Campbell *et al.* 1976).

The only way in which social and psychological well-being can be measured is by asking the people under study. Such surveys produce what have become known as *subjective social indicators*. Originally, many social scientists fought shy of such statistics and were particularly wary of the problems of reliability and validity involved in their collection. In practice, these problems have been found to be not much greater than is the case with so-called 'objective' indicators (e.g. the problem of deciding which census variables are reliable and valid measures of quality of life) and, as a result, the use of subjective social indicators is now widespread (Pacione 1982b). The hand of those advocating subjective surveys was in fact strengthened considerably when it became apparent that there was often a low correlation between subjective and objective indicators, thereby suggesting that the latter alone were an inadequate measure of well-being (Schneider 1975; Gans 1962).

The main problem inhibiting the use of subjective indicators to measure the quality of life of city dwellers is nowadays not so much the question of devising valid measures as the lack of an overall model describing the influence of the urban environment on well-being. In fact there are probably three competing models: *determinist theory* holds that city living leads to overstimulation, withdrawal, alienation, and low well-being; *compositionalist theory* argues that population size, density, and heterogeneity have little effect on well-being because individuals belong to small personal worlds that insulate them from the wider community; and *subcultural theory* suggests that it is membership of 'subcultures', most common in big cities, that most influences well-being. A test of these three models in London (UK), Los Angeles (USA), and Sydney (Australia) found little support for the first two but slight support for subcultural theory (Palisi and Canning 1983). This suggests that considerable attention should be paid to assessing the satisfaction of residents with the community and neighbourhood within which they live. Indeed, although some authorities dissent from this view and argue that health, friendship, work, finance, and marriage contribute far more to quality of life than does neighbourhood satisfaction (Marans 1976), it is now widely accepted that manipulation of the neighbourhood itself can have a major bearing on such integral components of well-being as a sense of belonging, personal relationships, and health (Carp and Carp 1982).

Surveys of subjective impressions of well-being have generally revealed high levels of satisfaction with the residential environment except where through traffic creates noise, pollution, and a threat to personal safety (Appleyard 1981). For example, in a major survey of 2164 adults in 40 states in the USA, Campbell *et al.* (1976) found that fewer than one in ten expressed dissatisfaction with the community or neighbourhood within which they lived and only 15% expressed dissatisfaction with housing (mainly complaints about the cost and size of dwellings). Despite this, it is not uncommon to find that 'perceived well-being' varies within the city. British work suggests that the areas of greatest satisfaction are inner city districts, new owner-occupied suburbs, and long-established public housing estates peopled by elderly households. In contrast the worst areas, in terms of lowest perceived well-being, tend to be privately rented inner city areas and peripheral public housing estates (Knox and MacLaran 1978). Curiously there does not seem to be much evidence for well-being varying with city size. Franck (1980), for example, studied friendship patterns (admittedly only one component of well-being) as assessed by in-migrants to New York City and to a town of 31,000 people and showed that, although New Yorkers did experience greater difficulty in initiating friendships, there were no differences between the two areas after eight months in either the number of friends or the frequency of contact with friends.

Associated with these spatial variations in perceived well-being, there are of course variations between different subgroups of the population in their satisfaction with the urban environment. Onibokun (1976), in a survey of Canadian public housing, found that satisfaction levels were lowest for big families, one parent families, the unemployed, new migrants, and the downwardly mobile. It has also been observed in the USA that neighbourhood satisfaction increases with age, is highest for the least well educated, and is greater for whites than for coloureds (Campbell *et al.* 1976). The reasons why different subgroups evaluate the urban environment in different ways are probably to be found in different perceptions of what is important, different aspirations, and different evaluations of neighbourhood provision, as well as 'real' differences from area to area (Marans and Rodgers 1975). For example, in a study of residential satisfaction in Cork (Eire), Hourihan (1984) showed that the effect of residents' personal characteristics on satisfaction levels was mediated through their perceptions and evaluations of neighbourhood attributes. Specifically, Hourihan found that length of residence and social class influenced how individuals evaluated neighbourhoods in terms of appearance (clean, neat, tidy, well planned), life style (interesting, friendly, active . . .), quality of life (tense, hazardous, crowded . . .), and stability (honest, balanced, healthy . . .) which all, in turn, influenced satisfaction levels. On top of this it has been found that there exists a direct relationship between a person's mobility rate (number of moves divided by age) and the amount of illnesses suffered by that individual. In particular highly mobile individuals tend to have high incidences of psychosomatic illness, a high rate of heart disease among males, a high incidence of depression among females, and a high mortality rate among the institutionalized aged (Stokols *et al.* 1983).

The subgroups of the population for whom satisfaction with the local environment is most critical are, of course, those sets of individuals who are relatively restricted in their mobility and who are therefore tied in no small measure to the neighbourhood in which they live. In some instances these subgroups have been labelled 'YOPHS' because they are comprised very largely of the young, old, poor, housewives, and sick (Clark 1972). This is not to say that all members of such subgroups are tied to their local areas. There is however a good deal of evidence that these subgroups are often less mobile than the population at large and evidence that the extent of mobility correlates positively with life satisfaction. Cutler (1972), for example, found that aged people with their own transportation have higher life satisfaction scores than similar individuals without their own transportation. There are of course problems in trying to assess the residential satisfaction and morale of immobile groups such as the aged (Bohland and Herbert 1983). Not the least of these problems relates to the tendency of individuals living in inadequate but inescapable surroundings to evaluate their situation more favourably than objective observers do. In other words, if the residential environment is inconsistent with an individual's self-image, and that individual is unable to improve the situation, one way for the individual to reduce feelings of inadequacy, and defend against anxiety, is to deny that the living situation is all that bad (Carp 1975). In short, an ego-defence mechanism may influence individuals in their assessment of their quality of life. It may also be that individuals adapt, over time, to their surroundings and learn to accept what may have been viewed initially as shortcomings. Certainly there is a good deal of evidence that individuals tend to adopt a neighbourhood view on political issues (Walmsley and Lewis 1984, 145–51). This 'neighbourhood effect' is most clearly seen in the tendency for individuals with similar voting preferences to cluster together. Undoubtedly this clustering derives in part from the segregation and clustering of city dwellers in terms of politically relevant characteristics like income, class, and race. However it also derives from a tendency for individuals to adapt to a prevailing neighbourhood point of view as a result of local social interaction. In some instances this adaptation to a neighbourhood view can operate in an almost subconscious way as peer group pressure, and a desire to conform, lead to a distinctive neighbourhood 'ethos'. It has been shown, for example, that the local residential environment can have a marked influence on educational achievement (Moulden and Bradford 1984). In particular, neighbourhood pressure can lead to a conformity in attitudes towards education that is independent of the influence of socio-economic status (Robson 1969).

5.2 CROWDING, STRESS AND MENTAL ILLNESS

The influence of the local environment on behaviour is not deterministic. That is to say, no one environmental feature (e.g. ethnicity) leads automatically to a certain type of behaviour (e.g. poor educational achievement). Nevertheless, when the incidence of things like mental illness, truancy, family breakdown, mumps, whooping cough, and suicide is examined, it is frequently found that such 'social pathologies', as they are often termed, are most common in inner city areas (Faris and Dunham 1939; McHarg 1969; Bagley *et al.* 1976). In some cases, inner city concentrations can be quite striking; Giggs (1973), for example, found that 70% of schizophrenics in Nottingham (UK) lived within 4 km of the city centre. Closer examination of other social pathologies reveals, however, that the pattern of incidence is in fact quite complex and defies simple description. For instance, Mintz and Schwarz (1964) noted that, although schizophrenia was concentrated in the underprivileged, substandard and largely central parts of the city, other mental illnesses such as manic depression were more or less random in incidence and seemed to be related to personality rather than environment. Likewise, Bagley and Jacobson (1976) differentiated several types of suicide (socio-pathic, depressive, physical illness) and showed that, although socio-pathic suicide was predominantly an inner city phenomenon, physical illness suicide occurred mainly in middle class suburbia.

It is not difficult to see how the inner city, with its high density living, may foster the spread of infectious and contagious disease (e.g. whooping cough). It is less easy to see the link between inner city living and mental illness. Indeed, it may be that it is not the inner city environment *per se* that causes mental illness and social problems generally. Rutter *et al.* (1974), for example, compared inner London and the Isle of Wight (UK) in a study of emotional disorders, conduct disorders, and specific retardation in reading among schoolchildren. Their results clearly showed that the incidence of social problems was very much higher in London. The authors were unable, however, to answer the question of what it is about life in the city that predisposes city residents to the development of disorder and deviance. Instead they concluded that social problems tend to be associated with two phenomena: marital breakdown, poverty, mental illness and antisocial behaviour on the part of parents, and schools with a high turnover of staff. Of course, it may well be that in some studies the difference between the inner city and the outer suburbs in the incidence of problems is more apparent than real. After all, there tends to be a greater number of hospitals, doctors, clinics and social workers in the inner city and hence it is not surprising to find that the per capita patronage of such facilities is higher than in outer suburbs (Freeman 1978). Consider the case of Sydney (Australia): per capita hospital patronage in the peripheral western suburbs is one-third of what it is in the inner city, a fact which may seem significant until it is realized that hospital provision (beds to population) is three times higher in the inner city than in the west (Walmsley and McPhail 1976).

The greater provision, in the inner city, of facilities for the treatment of social problems raises the interesting possibility that inner city areas may actually attract individuals seeking to use those facilities. In other words, it may be that people suffering from mental illness or social problems choose to live in inner suburbs in order to be near to the facilities on offer. A more likely explanation, however, is that individuals with problems often fail to compete successfully in the job market, in the housing market, and in the education system. They also tend to be unable to cope in personal relationships. As a result they tend to be forced out of 'normal' society and may well drift to those very areas that are least attractive to society as a whole, namely run-down, inner city areas. Additionally, individuals with a history of mental disorder may be rejected by the residents of middle-class suburbia who adopt the attitude that the de-institutionalization of mental health care is a good thing providing it does not involve the placement of 'patients' on their street (Dear and Taylor 1982). According to this general point of view, the cause of social problems and mental illness is to be found in the structure and functioning of society, and in the personality of the individual, rather than in the environment. It may be, in fact, that some neighbourhoods reduce mental illness by providing a therapeutic community that both encourages healthy human development and provides emotional support and friendship (Smith 1980). Despite the plausibility of this perspective, it is undoubtedly the case that inner city living can exacerbate whatever problems exist for residents. This is because the inner city environment is *stressful*.

Debate about the stressful nature of the inner city environment can be traced back to Wirth (1938). According to Wirth, high density living necessitates special modes of both interaction and social organization in order that individuals can cope with the vast array of situations which they encounter each day. Thus urban life, with its many transitory contacts, becomes segmented into distinct and often impersonal roles (Choldin 1978). Underlying Wirth's argument is the view that the inner city environment provides far more information than an individual can absorb (Lipowski 1975). The effects of this overload can be severe: individuals may well withdraw into anonymity with a result that the inner city becomes characterized by a lack of civility and by indifference in social interaction (e.g. a failure to help individuals in difficulty) (Levy-Leboyer 1982). A striking illustration of this diminished social responsibility in the inner city is to be found in Zimbardo's (1969) account of how a car, left in the Bronx (inner city New York), was stripped within 26 hours of everything that could be moved whereas another vehicle, in suburban Palo Alto, remained untouched after 64 hours. Other researchers have shown how the pace of life, as measured by pedestrian flows, increases in the centre of big cities (Bornstein and Bornstein 1976). This sort of evidence has led to the suggestion that, in certain parts of the inner city, the stress of urban living may be so intense that those areas become 'pathogenic', that is, they actually generate social problems. The evidence for this sort of proposition is however dubious. For one thing, the findings suggesting diminished social responsibility in the inner city are by no means universal. For example, the observation,

based on the United States, that city dwellers are much less coop-
erative than their small town counterparts in a variety of social situations (allowing the use of a telephone, posting a 'lost' letter,
speaking in the street, and helping strangers with streetmaps), was
found not to hold in the Netherlands (Korte and Kerr 1975). Moreover a focus on the inner city overlooks the substantial mental health
and stress-related problems that occur in outer suburbs. The
expression 'suburban neurosis' was first coined by Taylor as long ago
as 1938 to describe the stresses commonly associated with migration
to peripheral housing estates. Since then, writers such as Sennett
(1971) and Greenbie (1974) have drawn attention to the very real
feelings of grief and loss that can accompany a move to suburbia. This
has led to the point of view that outer suburbs, with their homo-
geneity and conformity, can be socially repressive and therefore just
as stressful as the inner city. Indeed, in some instances, the outer
suburbs may be even more stressful because they lack many of the
advantages that come with inner city living, notably exposure to
cosmopolitan life and innovative ideas and the easy availability of
alternative opportunities for indulging personal tastes and desires
(Hawley 1972).

Evidence for the proposition that inner city living is stressful is,
in other words, somewhat equivocal. Nevertheless, the image of the
inner city as a problem area is a very persistent one and, as a result,
a good deal of effort has gone into identifying just what it is about
the inner city that causes problems. The conventional approach was
well described by Kaplan and Kaplan (1982, 194): 'Among the
characteristics of the environment that seem to create problems are
crowding, confusion, coercion, and noise. These lead to a variety of
reactions which, in turn, raise other problems. People may become
insensitive and distrustful, constantly on guard, and withdraw from
the offending environment wherever possible. The result can be a
decline in communication, in trust, in helpfulness, in receptivity to
people and ideas.' Of course, in any enquiry into the stressful nature
of the urban environment, much hinges on what is meant by 'stress'.
Gans (1962) used the term to describe the feeling of discomfort that
individuals encounter when they go into unfamiliar neighbourhoods
that are distant from the routine of everyday life. Ley (1983) has gone
somewhat further and suggested that 'stress' is only one part of one
of a number of scales that can be used to differentiate parts of the
city (stress-security; stimulation-ennui; status-stigma). Stress, as used
in this sense, is a rather vague term. Indeed, in much of social science,
the term is used in a confusing manner to denote a psychological
precursor of illness, the result of pressure, and general feelings of
anxiety or discomfort. Despite this generality in usage, it is possible
to identify three factors that trigger stress: (1) cataclysmic phenomena

that affect great numbers of people (e.g. earthquakes); (2) illness or death (which are similar in effect but impact on only a few people); and (3) daily irritations associated with things like commuting, job dissatisfaction, and neighbourhood problems (Baum *et al.* 1983). The third of these is the one that impinges most directly on city dwellers.

Generally speaking, there are two sorts of models that attempt to account for the impact that stress has on individuals. These are *physiological* models and *psychological* models (Evans 1983). The former are associated mainly with the work of Selye (1956) who proposed a general adaptation syndrome (GAS) whereby internal organs (e.g. the endocrine system) help individuals to adjust to changes in the environment. Selye's GAS is based on the idea that the body can cope with stress but that this coping has costs for subsequent coping in that long-term exposure to stress or repeated instances of adaptation can deplete the body's reserves and lead eventually to physical dysfunction (Baum *et al.* 1983, 16). In short, the body can become exhausted if continually called upon to cope with stress, whereupon the individual becomes highly susceptible to physical and mental breakdown and disease. Although there is some support for this type of model in the study of stress and population regulation in the animal world (McClelland 1982), its direct relevance to urban living is as yet unproven. As a result, rather more attention has focussed on psychological models of stress. These models, stemming largely from the work of Lazarus (1966), propose that how individuals think about things has a major bearing on how stressful they prove to be. Stress, in other words, can be mediated cognitively and its impact thereby reduced. Thus in human as opposed to animal behaviour, stress results in anxiety and depression rather than morbidity and mortality. An example of cognitive mediation of stress is to be seen in cases where residents of a stress prone environment rate the stress as less important than do outsiders. A case in point is the tendency for individuals in hazard prone environments to reject information and suppress knowledge of risk in order to avoid damaging their prevailing value system (Walmsley and Lewis 1984, 115). It is not uncommon, for example, for people to devalue the threat of an earthquake in order not to appear to be silly for living in an earthquake area. Of course, psychological variables, like personality, also influence the way in which stress manifests itself in a particular case, irrespective of whether it be a somatic response (e.g. hormonal or cardiovascular changes), a verbal response (e.g. in a questionnaire), or a behavioural response (e.g. taking tranquillizers, paralysis through fear, or the use of body language such as notable facial expressions) (Lazarus and Cohen 1977).

Irrespective of individual capacities for mediating stress, the fact remains that not all environments are equally stressful. The question therefore arises as to which types of environment are most stressful. This, in turn, raises the problem of defining what it is that makes an environment stressful. Predictably, environmental designers have explored this issue is some detail in order to identify, and therefore avoid, the sorts of designs that thwart social interaction and the development of social networks, thereby contributing to anxiety, depression, anomie and asocial behaviour (Zimring 1981). Neighbourhoods, for instance, can be designed in such a way as to promote a sense of security, a sense of place, and socialization. Alternatively, carelessness in design can promote 'incivilities', both of a physical nature (e.g. abandoned housing, vandalism) and of a social nature (e.g. groups loitering on corners, drunks) (Taylor 1983). Possibly the most studied of all elements of design is the impact of high-rise living. For example, in Britain the incidence of psychoneurotic disorders was found to be three times higher among residents of multi-storeyed dwellings than among those living in detached houses. Moreover, the same study noted that psychological strain seems to vary directly with the floor level on which residents live, implying that the incremental effect of high-rise living becomes more severe as height increases (Fanning 1967). Similar findings have been made in New York. Again high-rise residents felt more crowded, had lower levels of residential satisfaction, and experienced greater difficulty in social relationships with neighbours and outsiders than did residents of low-rise dwellings (McCarthy and Saegert 1976). The usual explanation offered for this sort of finding is that high-rise living imposes an overload of information on individual residents. In other words, the number of social interactions that need to be monitored by the high-rise dweller far exceeds that individual's 'attentional capacity' with a result that 'cognitive fatigue' sets in and the individual copes less well with day-to-day living (Cohen and Sherrod 1978). According to this view, then, stress sets in because of a failure of coping mechanisms.

Of course, it may not be high-rise living *per se* that is the stressor, so much as some other feature of the sort of environment in which high-rise dwellings are found. Given that high-rise dwellings tend to be in inner city areas, it may be that *noise levels* are important. Certainly there is evidence that the reading and auditory discrimination skills of children can be diminished by high noise levels in and around the residential environment (Cohen *et al.* 1973). Similarly, pedestrians in Dundee (UK) have been found both to walk more quickly, and to notice oddities less readily (e.g. comical hats on passers-by, balloons tied to trees), in high noise as opposed to low noise environments (Korte and Grant 1980). The supposition is that people find noise unpleasant and walk quickly in order to escape from it. This can have profound implications for the nature of social interaction in high noise areas. Page (1977), for example, studied a large store near a noisy building site and found that the willingness of individuals to help strangers (by picking up dropped parcels or by giving change for a telephone call) decreased at times when the noise level increased. According to Page, there are five possible explanations for this type of behaviour: (1) the individuals concerned were suffering from information overload and therefore filtered out 'unnecessary' information; (2) noise is distracting and therefore causes individuals not to notice people needing help; (3) noise prevents communication with a result that individuals terminate an exchange as quickly as possible, often by a simple refusal to help; (4) noise is unpleasant and puts individuals in an uncooperative mood; and (5) noise is a negative stimulus from which individuals strive to escape. It is impossible to say which of these explanations is the most plausible because of a number of problems that have been found to be involved in the study of noise. The impact of noise, for example, may not manifest itself until a certain cumulative level of exposure has occurred (Glass and Singer 1972). Likewise, noise, unless at extreme levels, may be less of a stressor than is commonly imagined because it has been shown that 95% of people can habituate to meaningless noise, thereby reducing its annoyance (McLean and Tarnopolosky 1977). Noise may in fact only be disturbing where it is perceived to be unjust, when its timing is particularly irksome, or when it fluctuates markedly in level (Levy-Leyboyer 1982, 109). Perhaps this is why traffic noise is an irritant to people who see their streets used by a high volume of non-local traffic (Appleyard and Lintell 1972).

Another feature which may account for the significant level of social pathology in high-rise buildings is the high level of population density and crowding often associated with such buildings. For example, de Lauwe (1959) has suggested that stress-related illness and social problems begin to appear when individuals average less than 8 m² of space in a dwelling. Likewise family equilibrium is disturbed at less than 12 m² (although, obviously, both these figures are culturally determined and are therefore likely to vary somewhat from country to country). More generally, high population densities and crowding have been cited as the cause of 'physical effects (mass starvation, famine, environmental pollution, slums, disease and physiological breakdowns), social effects (deterioration of educational and service systems, increased crime, riots, war, economic stress and increased centralized control), and interpersonal and psychological effects (mental illness, increased drug addiction and alcoholism, family disorganization, reduced freedom and decreased quality of life)' (Boots 1979, 13). In this context it is important to note that the terms 'density' and 'crowding' are sometimes used interchangeably although, strictly speaking, the former refers to a physical variable (people per unit area) while the latter refers to a subjective feeling that there are too many people in a given situation (Stokols 1972).

Much of the work on density has drawn an analogy with high density and pathology in animal behaviour (Choldin 1978). Thus it has sometimes been suggested that there can arise a point where density becomes so great that it leads to bodily malfunction, excessive aggression, and a breakdown of nurturing (Calhoun 1966). Thankfully, there are no close parallels with such 'behavioural sinks' to be observed in human behaviour. There have, nevertheless, been researchers who have claimed to find clear links between density and pathology. Schmitt (1966), for example, found that density correlated significantly with family disorganization, physical illness, and mental breakdown in Honolulu. Likewise, in the Netherlands, Levy and Herzog (1974) found that density was related to the death rate, hospital admissions, delinquency and illegitimacy. Other researchers have been more sceptical. Fischer (1976), for one, has argued that there is no convincing evidence that density causes or is related to mental disorder, pathology, or social disorganization. In other words, it may be that the sorts of areas that have high density just happen, in some cities, to be the same areas that have high levels of social pathology, there being no causal link between the two variables. Certainly it is not difficult to find situations where cultural considerations, such as relatively rigid rules of behaviour and strong family ties, militate against any impact that density might otherwise have (Kirmeyer 1978). Hong Kong, for example, has relatively low levels of morbidity, delinquency, and mental illness despite individuals having as little as 4 m^2 residential space each (Schmitt 1963; Mitchell 1971).

The same scepticism that surrounds the impact of density on behaviour has also led some authorities to question whether *crowding* has any harmful effects on behaviour (Booth 1976). Thus it has been argued that people who experience crowding are just as happy and productive as those who do not (Freedman 1975). Others are less sure. Part of the problem is that there exists a number of models of the supposed impact of crowding. Aiello *et al.* (1975), for example, have pointed out that it is possible to adopt many different approaches to the study of crowding. Among these are demographic approaches (based on simple correlation between persons per dwelling and pathology), phenomenological approaches (which seek to empathize with individuals in order to understand why situations are construed as crowded), physiological approaches (like Lundberg's (1976) measurement of adrenalin in the urine of Stockholm commuters), and nonverbal approaches (that focus on proxemic behaviour and eye contact in crowded situations). The most common approach has probably been to look at persons per room and to relate this to self-assessed indi-

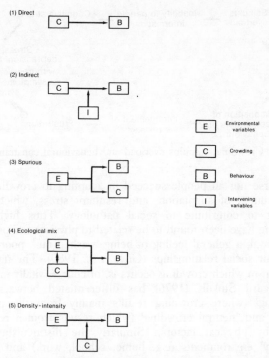

(1) Direct

C ⟶ B

(2) Indirect

C ⟶ B
↑
I

E	Environmental variables
C	Crowding
B	Behaviour
I	Intervening variables

(3) Spurious

E ⟶ B / C

(4) Ecological mix

E / C ⟶ B

(5) Density - intensity

E ⟶ B
↑
C

Fig. 5.2 Models of the impact of crowding on behaviour. *Source*: Boots (1979)

cators of pathology. This is, however, more difficult than it sounds, as is demonstrated by Boots' (1979) identification of five different models of crowding, ranging from the simple direct effect, to the indirect effect model (where intervening variables like family structure are implicated), to the spurious model (where crowding and behaviour appear to be related because they are both influenced by environmental factors like housing conditions), to models that emphasize that crowding only has effects when it acts in concert with other variables, to the density-intensity argument (which suggests that crowding only serves to amplify whatever relationship already exists between environment and behaviour) (Fig. 5.2).

Notwithstanding this variety of models, the influence of crowding on behaviour can be seen as operating in one or both of two ways: (1) an overload of stimulation, and (2) an infringement on privacy through the imposition of constraints on behaviour (Gove *et al.* 1980; Cox *et al.* 1984) (Fig. 5.3). The critical antecedents, emotional concomitants, and adaptive responses to the 'stimulus overload' and 'behavioural constraint' views of crowding are set out in Table 5.1.

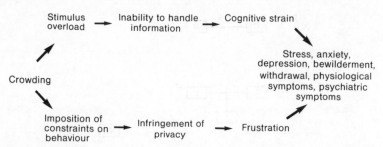

Fig. 5.3 Crowding, stimulus overload and behavioural constraint

Of course not all people succeed in adapting to crowding. Indeed, it is failures of adaptation, and resultant stress, which are often thought to contribute to social pathology. Thus high levels of crowding have been found to be related to physical and psychological withdrawal, a general feeling of being 'washed out', poor child care, and poor social relationships (Gove *et al.* 1980). The nature of the situation in which crowding occurs is, of course, vitally important. In this regard Stokols (1976) has differentiated between 'personal crowding' (where crowding results mainly from the presence of others) and 'neutral crowding' (which results from a restriction of space by physical factors). Similarly, he distinguished between 'primary' environments (e.g. home, school, work) and 'secondary' environments with which contact is transitory (e.g. shops, public transport). Obviously, crowding in the home environment is likely to be more threatening than the type of crowding that occurs at a pop

Table 5.1 Alternative views on the effects of crowding

Theoretical perspective	Critical antecedent of crowding	Emotional concomitants	Primary adaptive processes
stimulus overload	excessive stimulation	confusion fatigue	escape stimulation; behavioural or psychological withdrawal; architectural intervention
behavioural constraint	reduced behavioural freedom	psychological reactance, infringement	leave situation or improve co-ordination and relations with others

Source: Stokols (1976)

concert. This suggests that perceived loss of controllability over the environment may be a critical consideration (in that transitory crowding can be easily controlled by withdrawal). Certainly there is experimental evidence to suggest that crowding in uncontrolled situations results in diminished frustration tolerance levels compared to crowding in situations that are perceived to be controlled (Sherrod 1974). Similarly, elementary design features such as signs (Wener and Kaminoff 1983) and partitions (Desor 1972) can do much to reduce perceived levels of crowding. Culture, too, seems to be a variable that helps militate against the adverse effects of crowding. The Japanese, for example, have adapted successfully to crowding (Canter and Canter 1971). It would be wrong to overplay the importance of culture, however, because the Chinese, who successfully adapt to crowding in Hong Kong, suffer harmful side-effects as a result of crowding in San Francisco (Loo and Ong 1984). This suggests that social expectations may override subcultural values.

Unlike other stressors such as noise and pollution, crowding is very much a *group* phenomenon. 'If an individual were to be placed alone in an extremely small and confined environment, he or she would be cramped but not crowded. To be crowded, one must share an environment with others. The problems created by crowding are problems arising from difficulties in interaction and the coordination of activities with others' (Epstein 1983, 143). In particular, the capacity of an individual for coping with crowding seems to be dependent on that individual's ability to set up 'boundaries' for regulating social contact and maintaining privacy (Altman 1975). Personal space can be thought of as providing one such boundary because such space serves to prevent stress by (1) preventing over-stimulation, (2) constraining the behaviour of others thereby providing an optimal level of behavioural freedom, and (3) ensuring freedom from physical attack (Aiello and Thompson 1980). The significance of this lies in the fact that there are notable differences between cultures in the size and extent of personal spaces maintained by their members. Hall (1966), for example, distinguished between 'contact cultures' where members touch each other frequently (e.g. Arabs, Latins) and 'non-contact cultures' where touching is frowned upon other than in intimate situations (e.g. North America), the former being able to tolerate much higher levels of crowding than the latter. However, there also appears to be considerable variability within any one culture in the extent to which people cope with crowding. In some cases this variability follows a predictable pattern. Gender, for instance, seems to be important in that females respond more favourably to crowding than do males. This has been shown both in experimental situations where subjects rated their feelings after exposure to different levels of crowding (Ross *et al.* 1973) and also in real world situations such as Edwards *et al.*'s (1982) study of apartment living in Toronto which showed that the effects of high rise (e.g. discordant marital relations, psychiatric impairment) were more marked for males than females.

Further evidence that the effects of crowding tend to be mild has come from Rohe (1982) who showed that high-density living can affect residential satisfaction and attitudes but has little impact on health. This seems to imply that many people are remarkably good at adjusting to crowding and thereby vitiating its detrimental consequences. In fact whether or not an individual is affected by crowding seems to be influenced largely by that individual's expectations about the environment (Schmidt *et al.* 1979). People who feel themselves to be effective manipulators of the environment develop a sense of self-efficacy which increases their competence in the face of environmental stress. Conversely, people who experience inescapable environmental stress develop the expectancy that their own responses will be ineffective in producing desirable outcomes (Walmsley and Lewis 1984, 133). In other words, it may not be crowding *per se* but only *uncontrollable* crowding which is responsible for the negative effects popularly associated with crowding (Cohen and Sherrod 1978). Indeed it is likely to be *powerlessness* to control a situation which leads to a sense of crowding. This, in turn, relates to the way in which meaning and expectation are ascribed to the environment. After all, space develops a social nature in two ways: (1) groups gradually define what roles, activities and behaviours are deemed appropriate in their territories; and (2) space takes on general meaning through socialization (Baldassare 1978). It is not surprising therefore that those outside mainstream socialization processes tend to be most prone to the effects of crowding. Conversely, of course, the detrimental effects of crowding can be combatted by deliberately providing information about the environment thereby diminishing its perceived uncontrollability. Langer and Saegert (1977), for example, gave individuals a task to perform in busy New York supermarkets (viz. selecting the cheapest items for a shopping list). What was found was that individuals who were forewarned about the feelings of anxiety encountered by many supermarket shoppers, and hence those who had an expectation that the crowding would make them feel uncomfortable, performed better on the task in question.

In summary, then, the impact of crowding and high density living on human behaviour appears to be very variable. The popular image of crowding leading inexorably to social pathology is certainly not borne out by the evidence. This had led some researchers to claim that 'those who draw firm conclusions about density and behaviour are either speculating or making astounding inferences from flimsy evidence' (Fischer *et al.* 1975, 415). It would be wrong, however, to dismiss entirely the possibility that crowding does have negative effects largely because there are still important methodological problems to be resolved in defining accurately both crowding and density (Boots 1979).

5.3 URBANIZATION, ALIENATION AND CRIME

The incidence of crime and delinquency in the city appears to vary in much the same way as the incidence of mental illness. That is to say, inner city areas are generally characterized by high incidences. In the case of crime, however, the data on which such generalizations are based are far from perfect. Although official crime statistics are published in many countries (e.g. *Uniform Crime Reports* in the USA, *Criminal Statistics* in the UK), these figures fail to capture the true extent of crime. This is because many crimes are not reported to the police. For example, a large survey in Australia in 1983 showed that only 69% of break-ins and only 26% of sexual assaults were reported to the police (Australian Bureau of Statistics 1984). Additionally, the police have a certain amount of discretion in deciding whether or not to record and act upon whatever reports they do receive. Many crimes are therefore dealt with 'on the spot', rather than being recorded in official statistics (e.g. many cases of domestic violence). In other words, official statistics provide a distorted view of offences, offenders, and victims. Some of this distortion may be systematic: different social groups may report crimes to different degrees or be labelled as offenders to different extents (as when ethnic minorities are stigmatized as 'criminals') (Lowman 1982). Thus one of the fundamental problems in the study of crime is the fact that inaccurate

Table 5.2 Crime victimization rates, Australia 1975

Crime victims per 1000 population (overall average 117)					
Age		Workforce status		City size	
15–20	113	Not in labour force	88	>1 million	128
20–25	174	Unemployed	199	½–1 million	130
25–30	152	Full-time employed	139	100–500,000	125
30–40	135			50–100,000	72
40–50	119			<50,000	80
50–60	85				
>60	59				

Source: Australian Bureau of Statistics (1979)

stereotypes may cloud real patterns. Thus the popular image of old people as the victims of crime fails to match the picture uncovered by crime victimization surveys (Table 5.2). Despite this, there can be little doubt that crime rates are increasing in many areas: for instance, between 1955 and 1965 crime rates in both the USA and the UK more or less doubled and since that time crime rates have continued to increase (see Herbert 1982) although the precise figures vary from both crime to crime and from area to area (Walmsley *et al.* 1982). Nor can there be much doubt that large cities have higher crime rates than small towns and country areas. Ley (1983, 347), for example, has claimed that metropolitan areas over 250,000 population have three times the murder rate, five times the rate of property crime, ten times the rate of violent crime, and almost fifty times the rate of robbery found in small towns. The relationship between city size and crime is further elaborated in Fig. 5.4. Clearly, the relationship between size and crime is not a linear one.

Traditionally, high levels of crime in big cities have been explained

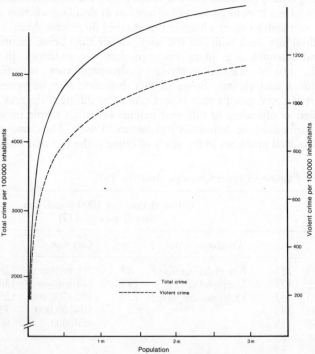

Fig. 5.4 City size and crime rate. *Source*: Calculated from data in Harries (1974)

in terms of the alienation and social isolation of residents, especially those living close to the town centres. In short, the assumption has been (1) that large cities attract migrants and (2) that the act of migration causes social ties to be ruptured with a result that new arrivals in cities are without the support mechanisms that would otherwise see them through times of crisis. Moreover the absence of ties implies an absence of social constraints and therefore an increased opportunity for indulgence in what might hitherto have been considered anti-social behaviour. Thus, migrants tend to be attracted to rental areas around the central business district. Once there, according to this explanation, they encounter economic stress which they remedy by turning to crime. This explanation is, of course, altogether too simplistic. For one thing, different crimes describe different spatial patterns with shoplifting most in evidence in the commercial centre, burglary in the poor, old parts of the city, and violence in rented accommodation (Davidson 1981). For another thing, not all parts of the inner city are the same. A distinction can be made, for example, between working class slums (where there may be a tradition of petty thieving, violence, criminal networks, and rejection of the law) and transitional neighbourhoods (characterized by weak social control and anomie); in the former crime may be normal behaviour during adolescence whereas in the latter crime may be very much a plea for help in that it reflects a failure to achieve adequate economic and social status (Davidson 1981, 91). The idea of the 'drifter' turning to crime to rectify perceived injustices is, in other words, no more than a caricature. It is inadequate as an explanation of inner city crime just as it is inadequate as an explanation of rioting in British and American cities (McPhail 1971; Sim 1983; Keith and Peach 1983). It is important, therefore, to break away from stereotypes and to look at inner city crime in detail.

It is often claimed that variations in the incidence of offences *within* cities are greater than variations between cities (Davidson 1981, 26). Certainly inner city areas seem to have far higher crime rates, as revealed in official statistics, than suburban areas. Nowhere is this pattern better seen than in the case of violent crime which tends to be concentrated to a remarkable degree in inner city areas. To be specific, violent crime is most often found in areas having character-istics usually associated with the inner city: low income, physical deterioration, dependency, ethnic concentration, broken homes, working mothers, low levels of education and vocational skills, high unemployment, high proportions of single males, overcrowding and substandard housing, low rates of home ownership, multiple occu-pancy of dwellings, mixed land use, and high population density (Murray and Boal 1979). Moreover, no less than 60% of violent crime has been found to be committed within one mile of the offender's residence (Baldwin and Bottoms 1976). The incidence of violent crime, in other words, correlates with a number of indicators of poor physical and social living conditions. Such correlations, however, reveal little about the causes of violent crime. As a result, it is not surprising to find that the study of the cause of violent crime is still very much a speculative exercise with no fewer than eight 'theories' having been put foward: (1) the *differential opportunity* theory which postulates that certain types of micro-environment (e.g. bars, underpasses) attract or facilitate violent crime; (2) the *differential drift* theory according to which individuals with violence-prone life-styles and personalities tend to be rejected by society and forced to drift to those areas that society as a whole rates lowly, namely the inner city; (3) theories which suggest the existence and persistence of *subcultures* for which violence is normal; (4) *social alienation* theories which argue that a minority group, such as an ethnic community, can experience powerlessness and frustration which is vented in hostility towards the host community; (5) *stress* theories which suggest that, in times of economic hardship, individuals turn to violent crime (e.g. robbery) simply to make ends meet; (6) theories highlighting *frustration and relative deprivation* according to which individuals turn to violence when they are prevented from satisfying some need that they expected to gratify; (7) *social disorganization* theories which identify lack of social and community support as predisposing factors in violent crime; and (8) *labelling* theories which suggest that giving an area a bad name can stigmatize the area to the extent where, because of differential policing, the area appears to live up to its reputation (Murray and Boal 1979).

In short, then, there are no simple causes underlying violent crime. The same is true of crime in general. Although non-violent crime tends to be concentrated in areas of low social cohesion, weak family life, low socio-economic status, physical deterioration, high density, and high population turnover (Schmid 1960; Roncek 1981), the causes of such crime are not clear. Indeed, the explanations that have been offered in the literature parallel very closely those suggested in relation to violent crime. For example, it has been noted that certain micro-environments are particularly prone to crime (notably blocks on the periphery of an estate where anonymity is more assured (Brantingham and Brantingham 1975)), that offenders tend to drift to inner city areas, that crime prone subcultures serve to initiate many offenders into a life of crime, and that social alienation and anomie are predisposing factors (Schmid, 1960). In other words, it is wrong to label one particular group or social class as criminals. In Britain, for example, Commonwealth immigrants are over-represented in offence rates for certain crimes (e.g. domestic disputes) but under-represented in other cases (e.g. fights in pubs) with a result that certain immigrant areas, although within the traditional inner city, have relatively low crime rates (Davidson 1981). Despite this, explanations that interpret crime in 'class' terms are common. Baldwin and Bottoms (1976), for instance, have suggested that 'housing class' may be important to the extent that renters are far more crime prone than owner-occupiers. Although this finding is undoubtedly true, housing class alone cannot account for variations in crime rates. This is because the local environment is also significant in that it contains the immediate 'cues' to which the individual responds, as well as significant reference groups (Herbert 1979, 127). This importance of local conditions was clearly demonstrated in the Power *et al.* (1972) study of delinquency in Tower Hamlets (UK) which showed that the variability that existed in delinquency rates between schools was independent of education attainment, type of school, and attributes of the school catchment areas and hence was presumably linked to the prevailing character of the school 'environment'.

Many of the 'theories' that have been advanced to explain crime have been based on little more than speculation. In fact, it is only relatively recently that an attempt has been made to understand the motivation and spatial behaviour of offenders as a first step in explaining patterns of crime (Brantingham and Brantingham 1981). Increasingly, it is recognized that crime depends on the convergence in space and time of (1) likely offenders, (2) suitable targets, if only in the form of generally attractive target 'areas' (Herbert and Hyde 1985), and (3) an absence of capable guardians (Cohen and Felson 1979). In other words, there has emerged what can be thought of as the *opportunity* theory of crime (Jackson 1984). According to this, the changing lifestyles of urban dwellers are creating a situation where homes are left unattended for considerable periods and where people necessarily travel in dangerous parts of the city. It is not surprising, therefore, according to this theory, that crimes against property and crimes against the person are both increasing. After all, criminals are rational beings who have needs (e.g. the physiological need for drugs, monetary needs), perceive opportunities, and act accordingly (Rengert 1980). As a result, a good deal may be gained from looking at the mental image that criminals have of the differential opportunity structure of the city (Carter and Hill 1980).

The significance of environmental imagery in criminology is not confined to the images held by offenders. Victims also have images of what they consider to be crime prone environments and such images may have a big bearing on behaviour, especially travel patterns. In particular, the perception of crime as a social problem can lead to a fear of crime which, in turn, can reach quite remarkable proportions. In fact, worldwide, fear of crime seems to be growing more quickly than crime itself (S. Smith 1984). Davidson (1981), for example, quotes a study in Minneapolis (USA) where a quarter of households in a survey rated their chance of being burgled as 50:50, when in reality it was approximately 1 in 1400. Such irrational fear might not be important were it not for its impact on behaviour. An unwillingness of many people to move to the inner city, because of fear of crime, can both depress inner city residential land values and also fuel suburban sprawl, thereby contributing to both fiscal and planning problems in cities (Katzman 1980). A fear of crime can also restrain many urban dwellers in their travel behaviour and limit them to the home for a good part of the day (Lavrakas 1982). Of course, fear of crime is not uniform over all categories of urban dwellers. Nor do differences between groups in their levels of fearfulness reflect differences in their respective rates of victimization. Those with most to lose, and those least able to protect themselves, have been suggested by Davidson (1981) as the most fearful. The first of these categories is a little questionable because low income earners have been found to be more fearful than high income earners (Clemente and Kleiman 1976). There can be no doubt, however, that the old, who are little able to protect themselves, experience levels of fear quite out of proportion with their chances of being victimized (see Table 5.2). The level of fear, even among the aged, does of course vary between different residential areas. Sundeen and Mathieu (1976) compared aged subjects in retirement villages, suburbs, and central city areas and showed quite clearly that the highest levels of fear, and the greatest number of security precautions (special locks, dogs, staying home), were to be found in the inner city. Despite this variability, it seems that fear increases with age. Clemente and Kleiman (1976), for example, demonstrated, in a national survey in the USA, that 51% of respondents aged over 65 were fearful of walking in their neighbourhood at night, a figure which contrasts with 41% for the under 65 age groups. This level of fear is by no means exceptional. Harries (1974), for example, quotes a *Life* magazine survey of 43,000 Americans in 1970 which suggested that in big cities up to 70% of respondents were afraid to go out after dark.

In addition to the aged, significant differences in fear levels have been found between males and females and between long-term city dwellers and rural in-migrants to the city. Pyle's (1980) study of the perception of crime in Akron (USA) showed that females have more exaggerated perceptions than males while Kennedy and Krahn's (1984) examination of Winnipeg and Edmonton (Canada) revealed not only this gender difference but also a difference whereby in-migrants from small rural settlements had higher fear levels, for at least two years after migration, than long-term city dwellers. Interestingly, the gender effects were twice as strong for those who grew up in urban areas as for those from rural areas. Not all parts of the city are of course equally prone to fear. Ley (1983) has demonstrated that fear, and associated stress, can peak quite sharply, thereby demarcating areas that many people try to avoid (see Fig. 3.1). A similar finding has been made by Smith and Patterson (1980). They found that, in Norman (USA), areas of fear focussed on the city centre, the mental hospital and the university. Gender differences were again apparent: *males* tended to fear *unknown parts* of the city and the people they encountered in such places whereas *females* were more fearful of the areas they *knew to be dangerous*. Once areas become feared, they tend to become labelled as 'problem areas'. This is particularly true of housing estates that develop a bad reputation. Herbert (1982) has investigated this labelling process in some detail and shown that, although some estates get their bad reputation initially by accident (e.g. problem families happen to be there), the labels persist because of (1) the tendency for urban managers to neglect such estates which thus become little more than a repository for 'hard cases', and (2) a self selection process among residents whereby 'good' tenants tend to move away, thereby leaving a rump of problem families whose very existence serves to perpetuate the bad reputation of the area (Fig. 5.5).

In some cases, the labelling of an area as crime-prone may be accurate. The same can be said of certain sections of the population because, as has already been pointed out, working class, poorly educated, adolescent males from problem estates are proportionally overrepresented among the ranks of convicted criminals. However, such labelling is very often unjustified. A case in point is ethnic stereotyping, particularly the tendency to attribute crime to racial minorities within a population. The relationship between race and crime, although prominent in the public mind, is in fact far from clear-cut. For example, in the case of American blacks, the link between race

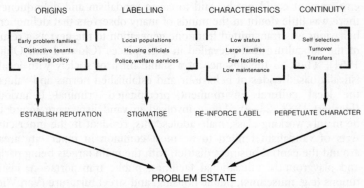

Fig. 5.5 The labelling of problem estates. *Source*: Herbert (1982)

and crime is spurious and derives simply from the numerical predominance of blacks among the least-paid, poorest-housed sections of the community (Davidson 1981, 66). Why then does ethnic stereotyping exist? According to S. Smith (1984), who conducted a major survey of crime victims in Birmingham (UK), such stereotyping can be interpreted simply as a pragmatic means of managing the dangers inherent in urban life. In other words, city dwellers distance themselves socially and physically from places and people that are perceived as harmful or threatening. Given the fleeting nature of most urban encounters, and the resultant lack of intimate information, such distancing has to be based on visible traits, like skin colour, which act as readily identifiable cues that signal either acceptable degrees of proximity or warning of the need for evasion (S. Smith 1984, 438). Stereotyping is, in short, one means that city dwellers employ to reduce the uncertainty in their environment; in the absence of accurate information on the causes of social problems, people resort to simple rules of thumb which, no matter how inaccurate, give a certain reassurance in day-to-day life.

Nowhere in criminology is stereotyping more prominent than in relation to *vandalism* and *delinquency*. There can be no doubt that vandalism is increasing: in the USA, for example, acts of vandalism went up by 70% between 1970 and 1979 (Van Vliet 1984). Vandalism is not, however, a new phenomenon. The very word derives from wanton acts of destruction committed over fifteen hundred years ago. Despite this long history, it was not until the 1930s, and the work of the Chicago School of Urban Ecology, that vandalism really became the focus of serious academic attention. Studies by the Chicago School found that vandalism tended to be highest in areas characterized by high population turnover, poor housing quality, poverty, unemployment, and concentrations of ethnic minorities (Shaw and McKay 1942). Although these features of the physical and social environment could not be said to cause vandalism and delinquency, there was little doubt in the minds of many observers that delinquent behaviour was transmitted from one generation to the next as a result of the subculture that prevailed in such places (Cloward and Ohlin 1961). Thus, in the absence of a stable form of society with legalistically based codes of behaviour and established norms and values, the local cultural environment precipitated criminal behaviour (Herbert 1982, 23–4). Those involved in vandalism were found to be mainly working class, male adolescents, resident in the inner city. Acts of vandalism tended to be most common in inner city areas around the central business district, with the main targets being parks and playgrounds, educational facilities, public transportation, institutions (e.g. museums), public housing, and street furniture (Van Vliet 1984).

There can be no doubt as to the validity of these descriptions of vandalism in big cities because they have been corroborated in many instances. For example, in a major study of young men in London in the 1960s and 1970s, West (1982) found a familiar list of predictors of delinquent behaviour: low family income; large families; low intelligence; parents with criminal records; parents deemed to be bad at childrearing. The weight of such evidence has been instrumental in encouraging the development of a stereotype of a vandal and a delinquent. It should be noted, however, that not all vandals are poorly educated inner city residents. Short and Nye (1957) have shown, for example, that supposed socio-economic differences in delinquency rates disappear when self-report data (i.e. survey data in which individuals acknowledge whether or not they have ever been involved in vandalism) are substituted for official statistics. Likewise, self-report data suggest that vandalism in rural areas may be more common than is often believed (Donnermeyer and Phillips 1984). One unfortunate consequence of the development of a stereotyped image of a vandal is that such stereotyping may actually *amplify* patterns of deviance within the city. Criminal labelling may encourage people in some areas to report offences more than people in other areas. At the same time, the mobilization of social control apparatus (e.g. police) may lead to both more arrests and to a tendency for individuals under suspicion in an area to believe that they have to live up to the area's reputation (Matza 1969; Lowman 1982).

The stereotyped image of vandalism holds that the acts that are committed are 'senseless' to the extent that the perpetrator makes no personal gain or profit (Levy–Leboyer 1984). In practice, of course, no crime is 'senseless'. All crimes can be understood once the underlying motivation is comprehended. In this context, it is perhaps best to view vandalism as an *environmental crime*. Indeed, vandalism is probably the ultimate environmental crime (1) because it is always against some aspect of the physical environment and (2) because those who commit vandalism are often spurred on by environmental reasons (e.g. they may be reacting to physical, managerial, social, or economic aspects of the environment) (Perlgut 1983a). Despite this, it is often very difficult to define vandalism. This is because 'vandalism' is not a legal term in some countries and hence official statistics merely record what is termed 'wilful damage'. Additionally, the definition of what constitutes vandalism is very much an attitude of mind: certain sorts of wilful damage are sometimes condoned provided financial recompense is made (e.g. damage done at stag parties) or provided the end is justified (e.g. graffiti against unhealthy products) (Biles 1984). Perhaps it is best, therefore, to think in terms of different categories of vandalism. Thus it is possible to identify no fewer than five types of vandalism: acquisitive vandalism done in order to acquire money or property (e.g. robbing phone boxes, removing street signs); tactical vandalism where the act in question serves as a means of achieving some other end, such as publicity for a cause (e.g. graffiti); vindictive vandalism where damage is done in order to obtain revenge and settle some real or imagined grievance; malicious vandalism where a sense of anger, frustration, or anomie manifests itself in destructive acts, like pulling out trees; and vandalism as play when damage results through either hard use (e.g. equipment failures in children's play-grounds) or competitive play (Lander 1954; Perlgut 1983a; Cohen 1984).

Given the extent of vandalism, it is not surprising that a good deal of attention has focussed on strategies for preventing such crime. The pioneering work in this field came from Newman (1972) who developed the idea of *defensible space*. Newman was concerned with crime in general, not just vandalism, and his central thesis was that the physical arrangement of the built environment, particularly housing estates, can be manipulated in such a way as to promote social inter-action, thereby fostering community spirit among residents and a willingness to keep an eye on what might otherwise be anonymous public spaces. In his work, Newman 'produced empirical evidence from surveys of American public housing projects to support his contention that areas will be generally well defended if they are visible to poss-ible witnesses, if a community spirit is developed whereby neighbours are encouraged to guard neutral territory, if design is such that a constant stream of potential witnesses is present, and if private territory is clearly demarcated, physically or symbolically' (Herbert 1979, 125). Predictably, Newman's views have been attacked as archi-tectural determinism. Examples have been found of estates that do not fit his generalizations and much has been made of the point that Newman did not consider offender behaviour (e.g. making a site busy might well increase the risk of an offender being seen but it also increases the range of potential targets) (Mawby 1977). Despite this, Newman's views have been quite influential because, although crime in housing projects is not caused by bad design *per se*, a poor design can undoubtedly aggravate potential security problems. Increasingly, therefore, urban planners have sought to develop *manageable spaces* where resident participation in management procedures can be combined with defensible architectural layout to produce a less crime-prone environment (Perlgut 1982).

Two problems are encountered in trying to use the idea of defens-ible space in the fight against vandalism. The first stems from the fact, already noted, that Newman's work pays little attention to the behaviour of the offender. The second arises because 'target hard-ening' may serve to *displace* rather than prevent crime. Sadly very little is known about the motivation of vandals despite the insights provided by Ward (1973). Indeed, vandalism is still seen very much as an absurd, unreasonable, or even pathological form of behaviour in so far as it produces no advantage to the perpetrator and may in fact produce disadvantages to the extent that the environment is despoiled. Such explanations as there are of vandalism tend to emphasize the role of a youth subculture in directing hostility towards symbols of adult or institutional authority (Levy–Leboyer 1984). Unfortunately such explanations say nothing about why some environments are more vandalized than others (e.g new or poorly maintained environments). However, a bewildering array of possible motivations emerges when an attempt is made to probe the causes of vandalism more deeply. Vandalism, it seems, can result from (1) a desire to wreak revenge on a society that is failing to produce opportunities for youth, (2) anger at not being able to get one's own way, (3) a need to have some excitement in an otherwise boring existence, (4) a need to acquire money, (5) a desire to 'break' a bit of the physical and social system on which society is based in order to see how the system works and to 'test its limits', (6) a desire for aesthetic stimulation (i.e. 'creative' destruction), and (7) a desire for free expression which enables an individual to define his or her 'self' (Canter 1984). Given this variety of motivations, it is easy to see why Newman's idea of defensible space is inadequate as a strategy for eradicating vandalism. Manipulation of the physical layout of a particular housing estate may prevent or diminish vandalism in that instance, but perhaps only at the expense of other areas. Vandalism, and crime in general, may, in other words, simply be displaced from one area to another. Alternatively displacement may be temporal (e.g. change the characteristic time of the crime), typological (e.g. change the type of crime committed), tactical (e.g. change the *modus operandi* of the crime rather than the target), or any combination of these (Reppetto 1976). Consideration of displacement, of course, introduces the whole issue of environmental strategies for crime prevention generally (see Perlgut 1983b), a topic which, although the subject of a great deal of research (see, for example, Jeffery 1977), lies outside the scope of the present book.

Chapter

6

Conclusion

Given projections that 3.2 *billion* people will be living in cities by the turn of the century, and 5.7 *billion* by the year 2025 (Table 1.1), this book has asked how individuals cope with city living. It has therefore addressed a topic that has been largely ignored in the literature on urban affairs. The preceding chapters have not, of course, provided comprehensive coverage of the field. Instead they focussed on selected topics. Despite this limited scope, it has become readily apparent that the coping behaviour exhibited by city dwellers is very complex, with the result that it is difficult to come up with simple and yet meaningful generalizations. For instance, there may well be variations from individual to individual in coping behaviour that stem from personality and other personal variables such as age, intelligence, and gender. Similarly, there are, in all probability, variations from group to group that derive from the influence of culture on the coping process. This is particularly the case with the way in which different societies accommodate crowding and high density living (Section 5.2). Other illustrations can be found in the impact of culture on the definition and use of personal space (Section 4.1), on travel patterns (Section 4.2), on the use of time (Section 4.3), and on the emergence of different lifestyles (Section 5.1). Despite this variability, the chapters in this book have cited a good deal of evidence that, on a 'deeper' level, human nature may also have an important bearing on the way in which individuals cope with city living. It may be, for example, that humans have basic needs which they expect the city to fulfil (Section 3.2), possibly involving emotional attachment to place (Section 3.3). It may be that children go through distinct phases of environmental awareness that match their stages of intellectual development (Section 2.1). And it may even be that the structure of the brain influences landscape appreciation, as is posited by habitat theory (Section 3.4).

The significance of human nature as an influence on the way in which individuals cope with city living lies in the fact that it is relatively immutable: if there is a hierarchy of innate human needs, then that hierarchy will be experienced similarly by all urban dwellers; if there are discrete stages in human intellectual development, then these stages will manifest themselves in the lives of all city children; and if the brain has been conditioned to appreciate certain configurations of landscape features, then that appreciation will obtain in a wide variety of environments. This is not to say that the study of how humans cope with city living is easy. Far from it. It is not simply a case of identifying components of human nature and 'applying' these in an urban context. For one thing, the behaviour of city dwellers is very highly constrained by such things as age, gender role, money, time, class, and health (Section 4.4), thereby rendering whatever links exist between human nature and behaviour at best hazy. Above all, though, it needs to be remembered that the environment is not simply a container within which behaviour is acted out. The environment is not a static and unchanging milieu to which city dwellers simply learn to adapt. Rather, the urban environment is continually in a state of flux.

Changes in the urban environment reflect, in large measure, changes in the overall nature of a society and economy. Probably the most notable changes to have affected the urban scene came with the Industrial Revolution and the concomitant shift from *gemeinschaft* to *gesellschaft* society (Chapter 1). These developments, incorporating both large factories and vast new residential tracts, changed the physiognomy of cities and led to the urban environment being distinctly different from the rural (Conzen 1983). In the eyes of many commentators, however, the cities of today, particularly those in advanced western countries, are about to undergo changes the impact of which will be every bit as far-reaching as the changes ushered in by the Industrial Revolution. Unfortunately, however, a great deal of writing on the nature of future cities is extremely speculative. Moreover, the tone of speculation has changed dramatically in a relatively few years. For example, in the 1960s a note of optimism pervaded writings on the future of cities as urban renewal and low density suburbia seemed to herald a new era of urban life. By the 1980s this had changed. Pessimism is now the order of the day with a result that there is little active debate about the future of the city other than the projection of current doubts and anxieties into the near future (Gold 1985, 92). One particular weakness of much contemporary writing is a tendency to view cities as a homogeneous class of settlement and to predict a common future, thereby glossing over significant differences between cities. Nevertheless, certain important trends are apparent. Most of these derive from the advent of computers and telecommunications which, in the eyes of many, constitute the basis for a Second Industrial Revolution that will extend society's brain-power in a similar way to that in which the first Industrial Revolution extended society's muscle-power (Kellerman 1984).

Predictions abound as to the impact of 'information technology' in the labour market. In simple terms, the best that can be said about such predictions is that they hint at a future that will be based on very different lifestyles from the ones that have dominated the urban scene in the last couple of decades. Although forecasts vary, consensus holds that employment in manufacturing will fall whereas employment in the information-rich quaternary sector of the economy will grow. What is not always made clear, unfortunately, is that workers displaced from one sector of the economy may not be easily redeployed in expanding sectors. Thus, new information may well serve to increase the gulf between the 'winners' and the 'losers' in society. If unemployment increases as a result, a situation may be reached where vast areas of cities become disadvantaged. Without a job, with limited resources and work skills of diminishing value, and with, in many cases, a millstone of capital investment in housing stock around their necks, it may be extremely difficult for such people to move in search of better prospects. New technology, in other words, may do much to fossilize the existing structure of cities. Such a viewpoint may, of course, be unnecessarily bleak, not least because an 'information economy' may well be a job generator. Indeed many commentators have taken a positive view of technological change and argued that improved information handling techniques will foster forms of settlement other than the present suburbia. Thus it is commonly envisaged that telecommunications will provide a substitute for transportation enabling people to work, shop, and bank from home, thereby creating an out-of-town population rejoicing in spaciousness and proximity to nature (Kellerman 1984, 234). In short, the concept of 'flexispace' may be as relevant to the labour market of the 1990s as 'flexitime' has become in the 1980s.

The intriguing question is how well human beings would cope with such a domicentric lifestyle if it were to come into being. Would home-based work and home-based shopping provide individuals with enough opportunities for social interaction? Would the fact that individuals work at home create a reciprocal need for leisure and entertainment activities outside the home? And what would be the implications for people's sense of community if life were to become increasingly domicentric? One of the first writers to ponder these questions was Webber (1964) who argued that interaction, not place, was becoming the essence of city life. Put slightly differently, Webber (1968) claimed that, as a result of the decreasing importance of distance and place, we are passing through a revolution which is unhitching the social processes of urbanization from the locationally fixed city and region. That is to say, in the past people chose to live in high density settlements because space was costly to overcome. This is no longer true. As a result the bonds that once held spatial settlements together are now, according to Webber (1968), dissolving, thereby dispersing settlement over an ever widening area. A similar view has been popularized by Toffler (1971). His premise is that never in history has distance meant less. Never have human relations with place been more numerous, fragile, and temporary. In consequence we are witnessing a historic decline in the significance of place to human life as there emerges a new race of 'nomads' (Toffler 1971, 76). Toffler noted that change was so rapid as to induce culture shock which might very well manifest itself, at the level of the individual, in increasing anxiety and depression, increasing self preoccupation, and an increase in psychosomatic illness. The crux of Toffler's (1971, 92) argument was that, as a result of mobility, social and emotional commitments are shifting from place-related social structures (such as cities and neighbourhoods) to more fluid and placeless social relationships (such as those provided by membership of business corporations and professional associations). In support of his arguments on mobility, Toffler cited the fact that, in seventy major United States cities, the average length of residence in one place is less than four years. Toffler's views are, then, very similar to Webber's notion of 'community without propinquity'. Basically Webber contended that, as a result of increased leisure time and increased mobility, people would no longer be forced to have their greatest involvement (i.e. their greatest sense of community) with those amongst whom they lived (i.e. their neighbourhood, as delimited on the basis of propinquity). Instead 'communities' might well be spatially dispersed but nevertheless close-knit, intimate, and held together by shared interests and values (i.e. communities based on common interest rather than propinquity). Initially, according to Webber, this development of community without propinquity would occur in the relatively more affluent sections of society but would eventually spread to the whole of society. Predictably, such views have come in for stern criticism, notably from researchers who have claimed that place and locality are still crucial variables in urban life (Blowers 1973). Moreover, it may well be that increasing mobility creates a reciprocal need for a firm home base, thereby strengthening place attachment with the result that the local area may come to serve as a repository of social traditions and as a haven in an uncertain world (Walmsley and Lewis 1984, 34).

Webber's views relate very much to changing societal behaviour and values. To a considerable extent these changes are brought about by new technology. It is therefore important to note, in this context, that just as there is an extensive literature on the changes in society that are likely to flow from technological change, so too there is an extensive literature on how new technology might change the form and function of cities (Brotchie *et al*. 1985; Castells 1985). Much of this work serves to expose the tension inherent in the need to plan a new social order at a time when many urban dwellers either cling to the status quo or indulge in nostalgia and hanker after what are commonly perceived to be more certain times (Gappert and Knight 1982). Conservatism in the face of technological change is, of course, understandable. Uncertainty about future urban lifestyles is widespread. The impact of change is difficult to predict. What can be said with a fair degree of certainty is, however, that leisure time is likely to increase, both in enforced terms and as a result of reductions in the length of the working week brought about by increased productivity and also possibly by a desire to share the work that is available among an otherwise under-employed workforce (e.g. work-sharing programmes). Retailing, too, will change (Guy 1985). Changes here will range from relatively simple ones such as EFTPOS (electronic funds transfer at point of sale) which will hasten the advent of the cashless society, to initiatives like home-based shopping (using two-way cable television systems) that might have potentially profound implications on the size and location of shopping centres. The city centre, for example, may become much less attractive as a venue for retail activity which in turn may lead to fewer opportunities for new investment or redevelopment (Champion 1983). Above all, though, the nature of work will change. The rise of what is described as 'telecommuting' has already been mentioned. Estimates have been made that improved telecommunications may replace 20–60% of local business travel (Nilles *et al*. 1976). The extent of such 'telecommuting' remains unclear however and it seems likely that a distinction between home and workplace will continue to apply for large numbers of workers. In this connection it is important to note that, in terms of industrial location, much hi-tech industry is likely to favour locations, particularly 'out-of-town', that offer characteristics different from those traditionally considered in factory location. In short, the impact of new technology on the labour market will be spatially selective. Some areas will grow, others decline. At a regional scale, a distinction has already been drawn in the United States between a growing 'sunbelt' and a stagnating 'snowbelt'. Similarly, Britain is often portrayed as two nations: a prosperous southeast and a depressed north. At an urban level, some cities will grow while others decline. Particularly favoured are likely to be those capital cities in which the headquarters of the major firms concerned with information technology are located. Paris, for example, has the headquarters of 90% of France's major corporations, London the headquarters of 62% of the United Kingdom's top 500 corporations (Ley 1983, 389). Within the city, inner suburban areas are likely to be hit hardest by changes in the labour market, particularly those associated with de-industrialization. Of course, there is nothing terribly new in the inner city being viewed as a 'problem area': such was the case in the late nineteenth century, the major difference being that cities at that time had dynamic economies. Nowadays the most optimistic scenario painted for the inner city is one of low growth with greater equality of service provision, brought about largely by government intervention (Hall 1981, 116). Despite this, some inner city areas, even in advanced economies, are characterized by unemployment rates as high as 40% and by derelict land that can occupy as much as 10% of the total area (Ley, 1983, 387).

Appreciation of the changes that are afoot in some advanced economies has led several commentators to suggest that cities are redundant in so far as improved telecommunications will free people from the need for face-to-face contact. There are, however, a number of strong arguments against such a view: *in situ* information exchange will not satisfy people's needs for work and leisure; isolation, even with improved communications, will be wholly unacceptable to many people; personnel management will not be able to be sustained properly in a decentralized and dispersed organization; and dispersal will not be cost-effective in terms of energy and transport (Kellerman 1984). In the light of these arguments, it seems likely that the city of the foreseeable future will be a variant on the existing city rather than something radically different. The most popular scenario seems to be one of continued urban sprawl. Various names have been applied to this phenomenon. Muller (1981) coined the term 'exurbia' to describe suburban sprawl beyond city limits and Berry (1980) used the expression 'counter-urbanization' to denote the decentralization of population and employment away from large metropolitan areas and into adjoining regions. The end product of this sort of sprawl may conceivably be the 'megalopolis' described by Gottmann (1961) in his study of urbanized settlement on the northeastern seaboard of the United States. Such megalopolitan development arises from the coalescence of individual metropolitan areas as they spread outwards, and is well illustrated in the so-called 'Boswash' megalopolis stretching from Boston to Washington along a north-south axis of nearly 1000 kilometres (600 miles) and an east-west axis of 80–240 kilometres (50–150 miles) (Ley 1983, 39). The notion of dispersed cities is not, of course, new (Scargill 1979). It found expression, for example, in Wright's (1958) version of 'Broadacre City'. The difference between Wright and Gottmann is, however, that the former saw dispersed urban living as a utopian idea whereas the latter saw it as a reality. In the megalopolitan areas of today, urban dwellers are 'voting with their wheels' in the sense that they are choosing to live outside cities, thereby escaping some of the problems (noise, congestion, pollution, crowding) often associated with cities (Davie 1972). Predictably, megalopolis has its detractors, principally among those who see it as both ugly and an unnecessary alienation of rural land. Others have defended it, claiming that, if properly planned, such development may be superior to past standards of urban living (Lynch 1968). What remains to be seen, however, is whether megalopolis is an emerging universal urban form or whether it is merely an American cultural extravaganza, highly dependent on the private car and a passion for space.

Implicit in many discussions of urban sprawl is the idea that urban development will have about it a certain 'sameness'. Architecturally, this may be true, given standardized building materials and techniques. Nevertheless, it is equally possible to argue that the city of the future will become internally more differentiated than is the case at present. In particular, the residential segregation of social classes that came to the fore with the rise of industrial capitalism (Harris 1984) may give way to differentiation on the basis of other variables such as lifestyle. Indeed, one possible way for planners and policy-makers to cope with the turbulence and uncertainty of the so-called 'post-industrial society' might be to encourage diversity based on public participation, open planning, and the decentralization of decision-making (Walmsley 1980). Such variety might herald an urban renaissance (Cybriwsky and Western 1982). In this way there might be increasing residential choice, at least for those with enough social 'power' to have a choice. This raises the question of what people want. What are their preferences for urban living? How will they accommodate change? How will people cope if they are uprooted? Will they seek to maintain a sense of community in the face of a changing urban fabric? Of course, knowing what people want will not reveal everything about living in the cities of the future because much hinges, not on what people want, but on what is provided by development and regulatory agencies. However, even in the policy area, it cannot be claimed that what will happen is what governments allow to happen because this attributes too much power and influence to government. Governments are undoubtedly important but, in respect of urban policy, they are always faced by constraints: economic constraints (notably the fact that there is never enough money to do everything that is needed); political constraints (such as the need to arrive at a trade-off between liberty, equality, and efficiency); and cultural constraints (exemplified by the fact that cities tend to have been 'bureaucratized' and their development guided by principles of organizational efficiency and rationality) (Ley 1983). In short, governments might have little room to manoeuvre in urban policy, especially when many of the issues (e.g. new technology) and institutions (e.g. trans-national corporations) with which they have to deal are beyond their control.

Clearly, the question of what it will be like to live in cities for the remainder of this century and beyond is so complex that no one approach can, in isolation, provide a sufficient level of understanding. The student of urban affairs obviously needs to take stock of the changing spatial organization of society and, in particular, of shifting power bases within cities because these will have a major bearing on 'who gets what when where and how'. Power, after all, influences resource allocation which in turn influences the way in which cities are structured. In short, it is undeniable that cities around the world are in a state of flux that will cause their character and function to change markedly, even before the end of this century. It follows from this that the student of urban affairs needs to know about the forces that are changing the structure of cities. Such a 'structuralist' approach will not, however, provide a full understanding of what city life will be like in coming decades. This is because city dwellers are not mere automatons that respond predictably to the conditions in which they find themselves living. Rather, city dwellers are caring, feeling individuals who both adapt environments and adapt to environments. Any understanding of urban life, both now and in the future, therefore needs to take stock of how individual city dwellers cope with the urban environment. The present book has tried to shed light on this issue. It has shown, in particular, that, in recent years, a good deal has been learnt about how individuals cognize the urban environment, how they learn about the environment to the point where they build up images which may influence their subsequent behaviour, how they attach meaning to places and landscapes, and how the city environment can be instrumental in filling a number of basic human needs. The book has also provided some insights into how people decide where to go and what to do with their time in cities. The book has not, however, set forward a set of hard and fast principles according to which city dwellers act out their lives. Such an undertaking would be an impossibility for a number of reasons, not least the fact that our understanding of the causes and characteristics of the behaviour of city dwellers is still at a very tentative stage. The present book has therefore been able to do no more than point out the more salient findings to have emerged in a vast volume of research in the last couple of decades. No doubt progress in our understanding of city life will be enhanced as more research is undertaken in the future. Thus, the nature of environmental images may become better understood, the link between images and behaviour better elucidated, the mobility of city dwellers better documented, and the nature of human territoriality better defined, all within the bounds of mainstream social science. Equally, advances in humanistic approaches may lead to new insights into the emotional bonding that develops between people and their surroundings, a bonding presently all too often detailed only in anecdote. There is, in other words, a vast amount of research waiting to be done that will almost certainly provide a clearer picture than we presently have of how individuals cope with city living. It would be wrong, however, to view this research as involving no more than the discovery and piecing together of new bits of information, much in the manner of a jigsaw puzzle. Human behaviour is astonishingly varied and one of the paramount problems to be faced by researchers is that of providing a theoretical framework which explains how this variability comes about and how city dwellers trade off their own preferences, wants and desires against the constraints imposed by the society in which they live. Hopefully the present book will stimulate research that may lead us towards such a theoretical framework.

References

Agrest, D. and **Gandelsonas, M.** (1977) Semiotics and the limits of architecture, in **T. A. Seboek** (ed.) *A Perfusion of Signs*, Indiana University Press, pp. 90–120.

Aiello, J. R., **Epstein, Y. M.** and **Karlin, R. A.** (1975) Effects of crowding on electrodermal activity, *Sociological Symposium* **14**, 45–58.

Aiello, J. R. and **Thompson, D. E.** (1980) Personal space, crowding, and spatial behaviour in a cultural context, in **I. Altman, A. Rapoport** and **J. F. Wohlwill** (eds) (1980) *Human Behaviour and Environment: Advances in Theory and Research, Vol. 4: Environment and Culture*, Plenum, New York, pp. 107–78.

Altman, I. (1975) *Environment and Social Behaviour*, Brooks-Cole: Belmont.

Altman, I. and **Gauvain, M.** (1981) A cross-cultural and dialectic analysis of homes, in **L. S. Liben** *et al.* (eds) *Spatial Representation and Behaviour Across the Life Span*, Academic Press, New York, pp. 283–320.

Amato, P. R. (1981) The impact of the built environment on prosocial and affiliative behaviour: a field study of the Townsville City Mall, *Australian Journal of Psychology* **33**, 297–303.

Anderson, M. (1971) *Family Structure in Nineteenth Century Lancashire*, Cambridge University Press: Cambridge.

Anderson, R. (1975) *Leisure–An Inappropriate Concept for Women?* AGPS: Canberra.

Appleton, J. H. (1975a) *The Experience of Landscape*, Wiley: London.

Appleton, J. (1975b) Landscape evaluation: the theoretical vacuum, *Transactions of the Institute of British Geographers* **66**, 120–3.

Appleyard, D. A. (1969a) Why buildings are known, *Environment and Behaviour* **1**, 131–56.

Appleyard, D. (1969b) City designers and the pluralistic city, in **L. Rodwin** (ed.) *Planning Urban Growth and Regional Development*, MIT Press: Cambridge, Mass., pp. 422–52.

Appleyard, D. (1970) Styles and methods of structuring a city, *Environment and Behaviour* **2**, 100–17.

Appleyard, D. (1973) Notes on urban perception and knowledge, in **R. M. Downs** and **D. Stea** (eds) *Image and Environment*, Aldine, Chicago, pp. 109–14.

Appleyard, D. (1976) *Planning a Pluralistic City*, M.I.T. Press: Cambridge, Mass.

Appleyard, D. (1979) The environment as a social symbol, *Ekistics* **46** (278), 272–80.

Appleyard, D. (1981) *Livable Streets*, University of California Press: Berkeley.

Appleyard, D. and **Lintell, M.** (1972) The environmental quality of city streets: the residents' viewpoint, *Journal of the American Institute of Planners* **38**, 84–101.

Ardener, S. (1981) Ground rules and social maps for women: an introduction, in **S. Ardener** (ed.) *Women and Space: Ground Rules and Social Maps*, Croom Helm, London, pp. 11–34.

Ardrey, R. (1967) *The Territorial Imperative*, Fontana: London.

Australian Bureau of Statistics (1979) *General Social Survey: Crime Victims, May 1975*, Australian Bureau of Statistics: Canberra.

Australian Bureau of Statistics (1984) *Crime Victims Survey, Australia 1983, Preliminary*, Australian Bureau of Statistics: Canberra.

Bagley, C. and **Jacobson, S.** (1976) Ecological variation in three types of suicide, *Psychological Medicine* **6**, 423–7.

Bagley, C., Jacobson, S. and **Rehin, A.** (1976) Completed suicide: a taxonomic analysis of clinical and social data, *Psychological Medicine* **6**, 429–38.

Baldassare, M. (1978) Human spatial behaviour, *Annual Review of Sociology* **4**, 29–56.

Baldwin, J. and **Bottoms, A. E.** (1976) *The Urban Criminal*, Tavistock: London.

Bardo, J. W. (1984) A re-examination of the neighbourhood as a socio-spatial schema, *Sociological Inquiry* **54**, 346–58.

Barker, R. (1968) *Ecological Psychology*, Stanford University Press: Stanford.

Barthes, R. (1964) *Elements of Semiology* [trans. A. Lavers and C. Smith], Hill and Wang: New York.

Bartlett, F. C. (1932) *Remembering*, Cambridge University Press: Cambridge.

Bauer, R. A. (ed.) (1966) *Social Indicators*, MIT Press: Cambridge, Mass.

Baum, A., Singer, J. E. and **Baum, C. S.** (1983) Stress and the environment, in **G. W. Evans** (ed.) *Environmental Stress*, Cambridge University Press, Cambridge, pp. 15–44.

Beck, R. and **Wood, D.** (1976) Cognitive transformation of information from urban geographic fields to mental maps, *Environment and Behaviour* 8, 199–238.

Becker, F. D. (1977) *Housing Messages*, Dowden, Hutchinson and Ross: Stroudsburg.

Bell, W. (1958) Social choice, life style and suburban residence, in **W. Dobriner** (ed.) *The Suburban Community*, Putnam, New York, pp. 225–47.

Bell, C. and **Newby, H.** (1971) *Community Studies: An Introduction to the Sociology of the Local Community*, Allen and Unwin: London.

Berger, B. M. (1960) *The Working-Class Suburb: A Study of Auto Workers in Suburbia*, University of California Press: Berkeley.

Berk, R. A. and **Berk, S. F.** (1980) *Labour and Leisure at Home: Content and Organization of the Household Day*, Sage: London.

Bernstein, B. (1959) A public language: some sociological implications of a linguistic form, *British Journal of Sociology* 10, 311–26.

Berry, B. J. L. (1980) Inner city futures: an American dilemma revisited, *Transactions of the Institute of British Geographers* 5, 1–28

Biles, D. (1984) Vandalism: An Australian view, in **M. Campbell** (ed.)(1984) *Vandalism in the A.C.T.: Problems and Strategies*, Canberra CAE Series in Administrative Studies Seminar Proceedings 6, pp. 17–32.

Billinge, M. (1983) The Mandarin dialect: an essay on style in contemporary geographical writing, *Transactions of the Institute of British Geographers* 8, 400–20.

Blacksell, M. and **Gilg, A.** (1975) Landscape evolution in practice – the case of south-east Devon, *Transactions of the Institute of British Geographers* 66, 135–40.

Blaut, J. M. (1983) Assimilation versus ghettoization, *Antipode* 15(1), 35–41.

Blaut, J. M., McCleary, G. S. and **Blaut, A. S.** (1970)

Environmental mapping in young children, *Environment and Behaviour* **2**, 335–50.

Blowers, A. (1973) The neighbourhood: explorations of a concept, in *The City as a Social System*, Open University, Milton Keynes, pp. 49–90.

Bohland, J. R. and **Herbert, D. T.** (1983) Neighbourhood and health effects on elderly morale, *Environment and Planning A* **15**, 929–44.

Boles, J. K. (1983) Making cities work for women, *Urban Affairs Quarterly* **19**, 573–80.

Bonnes-Dobrowolny, M. and **Secchiaroli, G.** (1983) Space and meaning of the city-centre cognition: an interactional-transactional approach, *Human Relations* **36**, 23–37.

Booth, A. (1976) *Human Crowding and Its Consequences*, Praeger: New York.

Boots, B. N. (1979) Population density, crowding and human behaviour, *Progress in Human Geography* **3**, 13–63.

Bornstein, M. and **Bornstein, H.** (1976) The pace of life, *Nature* **259** (5544), 557–9.

Boulding, K. E. (1956) *The Image*, University of Michigan Press: Ann Arbor.

Boulding, K. E. (1973) Foreword, in **R. M. Downs** and **D. Stea** (eds) *Image and Environment*, Aldine, Chicago, pp. vii–xi.

Bowlby, S. (1978) Accessibility, shopping provision and mobility, in **A. Kirby** and **B. Goodall** (eds) *Resources in Planning*, Pergamon, Oxford.

Boyle, M. J. and **Robinson, M. E.** (1979) Cognitive mapping and understanding, in **D. T. Herbert** and **R. J. Johnston** (eds) *Geography and the Urban Environment: Progress in Research and Applications, Vol. 2*, Wiley, London, pp. 59–82.

Bradshaw, J. (1972) The concept of social need, *New Society* **19** (496), 640–3.

Brantingham, P. J. and **Brantingham, P. L.** (1975) Residential burglary and urban form, *Urban Studies* **12**, 273–84.

Brantingham, P. J. and **Brantingham, P. L.** (eds) (1981) *Environmental Criminology*, Sage: Beverly Hills.

Briggs, R. (1973a) Urban cognitive distance, in **R. M. Downs** and **D. Stea** (eds) *Image and Environment*, Aldine, Chicago, pp. 361–88.

Briggs, R. (1973b) On the relationship between cognitive and objective distance, in **W. F. E. Preiser** (ed.) *Environmental Research Design*, Dowden, Hutchinson and Ross, Stroudsburg, pp. 186–99.

Briggs, R. (1976) Methodologies for the measurement of cognitive distance, in **G. T. Moore** and **R. G. Golledge** (eds)

Environmental Knowing, Dowden, Hutchinson and Ross, Stroudsburg, pp. 325–34.

Broadbent, G. (1976) A plain man's guide to the theory of signs in architecture, *Architectural Design* **47**, 474–82.

Brookfield, H. C. (1969) On the environment as perceived, *Progress in Geography* **1**, 51–80.

Brotchie, J. *et al.* (eds) (1985) *The Future of Urban Form: The Impact of New Technology*, Croom Helm: Beckenham.

Brower, S. N. (1980) Territory in urban settings, in I. Altman, A. Rapoport, and J. F. Wohlwill (eds) *Human Behaviour and Environment: Advances in Theory and Research, Vol. 4: Environment and Culture*, Plenum, New York, pp. 179–207.

Bruegmann, R. (1982) Two postmodernist visions of urban design, *Landscape* **26**, 31–7.

Bryant, P. (1974) *Perception and Understanding in Young Children: An Experimental Approach*, Methuen: London.

Bunting, T. E. and Guelke, L. (1979) Behavioural and perception geography: a critical appraisal, *Annals of the Association of American Geographers* **69**, 448–62.

Burgess, J. (1982) Filming the Fens: a visual interpretation of regional character, in J. Gold and J. Burgess (eds) *Valued Environments*, Allen & Unwin, London, pp. 35–54.

Burgess, J. and Gold, J. (1982) On the significance of valued environments, in J. Gold and J. Burgess (eds) *Valued Environments*, Allen & Unwin, London, pp. 1–9.

Burnett, P. (1976) Behavioural geography and the philosophy of mind, in R. G. Golledge and G. Rushton (eds) *Spatial Choice and Spatial Behaviour*, Ohio State University Press, Columbus, pp. 23–48.

Burton, I. (1963) The quantitative revolution and theoretical geography, *Canadian Geographer* **7**, 151–62.

Buttimer, A. (1972) Social space and planning of residential areas, *Environment and Behaviour* **4**, 279–318.

Buttimer, A. (1974) *Values in Geography*, AAG Commission on College Geography, Resource Paper No. 24, Washington.

Buttimer, A. and Seamon, D. (eds) (1980) *The Human Experience of Space and Place*, Croom Helm: London.

Cadwallader, M. (1976) Cognitive distance in intraurban space, in G. T. Moore and R. G. Golledge (eds) *Environmental Knowing*, Dowden, Hutchinson and Ross, Stroudsburg, pp. 316–24.

Cadwallader, M. (1979) Problems in cognitive distance: implications for cognitive mapping, *Environment and Behaviour* **11**, 559–76.

Calhoun, J. B. (1966) The role of space in animal sociology, *Journal of Social Issues* **22**, 46–58.

Campbell, A., Converse, P. E. and **Rodgers, W. L.** (1976) *The Quality of American Life: Perceptions, Evaluations, and Satisfactions*, Russell Sage Foundation: New York.

Canter, D. V. (1977) *The Psychology of Place*, Architectural Press: London.

Canter, D. (1984) Vandalism: overview and prospect, in **C. Levy-Leboyer** (ed.) *Vandalism: Behaviour and Motivations*, Elsevier, Amsterdam, pp. 345–56.

Canter, D. and **Canter, S.** (1971) Close together in Tokyo, *Design and Environment* **2**, 60–3.

Canter, D. V. and **Tagg, S. K.** (1975) Distance estimation in cities, *Environment and Behaviour* **7**, 59–80.

Carp, F. M. (1975) Ego-defense or cognitive consistency effects on environmental evaluation, *Journal of Gerontology* **30**, 707–11.

Carp, F. M. and **Carp, A.** (1982) Perceived environmental quality of neighbourhoods: development of assessment scales and their relation to age and gender, *Journal of Environmental Psychology* **2**, 295–312.

Carter, R. L. and **Hill, K. Q.** (1980) Area-images and behaviour: an alternative perspective for understanding urban crime, in **D. E. Georges-Abeyie** and **K. Harries** (eds) *Crime: A Spatial Perspective*, Columbia University Press, New York, pp. 193–204.

Castells, M. (ed.) (1985) *High Technology, Space and Society*, Sage: Beverly Hills.

Cavan, R. S. *et al.* (1949) *Personal Adjustment in Old Age*, Science Research Associates: Chicago.

Champion, A. G. (1983) Conclusion, in **R. L. Davies** and **A. G. Champion** (eds) *The Future for the City Centre*, Academic Press, London, pp. 283–9.

Chapin, F. S. Jr. (1974) *Human Activity Patterns and the City: Things People do in Time and in Space*, Wiley: New York.

Choldin, H. M. (1978) Urban density and pathology, *Annual Review of Sociology* **4**, 91–113.

Christensen, K. (1982) Geography as a human science: a philosophic critique of the positivist-humanist split, in **P. R. Gould** and **G. Olsson** (eds) *A Search for Common Ground*, Pion, London, pp. 37–57.

Cichocki, M. K. (1981) Women's travel patterns in a suburban development, in **G. R. Wekerle** *et al.* (eds) *New Space for Women*. Westview Press, Boulder, pp. 151–63.

Clark, N. (1972) Transport policy for Australian cities, *Australian Quarterly* **44** (3), 33–48.

Clark, W. A. V. and **Smith, T. R.** (1979) Modelling information use in a spatial context, *Annals of the Association of American Geographers* **69**, 575–88.

Clayton, S. (1983) Social need revisited, *Journal of Social Policy* **12**, 215–34.

Clemente, F. and **Kleiman, M. B.** (1976) Fear of crime among the aged, *Gerontologist* **16**, 207–10.

Cloward, R. A. and **Ohlin, L. E.** (1961) *Delinquency and Opportunity: A Theory of Delinquent Gangs*, Routledge and Kegan Paul: London.

Cohen, L. E. and **Felson, M.** (1979) Social change and crime rate trends: a routine activity approach, *American Sociological Review* **44**, 588–608.

Cohen, S. (1984) Sociological approaches to vandalism, in **C. Levy-Leboyer** (ed.) *Vandalism: Behaviour and Motivations*, Elsevier, Amsterdam, pp. 51–61.

Cohen, S., Glass, D. C. and **Singer, J. E.** (1973) Apartment noise, auditory discrimination and reading ability in children, *Journal of Experimental Social Psychology* **9**, 407–22.

Cohen, S. and **Sherrod, D. R.** (1978) When density matters: environmental control as a determinant of crowding effects in laboratory and residential settings, *Journal of Population* **1**, 189–202.

Conzen, M. P. (1983) Historical geography: changing spatial structure and social patterns of Western cities, *Progress in Human Geography* **7**, 88–107.

Cooper, C. (1974) The house as symbol of the self, in **J. Lang** *et al.* (eds) *Designing for Human Behaviour: Architecture and the Behavioural Sciences*, Dowden, Hutchinson and Ross, Stroudsburg, pp. 130–46.

Cooper, M. C. (1978) A tale of two spaces: contrasting lives of a court and plaza in Minneapolis, *American Institute of Architects Journal* **67**, 34–40.

Couclelis, H. (1983) Some second thoughts about theory in the social sciences, *Geographical Analysis* **15**, 28–33.

Cox, V. C., Paulus, P. B. and **McCain, G.** (1984) Prison crowding research: the relevance for prison housing standards and a general approach regarding crowding phenomena, *American Psychologist* **39**, 1148–60.

Craik, K. H. (1972a) Psychological factors in landscape appraisal, *Environment and Behaviour* **4**, 255–66.

Craik, K. H. (1972b) Appraising the objectivity of landscape dimensions, in **J. V. Krutilla** (ed.) *Natural Environments*, Johns Hopkins University Press, Baltimore, pp. 292–346.

Cressey, P. G. (1971) The Taxi-Dance Hall as a social world, in **J. Short** (ed.) *The Social Fabric of the Metropolis*, University of Chicago Press, Chicago, pp. 193–209.

Csikszentmihalyi, M. and **Rochberg-Halton, E.** (1981) *The*

Meaning of Things: Domestic Symbols and the Self, Cambridge University Press: Cambridge.

Cullen, G. (1971) *The Concise Townscape,* Architectural Press: London.

Culler, J. (1976) *Ferdinand de Saussure,* Penguin: Harmondsworth.

Cumming, E. and Henry, W. E. (1961) *Growing Old,* Basic Books: New York.

Cutler, S. J. (1972) The availability of personal transportation, residential location and life satisfaction among the aged, *Journal of Gerontology* **27**, 383–89.

Cybriwsky, K. A. and **Western, J.** (1982) Revitalizing downtowns: by whom and for whom? in **D. T. Herbert** and **R. J. Johnston** (eds) *Geography and the Urban Environment: Progress in Research and Applications, Vol.4,* Wiley, Chichester, pp. 343–65.

Dalton and **Dalton** (1975) *Community and its Relevance to Australian Society: An Examination of the Sociological Definition,* AGPS: Canberra.

Dangschat, J. *et al.* (1982) Action spaces of urban residents: an empirical study in the region of Hamburg, *Environment and Planning A* **14**, 1155–74.

Daniels, P. W. and **Warnes, A. M.** (1980) *Movement in Cities: Spatial Perspectives on Urban Transport and Travel,* Methuen: London.

Davidson, R. N. (1981) *Crime and Environment,* Croom Helm: London.

Davie, M. (1972) *In the Future Now: A Report from California,* Hamilton: London.

Day, R. A. (1976) Urban distance cognition: review and contribution, *Australian Geographer* **13**, 193–200.

Day, R. A. and **Walmsley, D. J.** (1978) Trendies and workers: inner suburban attitudes, *Royal Australian Planning Institute Journal* **16** (2), 72.

Day, R. A. and **Walmsley, D. J.** (1981) Residential preferences in Sydney's inner suburbs: a study in diversity, *Applied Geography* **1**, 185–97.

Dear, M. J. and **Taylor, S. M.** (1982) *Not on Our Street: Community Attitudes to Mental Health Care,* Pion: London.

Dearden, P. (1980) Landscape assessment: the last decade, *Canadian Geographer* **24**, 316–25.

de Lauwe, C. P. M. (1959) *Famille et Habitation,* Centre National de la Recherche Scientifique: Paris.

Department of the Environment (1976) *National Travel Survey 1972/73: A Comparison of the 1965 and 1972/73 Surveys,* HMSO: London.

Desbarats, J. (1983) Spatial choice and constraints on behaviour, *Annals of the Association of American Geographers* **73**, 340–57.

Desor, J. A. (1972) Toward a psychological theory of crowding, *Journal of Personality and Social Psychology* **21**, 79–83.

Donnermeyer, J. F. and **Phillips, G. H.** (1984) Vandals and vandalism in the USA: a rural perspective, in **C. Levy-Leboyer** (ed.) *Vandalism: Behaviour and Motivations*, Elsevier, Amsterdam, pp. 149–160.

Doob, L. W. (1940) *The Plans of Men*, Yale University Press: New Haven.

Downs, R. M. (1970a) Geographic space perception: past approaches and future prospects, *Progress in Geography* **2**, 65–108.

Downs, R. M. (1970b) The cognitive structure of an urban shopping centre, *Environment and Behaviour* **2**, 13–39.

Downs, R. M. (1976) Personal constructions of personal construct theory, in **G. T. Moore** & **R. G. Golledge** (eds) *Environmental Knowing*, Dowden, Hutchinson and Ross, Stroudsburg, pp. 72–87.

Downs, R. M. (1981) Cognitive mapping: a thematic analysis, in **K. R. Cox** and **R. G. Golledge** (eds) *Behavioural Problems in Geography Revisited*, Methuen, London, pp. 95–122.

Downs, R. M. and **Meyer, J. T.** (1978) Geography and the mind: an exploration of perceptual geography, *American Behavioural Scientist* **22**, 59–77.

Downs, R. M. and **Stea, D.** (1973a) Cognitive maps and spatial behaviours: processes and products, in **R. M. Downs** and **D. Stea** (eds) *Image and Environment*, Aldine, Chicago, pp. 8–26.

Downs, R. M. and **Stea, D.** (1973b) Cognitive representations, in **R. M. Downs** and **D. Stea** (eds) *Image and Environment*, Aldine, Chicago, pp. 79–87.

Downs, R. M. and **Stea, D.** (1973c) Preface, in **R. M. Downs** and **D. Stea** (eds) *Image and Environment*, Aldine, Chicago, xiii–xviii.

Downs, R. M. and **Stea, D.** (1977) *Maps in Minds: Reflections on Cognitive Mapping*, Harper & Row: New York.

Edney, J. J. (1976) Human territories: comment of function properties, *Environment and Behaviour* **8**, 31–48.

Edwards, J. N., Booth, A. and **Edwards, P. K.** (1982) Housing type, stress and family relations, *Social Forces* **61**, 241–57.

Eibl-Eibesfeldt, I. (1970) *Ethology: The Biology of Behaviour*, Holt: New York.

Ekman, G. and **Bratfisch,O.** (1965) Subjective distance and emotional involvement: a psychological mechanism, *Acta Psychologica* **24**, 430–7.

Epstein, Y. M. (1983) Crowding stress and human behaviour, in **G. W. Evans** (ed.) *Environmental Stress*, Cambridge University Press, Cambridge, pp. 133–48.

Evans, G. W. (1980) Environmental cognition, *Psychological Bulletin* **88**, 259–87.

Evans, G. W. (ed.)(1983) *Environmental Stress*, Cambridge University Press: Cambridge.

Everitt, J. C. (1976) Community and propinquity in a city, *Annals of the Association of American Geographers* **66**, 104–16.

Everitt, J. and **Cadwallader, M.** (1972) The home area concept in urban analysis, in **W. J. Mitchell** (ed.) *Environmental Design: Research and Practice*, University of California Press, Los Angeles.

Eyles, J. (1968) *The Inhabitants' Images of Highgate Village, London*, Discussion Paper No. 15, Department of Geography, London School of Economics.

Eyles, J. (1985) *Senses of Place*, Silverbrook Press: Warrington.

Fanning, D. M. (1967) Families in flats, *British Medical Journal* **18**, 382–6.

Faris, R. E. L. and **Dunham, H. W.** (1939) *Mental Disorders in Urban Areas*, University of Chicago Press: Chicago.

Faulkner, H. W. (1978) Locational stress on Sydney's metropolitan fringe, Unpublished Ph.D. thesis, Australian National University, Canberra.

Fines, K. D. (1968) Landscape evaluation: a research project in East Sussex, *Regional Studies* **2**, 41–55.

Fischer, C. S. (1976) *The Urban Experience*, Harcourt, Brace Jovanovitch: New York.

Fischer, C. S. (1981) The public and private worlds of city life, *American Sociological Review* **46**, 306–16.

Fischer, C. S., Baldassare, M. and **Oshe, R. J.** (1975) Crowding studies and urban life: a critical review, *Journal of the American Institute of Planners* **31**, 406–18.

Fishbein, M. and **Ajzen, I.** (1975) *Belief, Attitude, Intention and Behaviour: An Introduction to Theory and Research*, Addison-Wesley: Reading, Mass.

Fontana, A. (1977) *The Last Frontier: The Social Meaning of Growing Old*, Sage: Beverly Hills.

Franck, K. A. (1980) Friends and strangers: the social experience of living in urban and non-urban settings, *Journal of Social Issues* **36**, 3, 52–71.

Fransella, F. and **Bannister, D.** (1977) *A Manual for Repertory Grid Technique*, Academic Press: London.

Freedman, J. (1975) *Crowding and Behaviour*, Viking Press: New York.

Freeman, H. (1978) Mental health and the environment, *British Journal of Psychiatry* **132**, 113–24.

Fried, M. (1963) Grieving for a lost home, in **L. H. Duhl** (ed.) *The Urban Condition*, Basic Books, New York, pp. 151–71.

Gans, H. (1962) *The Urban Villagers*, Free Press: New York.

Gans, H. (1967) *The Levittowners: Ways of Life and Politics in a New Suburban Community*, Penguin: Harmondsworth.

Gans, H. J. (1968) *People and Plans*, Basic Books: New York.

Gappert, G. and **Knight, R. V.** (eds) (1982) *Cities in the Twenty-First Century*, Sage: Beverly Hills.

Garling, T., Book, A. and **Linberg, E.** (1984) Cognitive mapping of large-scale environments: the interrelationship of action plans, acquisition, and orientation, *Environment and Behaviour* **16**, 3–34.

Genereux, R. L., Ward, L. M. and **Russell, J. A.** (1983) The behavoural component of the meaning of places, *Journal of Environmental Psychology* **3**, 43–55.

Genovese, R. G. (1980) A women's self-help network as a response to service needs in the suburbs, *Signs* **5**(3) Supplement S 248–56.

Giggs, J. A. (1973) The distribution of schizophrenics in Nottingham, *Transactions of the Institute of British Geographers* **51**, 55–76.

Glass, D. C. and **Singer J.** (1972) *Urban Stress*, Academic Books: New York.

Godkin, M. A. (1980) Identity and place: clinical applications based on notions of rootedness and uprootedness, in **A. Buttimer** and **D. Seamon** (eds) *The Human Experience of Space and Place*, Croom Helm, London, pp. 73–85.

Golant, S. M. (1972) *The Residential Location and Spatial Behaviour of the Elderly: A Canadian Example*, Research Paper 143, Department of Geography, University of Chicago.

Gold, J. R. (1980) *An Introduction to Behavioural Geography*, Oxford University Press: Oxford.

Gold, J. R. (1982) Territoriality and human spatial behaviour, *Progress in Human Geography* **6**, 44–67.

Gold, J. R. (1985) The city of the future and the future of the city, in **R. King** (ed.) *Geographical Futures*, Geographical Association, Sheffield, pp. 92–101.

Gold, J. and **Burgess, J.** (eds) (1982) *Valued Environments*, Allen & Unwin: London.

Golledge, R. G. (1978) Learning about urban environments, in **T. Carlstein** *et al.* (eds) *Timing Space and Spacing Time, Vol. 1 Making Sense of Time*, Arnold, London, pp. 76–98.

Golledge, R. G., Briggs, R. and **Demko, D.** (1969) The configuration of distances in intraurban space, *Proceedings of the Association of American Geographers* 1, 60–5.

Goodchild, B. (1974) Class differences in environmental perception: an exploratory study, *Urban Studies* 11, 157–69.

Goodey, B. (1978) Where we're at: interpreting the urban environment, *Urban Design Forum* 1, 28–34.

Goodey, B. (1982) Values in place: interpretations and implications from Bedford, in J. Gold and J. Burgess (eds) *Valued Environments*, Allen & Unwin, London, pp. 10–34.

Goodman, R. (1972) *After the Planners*, Penguin: Harmondsworth.

Gottmann, J. (1961) *Megalopolis: The Urbanized Northeastern Seaboard of the United States*, The Twentieth Century Fund: New York.

Gould, P. (1966) *On Mental Maps*, Discussion Paper No. 9, Michigan Inter-University Community of Mathematical Geographers.

Gould, P. (1973) The black boxes of Jönköping: spatial information and preference, in R. M. Downs and D. Stea (eds) *Image and Environment*, Aldine, Chicago, pp. 235–45.

Gould, P. and White, R. (1974) *Mental Maps*, Penguin: Harmondsworth.

Gove, W. R., Hughes, M. and Galle, O. M. (1980) Overcrowding in the home: an empirical investigation of its possible pathological consequences, in C. Ungerson and V. Karn (eds) *The Consumer Experience of Housing*, Gower, Aldershot, pp. 124–55.

Greenbie, B. B. (1974) Social territory, community health, and urban planning, *Journal of the American Institute of Planners* 40, 74–82.

Greene, J. (1972) *Psycholinguistics: Chomsky and Psychology*, Harmondsworth: Penguin.

Grier, G. and Grier, E. (1977) *Movers to the City: New Data on the Housing Market for Washington, DC*, The Washington Center for Metropolitan Studies: Washington.

Guelke, L. (1981) Idealism, in M. E. Harvey and B. P. Holly (eds) *Themes in Geographic Thought*, Croom Helm, London, pp. 133–47.

Guest, A. M. and Lee, B. A. (1983) Consensus on locality names within the metropolis, *Sociology and Social Research* 67, 374–91.

Guy, C. (ed.) (1985) Special issue on information technology in retailing, *Environment and Planning B*, 12, 139–248.

Hägerstrand, T. (1970) What about people in regional science? *Papers and Proceedings of the Regional Science Association* 24, 7–21.

Haggerty, L. J. (1982) Differential social contact in urban

neighbourhoods: environmental vs. sociodemographic explanations, *Sociological Quarterly* **23**, 359–72.

Halford, G. S. (1972) The impact of Piaget on psychology in the seventies, in **P. C. Dodwell** (ed.) *New Horizons in Psychology 2*, Penguin, Harmondsworth, pp. 171–96.

Hall, D. R. (1982) Valued environments and the planning process: community consciousness and urban structure, in **J. R. Gold** and **J. Burgess** (eds) *Valued Environments*, Allen & Unwin, London, pp. 172–88.

Hall, E. T. (1959) *The Silent Language*, Doubleday: New York.

Hall, E. T. (1966) *The Hidden Dimension*, Doubleday: New York.

Hall, P. (1981) Retrospect and prospect, in **P. Hall** (ed.) *The Inner City in Context*, Heinemann, London, pp. 112–31.

Hallman, H. W. (1984) *Neighbourhoods: Their Place in Urban Life*, Sage: London.

Hanson, S. (1976) Spatial variation in the cognitive levels of urban residents, in **R. G. Golledge** and **G. Rushton** (eds) *Spatial Choice and Spatial Behaviour*, Ohio State University Press, Columbus, pp. 157–88.

Hanson, S. (1977) Measuring the cognitive levels of urban residents, *Geografiska Annaler* **59B**, 67–81.

Hanson, S. and Hanson, P. (1981) The travel activity patterns of urban residents: dimension and relationships to socio-demographic characteristics, *Economic Geography* **57**, 332–47.

Hareven, T. K. (1982) *Family Time and Industrial Time: The Relationship between the Family and Work in a New England Industrial Community*, Cambridge University Press: Cambridge.

Harries, K. D. (1974) *The Geography of Crime and Justice*, McGraw-Hill: New York.

Harris, L. J. (1981) Sex-related variations in spatial skill, in **L. S. Liben** *et al.* (eds) *Spatial Representation and Behaviour across the Life Span*, Academic Press, New York, pp. 83–125.

Harris, R. (1984) Residential segregation and class formation in the capitalist city: a review and directions for research, *Progress in Human Geography* **8**, 26–49.

Harrison, G. (1983) Gentrification in Knoxville, Tennessee: a study of the Fourth and Gill neighbourhood, *Urban Geography* **4**, 40–53.

Harrison, J. D. and Howard, W. A. (1980) The role of meaning in the urban image, in **G. Broadbent, R. Bunt** and **T. Llorens** (eds) *Meaning and Behaviour in the Built Environment*, Wiley, London, pp. 163–82.

Hart, R. A. (1979) *Children's Experience of Place*, Irvington: New York.

Hart, R. (1984) The geography of children and children's

geographies, in **T. F. Saarinen, D. Seaman** and **J. L. Sell** (eds) *Environmental Perception and Behaviour: An Inventory and Prospect*, Research Paper No. 209, Department of Geography, University of Chicago.

Hart, R. A. and **Moore, G. T.** (1973) The development of spatial cognition: a review, in **R. M. Downs** and **D. Stea** (eds) *Image and Environment*, Aldine, Chicago, pp. 246–88.

Hartshorne, D. and **Weiss, P.** (eds) (1974) *The Collected Papers of Charles Sanders Peirce. 8 Vols.*, Harvard University Press: Cambridge, Mass.

Hawley, A. H. (1972) Population density and the city, *Demography* **9**, 521–9.

Hediger, H. (1961) The evolution of territorial behaviour, in **S. L. Washburn** (ed.) *Social Life of Early Man*, Wenner-Gren Foundation for Anthropological Research, New York.

Herbert, D. T. (1979) Urban crime: a geographical perspective, in **D. T. Herbert** and **D. M. Smith** (eds) *Social Problems and the City*, Oxford University Press, Oxford, pp. 117–38.

Herbert, D. T. (1982) *The Geography of Urban Crime*, Longman: London.

Herbert, D. T. and **Hyde, S. W.** (1985) Environmental criminology: testing some area hypotheses, *Transactions of the Institute of British Geographers* **10**, 259–74.

Herbert, D. T. and **Peace, S. M.** (1980) The elderly in an urban environment: a study of Swansea, in **D. T. Herbert** and **R. J. Johnston** (eds) *Geography and the Urban Environment: Progress in Research and Applications Vol. 3*, Wiley, London, pp. 223–55.

Herbert, D. T. and **Raine, J. W.** (1976) Defining communities within urban areas, *Town Planning Review* **47**, 325–38.

Herz, R. (1982) The influence of environmental factors on daily behaviour, *Environment and Planning A* **14**, 1175–93.

Hillery, G. A. (1955) Definitions of community: areas of agreement, *Rural Sociology* **20**, 111–23.

Horton, F. and **Reynolds, D. R.** (1971) Effects of urban spatial structure on individual behaviour, *Economic Geography* **47**, 36–48.

Hourihan, K. (1984) Residential satisfaction, neighbourhood attributes, and personal characteristics: an exploratory path analysis in Cork, Ireland, *Environment and Planning A* **16**, 425–36.

Huckfeldt, R. R. (1983) Social contexts, social networks, and urban neighbourhoods: environmental constraint on friendship choice, *American Journal of Sociology* **89**, 651–69.

Ittelson, W. H. *et al.* (1974) *An Introduction to Environmental Psychology*, Holt, Rinehart & Winston: New York.

Jackson, P. (1983) Principles and problems of participant observation, *Geografiska Annaler* **65B**, 39–46.

Jackson, P. (1985) Urban ethnography, *Progress in Human Geography* **9**, 157–76.

Jackson, P. I. (1984) Opportunity and crime: a function of city size, *Sociology and Social Research* **68**, 172–93.

Jacobs, J. (1961) *The Death and Life of Great American Cities*, Random House: New York.

Janelle D. and Goodchild, M. (1983) Diurnal patterns of social group distributions in a Canadian city, *Economic Geography* **59**, 403–25.

Jeffery, C. R. (1977) *Crime Prevention through Environmental Design*, Sage: Beverly Hills.

Jencks, C. (1980) The architectural sign, in **G. Broadbent, R. Bunt** and **C. Jencks** (eds) *Signs, Symbols and Architecture*, Wiley, New York, pp. 71–118.

Johnson-Laird, P. N. (1983) *Mental Models: Towards a Cognitive Science of Language, Inference, and Consciousness*, Cambridge University Press: Cambridge.

Kamenka, E. (ed.) (1982) *Community as a Social Ideal*, Arnold: London.

Kaplan, S. (1973) Cognitive maps in perception and thought, in **R. M. Downs** and **D. Stea** (eds) *Image and Environment*, Aldine, Chicago, pp. 63–78.

Kaplan, S. (1976) Adaptation, structure, and knowledge, in **G. T. Moore** and **R. G. Golledge** (eds) *Environmental Knowing*, Dowden, Hutchinson and Ross, Stroudsburg, pp. 32–45.

Kaplan, S. and Kaplan, R. (1982) Stress and the failure of preference, in **S. Kaplan** and **R. Kaplan** (eds) *Humanscape*, Ulrich's Books, Ann Arbor, pp. 194–9.

Katzman, M. T. (1980) The contribution of crime to urban decline, *Urban Studies* **17**, 277–86.

Keith, M. J. A. and Peach, C. (1983) The conditions in England's inner cities on the eve of the 1981 riots: comment, *Area* **15**, 316–9.

Kellerman, A. (1984) Telecommunications and the geography of metropolitan areas, *Progress in Human Geography* **8**, 222–46.

Kelly, G. A. (1955) *The Psychology of Personal Constructs*, Norton: New York.

Kennedy, L. W. and Krahn, H. (1984) Rural-urban origin and fear of crime: the case for 'rural baggage', *Rural Sociology* **49**, 247–60.

King, L. J. and Golledge, R. G. (1978) *Cities, Space, and Behaviour*, Prentice-Hall: Englewood Cliffs.

Kirk, W. (1963) Problems of geography, *Geography* **48**, 357–71.

Kirmeyer, S. L. (1978) Urban density and pathology: a review of research, *Environment and Behaviour* 10, 247–69.

Knox, P. (1982) *Urban Social Geography: An Introduction*, Longman: London.

Knox, P. L. and **MacLaran, A.** (1978) Values and perceptions in descriptive approaches to urban social geography, in **D. T. Herbert** and **R. J. Johnston** (eds) *Geography and the Urban Environment: Progress in Research and Applications, Vol. 1*, Wiley, London, pp. 197–247.

Korte, C. and **Grant, R.** (1980) Traffic noise, environmental awareness, and pedestrian behaviour, *Environment and Behaviour* 12, 408–20.

Korte, C. and **Kerr, N.** (1975) Response to altruistic opportunities under urban and rural conditions, *Journal of Social Psychology* 95, 183–4.

Krampen, M. (1979) *Meaning in the Urban Environment*, Pion: London.

Krech, D., Rosenzweig, M. R. and **Bennett, E. L.** (1962) Relation between brain chemistry and problem-solving among rats raised in enriched and impoverished environments, *Journal of Comparative and Physiological Psychology* 55, 801–7.

Ladd, F. C. (1970) Black youths view their environment: neighbourhood maps, *Environment and Behaviour* 2, 74–99. Copyright ©, Sage Publications Inc., Beverly Hills, Ca., USA.

Lander, B. (1954) *Towards an Understanding of Juvenile Delinquency*, Columbia University Press: New York.

Langer, E. J. and **Saegert, S.** (1977) Crowding and cognitive control, *Journal of Personality and Social Psychology* 35, 175–82.

Laslett, P. (1965) *The World We Have Lost*, Methuen: London.

Lavrakas, P. J. (1982) Fear of crime and behavioural restrictions in urban and suburban neighbourhoods, *Population and Environment* 5, 242–64.

Lazarus, R. (1966) *Psychological Stress and the Coping Process*, McGraw-Hill: New York.

Lazarus, R. S. and **Cohen, J. B.** (1977) Environmental stress, in **I. Altman** and **J. Wohlwill** (eds) *Human Behaviour and Environment, Vol. 2*, Plenum Press, New York.

Lee, S-A. (1982) The value of the local area, in **J. R. Gold** and **J. Burgess** (eds) *Valued Environments*, Allen & Unwin, London, pp. 161–71.

Lee, T. R. (1962) 'Brennan's Law' of shopping behaviour, *Psychological Reports* 11, 662.

Lee. T. (1968) Urban neighbourhood as a social spatial schema, *Human Relations* 21, 241–67.

Lee T. R. (1970) Perceived distance as a function of direction in the city, *Environment and Behaviour* **2**, 40–51.

Lee T. R. (1976) *Psychology and the Environment*, Methuen: London.

Lenz-Romeiss, F. (1973) *The City: New Town or Home Town?* (trans. E. Kustner and J. A. Underwood), Pall Mall: London.

Levy, L. and **Herzog, A. N.** (1974) Effects of population density and crowding on health and social adaptation in the Netherlands, *Journal of Health and Social Behaviour* **15**, 228–40.

Levy-Leboyer, C. (1982) *Psychology and Environment* (trans. D. Canter and I. Griffiths), Sage: Beverly Hills.

Levy-Leboyer, C. (1984) Vandalism and the social sciences, in **C. Levy-Leboyer** (ed.) *Vandalism: Behaviour and Motivations*, Elsevier, Amsterdam, pp. 1–11.

Lewin, K. (1951) *Field Theory in Social Science: Selected Theoretical Papers* (ed. D. Cartwright), Harper: New York.

Lewis, P. F. (1979) Axioms for reading the landscape: some guides to the American scene, in **D. W. Meinig** (ed.) *The Interpretation of Ordinary Landscapes*, Oxford University Press, New York, pp. 11–32.

Ley, D. (1974) *The Black Inner City as Frontier Outpost: Images and Behaviour of a Philadelphia Neighbourhood*, Association of American Geographers Monograph Series No. 7, Washington DC.

Ley, D. (1978) Social geography and social action, in **D. Ley** and **M. S. Samuels** (eds) *Humanistic Geography: Prospects and Problems*, Maaroufa Press, Chicago, pp. 41–57.

Ley, D. (1981) Cultural/humanistic geography, *Progress in Human Geography* **5**, 249–57.

Ley, D. (1983) *A Social Geography of the City*, Harper & Row: New York.

Ley, D. and **Samuels, M. S.** (1978a) Methodological implications, in **D. Ley** and **M. S. Samuels** (eds) *Humanistic Geography: Prospects and Problems*, Maaroufa Press, Chicago, pp. 121–2.

Ley, D. and **Samuels, M. S.** (1978b) Epistemological orientations, in **D. Ley** and **M. S. Samuels** (eds) *Humanistic Geography: Prospects and Problems*, Maaroufa Press, Chicago, pp. 19–21.

Liben, L. A. (1978) Perspective-taking skills in young children: seeing the world in rose-coloured glasses, *Developmental Psychology* **14**, 87–92.

Linton, D. L. (1968) The assessment of scenery as a natural resource, *Scottish Geographical Magazine* **84**, 219–38.

Lipowski, A. J. (1975) Sensory and information inputs overload: behavioural effects, *Comprehensive Psychiatry* **16**, 199–221.

Litton, R. B. (1972) Aesthetic dimensions of the landscape, in **J. V**

Krutilla (ed.) *Natural Environments*, Johns Hopkins University Press, Baltimore, pp. 262–91.

Loo, C. and **Ong, P.** (1984) Crowding perceptions, attitudes, and consequences among the Chinese, *Environment and Behaviour* **16**, 55–88.

Lowenthal, D. (1961) Geography, experience, and imagination: towards a geographical epistemology, *Annals of the Association of American Geographers* **51**, 241–60.

Lowenthal, D. (1975) Past time, present place: landscape and memory, *Geographical Review* **65**, 1–36.

Lowenthal, D. (1982) Revisiting valued landscapes, in **J. Gold** and **J. Burgess** (eds) *Valued Environments*, Allen & Unwin, London, pp. 74–99.

Lowenthal, D (1985) *The Past is a Foreign Country*, Cambridge University Press: Cambridge.

Lowman, J. (1982) Crime, criminal justice policy and the urban environment, in **D. T. Herbert** and **R. J. Johnston** (eds) *Geography and the Urban Environment: Progress in Research and Applications, Vol. 5*, Wiley, London, pp. 307–41.

Lowrey, R. A. (1970) Distance concepts of urban residents, *Environment and Behaviour* **2**, 52–73.

Lowrey, R. A. (1973) A method for analysing distance concepts of urban residents, in **R. Downs** and **D. Stea** (eds) *Image and Environment*, Aldine, Chicago, pp. 338–60.

Lundberg, U. (1976) Urban commuting: crowdedness and catecholamine excretion, *Journal of Human Stress* **2**, 26–34.

Lynch, K. (1960) *The Image of the City*, MIT Press: Cambridge, Mass.

Lynch, K. (1968) The possible city, in **E. W. Ewald Jr** (ed.) *Environment and Policy: The Next Fifty Years*, Indiana University Press, Bloomington, pp. 139–48.

Lynch, K. (1971) *Site Planning*, MIT Press: Cambridge, Mass.

Maclennan, D. and **Wood, G.** (1982) Information acquisition: patterns and strategies, in **W. A. V. Clark** (ed.) *Modelling Housing Market Search*, Croom Helm, London, pp. 134–59.

Marans, R. W. (1976) Perceived quality of residential environments, in **K. H. Craik** and **E. H. Zube** (eds) *Perceiving Environmental Quality*, Plenum, New York.

Marans, R. W. and **Rodgers, W.** (1975) Toward an understanding of community satisfaction, in **A. H. Hawley** and **V. P. Rock** (eds) *Metropolitan America in Contemporary Perspective*, Halstead Press, New York, pp. 299–352.

Maslow, A. H. (1954) *Motivation and Personality*, Harper & Row: New York.

Matrix (1984) *Making Space: Women and the Man-made Environment*, Pluto Press: London.

Matthews, M. H. (1981) Children's perception of urban distance, *Area* **13**, 333–43.

Matthews, M. H. (1984a) Cognitive maps: a comparison of graphic and iconic techniques, *Area* **16**, 33–40.

Matthews, M. H. (1984b) Environmental cognition of young children: images of journeys to school and home area, *Transactions of the Institute of British Geographers* **9**, 89–105.

Matza, D. (1969) *Becoming Deviant*, Prentice-Hall: Englewood Cliffs.

Mawby, R. I. (1977) Defensible space: a theoretical and empirical appraisal, *Urban Studies* **14**, 169–79.

McArthur, L. Z. and **Baron, R. M.** (1983) Toward an ecological theory of social perception, *Psychological Review* **90**, 215–38.

McCarthy, D. and **Saegert, S.** (1976) Residential density, social overload and social withdrawal, *Human Ecology* **6**, 253–72.

McClelland, L. (1982) Crowding and territoriality, in **S. Kaplan** and **R. Kaplan** (eds) (1982) *Humanscape*, Ulrich's Books, Ann Arbor, pp. 202–11.

McGee, M. G. (1979) Human spatial abilities: psychometric studies and environmental, genetic, hormonal, and neurological influences, *Psychological Bulletin* **86**, 889–918.

McHarg, I. (1969) *Design with Nature*, Natural History Press: New York.

McLean, E. K. and **Tarnopolosky, A.** (1977) Noise, discomfort and mental health, *Psychological Medicine* **7**, 19–62.

McPhail, C. (1971) Civil disorder participation: a critical examination of recent research, *American Sociological Review* **36**, 1058–73.

Meinig, D. W. (ed.) (1979a) *The Interpretation of Ordinary Landscapes*, Oxford University Press, New York.

Meinig, D. W. (1979b) Introduction, in **D. W. Meinig** (ed.) *The Interpretation of Ordinary Landscapes*, Oxford University Press, New York, pp. 1–10.

Meinig, D. W. (1979c) The beholding eye: ten versions of the same scene, in **D. W. Meinig** (ed.) *The Interpretation of Ordinary Landscapes*, Oxford University Press, New York, pp. 33–48.

Meyer, G. (1977) Distance perception of consumers in shopping streets, *Tijdschrift voor Economische en Sociale Geografie* **68**, 355–61.

Michelson, W. (1976) *Man and His Urban Environment: A Sociological Approach*, Addison Wesley: Reading, Mass.

Michelson, W. (1977) *Environmental Choice, Human Behaviour, and Residential Satisfaction*, Oxford University Press: New York.

Michelson, W. (1980) Long and short range criteria for housing choice and environmental behaviour, *Journal of Social Issues* **36**(3), 135–49.

Milgram, S. (1970) The experience of living in cities, *Science* **167**, 1461–8.

Mintz, N. L. and **Schwartz, D. T.** (1964) Urban psychology and psychoses, *International Journal of Social Psychiatry* **10**, 101–17.

Mitchell, J. C. (1983) Case and situation analysis, *Sociological Review* **31**, 187–211.

Mitchell, R. E. (1971) Some social implications of high density housing, *American Sociological Review* **36**, 18–29.

Moore, E. G. (1972) *Residential Mobility in the City*, Resource Paper No. 13, Association of American Geographers Commission on College Geography, Washington DC.

Moore, G. T. (1976) Theory and research on the development of environmental knowing, in **G. T. Moore** and **R. G. Golledge** (eds) *Environmental Knowing*, Dowden, Hutchinson & Ross, Stroudsburg, pp. 138–64.

Morgan, B. S. (1976) The bases of family status segregation: a case study in Exeter, *Transactions of the Institute of British Geographers* **1**, 83–107.

Morris, D. (1977) *Manwatching*, Jonathan Cape: London.

Moser, C. and **Kalton, G.** (1983) *Survey Methods in Social Investigation*, Heinemann: London.

Moulden, M. and **Bradford, M. G.** (1984) Influences on educational attainment: the importance of the local residential environment, *Environment and Planning A* **16**, 49–66.

Mounin, G. (1980) The semiology of orientation in urban space, *Current Anthropology* **21**, 491–501.

Muller, P. O. (1981) *Contemporary Suburban America*, Prentice-Hall: Englewood Cliffs.

Mumford, L. (1961) *The City in History*, Secker & Warburg: London.

Murray, R. and **Boal, F. W.** (1979) The social ecology of urban violence, in **D. T. Herbert** and **D. M. Smith** (eds) *Social Problems and the City*, Oxford University Press, London, pp. 139–57.

Nachmias, D. and **Nachmias, C.** (1976) *Research Methods in the Social Sciences*, Arnold: London.

Newman, O. (1972) *Defensible Space – Crime Prevention through Urban Design*, Collier: New York.

Nilles, J. M. *et al.* (1976) *The Telecommunications-Transportation Trade-Off: Options for Tomorrow*, Wiley: New York.

Norberg–Schulz, C. (1971) *Existence, Space and Architecture*, Studio Vista: London.

Norberg–Schulz, C. (1980) *Genius Loci: Towards a Phenomenology of Architecture*, Rizzoli: New York.

Nourse, H. and **Phares, D.** (1975) Socioeconomic transition and housing values: a comparative analysis of urban neighbourhoods, in **G. Gappert** and **H. Rose** (eds) *The Social Economy of Cities*, Sage, Beverly Hills, pp. 183–208.

Ohta, R. J. and **Kirasic, K. C.** (1983) The investigation of environmental learning in the elderly, in **G. D. Rowles** and **R. J. Ohta** (eds) *Aging and Milieu: Environmental Perspectives on Growing Old*, Academic Press, New York, pp. 83–95.

O'Keefe, J. and **Nadel, L.** (1978) *The Hippocampus as a Cognitive Map*, Clarendon: Oxford.

Oliver, K. A. (1982) Places, conservation and the care of streets in Hartlepool, in **J. Gold** and **J. Burgess** (eds) *Valued Environments*, Allen & Unwin, London, pp. 145–60.

Onibokun, A. G. (1976) Social system correlates of residential satisfaction, *Environment and Behaviour* 8, 323–44.

Orleans, P. (1973) Differential cognition of urban residents: effects of social scale on mapping, in **R. M. Downs** and **D. Stea** (eds) *Image and Environment*, Aldine, Chicago, pp. 115–30.

Ornstein, R. E. (1972) *The Psychology of Consciousness*, Freeman: New York.

Pacione, M. (1975) Preference and perception: an analysis of consumer behaviour, *Tijdschrift voor Economische en Sociale Geografie* 66, 84–92.

Pacione, M. (1982a) Space preferences, locational decisions, and the dispersal of civil servants from London, *Environment and Planning A* 14, 323–33.

Pacione, M. (1982b) The use of objective and subjective measures of life quality in human geography, *Progress in Human Geography* 6, 495–514.

Page, R. A. (1977) Noise and helping behaviour, *Environment and Behaviour* 9, 311–14.

Pahl, R. E. (1968) Is mobile society a myth?, *New Society*, 11 January, pp. 46–8.

Palisi, B. J. and **Canning, C.** (1983) Urbanism and social psychological well-being: a cross-cultural test of three theories, *Sociological Quarterly* 24, 527–43.

Palm, R. (1985) Ethnic segmentation of real estate agent practise in the urban housing market, *Annals of the Association of American Geographers* 75, 58–68.

Palm, R. E. and **Pred, A.** (1974) *A Time-geographic Perspective on Problems of Inequality for Women*, Institute of Urban and Regional Development Working Paper No. 236, University of California at Berkeley.

Parkes, D. and **Thrift, N.** (1980) *Times, Spaces, and Places: A Chronogeographic Perspective*, Wiley: New York.

Percival, A. (1979) *Understanding Our Surroundings: A Manual of Urban Interpretation*, Civic Trust: London.

Perlgut, D. J. (1982) Manageable space: proposals for crime prevention in subsidized housing, in **H. J. Schneider** (ed.) *The Victim in International Perspective*, Walter de Gruyter, New York, pp. 453–71.

Perlgut, D. (1983a) Vandalism: the environmental crime, *Australian Journal of Social Issues* **18**, 209–16.

Perlgut, D. (1983b) *Manageable Space*, Social Impact Publications: Armidale.

Phipps, A. G. (1979) Scaling problems in the cognition of urban distances, *Transactions of the Institute of British Geographers* **4**, 94–102

Piaget, J. and **Inhelder, B.** (1956) *The Child's Conception of Space*, Norton: New York.

Piché, D. (1981) The spontaneous geography of the urban child, in **D. T. Herbert** and **R. J. Johnston** (eds) *Geography and the Urban Environment: Progress in Research and Applications, Vol. 4*, Wiley, Chichester, pp. 229–56.

Pickup, L. (1984) Women's gender-role and its influence on travel behaviour, *Built Environment* **10**, 61–8.

Pocock, D. C. D. (1978) The cognition of intra-urban distance: a summary, *Scottish Geographical Magazine* **94**, 31–5.

Pocock, D. C. D. (1982) Valued landscape in memory: the view from Prebends' Bridge, *Transactions of the Institute of British Geographers* **7**, 354–64.

Pocock, D. C. D. (1983) The paradox of humanistic geography, *Area* **15**, 355–8.

Pocock, D. and **Hudson, R.** (1978) *Images of the Urban Environment*, Macmillan: London.

Popenoe, D. (1973) Urban residential differentiation: an overview of patterns, trends and problems, *Sociological Inquiry* **43**, 35–46.

Popenoe, D. (1981) Women in the suburban environment: a US–Sweden comparison, in **G. R. Wekerle, R. Peterson** and **D. Morley** (eds) *New Space for Women*, Westview Press, Boulder, pp. 165–74.

Porteous, J. D. (1973) The Burnside Gang: territoriality, social space and community planning, *Western Geographical Series* **5**, 130–48.

Porteous, J. D. (1974) Social class in Atacama company towns, *Annals of the Association of American Geographers* **64**, 409–17.

Porteous, J. D. (1976) Home: the territorial core, *Geographical Review* **66**, 383–90.

Porteous, J. D. (1977) *Environment and Behaviour: Planning and Everyday Urban Life*, Addison-Wesley: Reading, Mass.

Porteous, J. D. (1985) Smellscape, *Progress in Human Geography* **9**, 356–78.

Potter, R. B. (1977) Spatial patterns of consumer behaviour and perception in relation to the social class variable, *Area* **9**, 153–6.

Potter, R. B. (1979) Perception of urban retailing facilities: an analysis of consumer information fields, *Geografiska Annaler* **61B**, 19–27.

Potter, R. B. (1982) *The Urban Retailing System*, Gower: Aldershot.

Powell, J. M. (1978) *Mirrors of the New World: Images and Image-makers in the Settlement Process*, Australian National University Press: Canberra.

Power, M. J., Benn, R. T. and **Morris, J. N.** (1972) Neighbourhood, school and juveniles before the courts, *British Journal of Criminology* **12**, 111–32.

Pred, A. (1981) Social reproduction and the time-geography of everyday life, *Geografiska Annaler* **63B**, 1–22.

Pred, A. (1984) Place as historically contingent process: structuration and the time-geography of becoming places, *Annals of the Association of American Geographers* **74**, 279–97.

Pred, A. and **Palm, R.** (1978) The status of American women: a time-geographic view, in **D. A. Lanegran,** and **R. Palm** (eds) *An Invitation to Geography*, McGraw-Hill, New York, pp. 99–109.

Proshansky, H. M. *et al.* (1970) Basic psychological processes and the environment, in **H. M. Proshansky** *et al.* (eds) *Environmental Psychology*, Holt, Rinehart & Winston, New York, pp. 101–4.

Proshansky, H. M., Fabian, A. K., and **Kaminoff, R.** (1983) Place-identity: physical world socialisation of the self, *Journal of Environmental Psychology* **3**, 57–83.

Punter, J. V. (1982) Landscape aesthetics: a synthesis and critique, in **J. Gold** and **J. Burgess** (eds) *Valued Environments*, Allen & Unwin, London, pp. 100–23.

Pyle, G. F. (1980) Systematic sociospatial variation in perceptions of crime location and severity, in **D. E. Georges-Abeyie** and **K. D. Harries** (eds) *Crime: A Spatial Perspective*, Columbia University Press, New York, pp. 219–45.

Rainwater, L. (1966) Fear and the house-as-haven in the lower class, *Journal of the American Institute of Planners* **32**, 23–31.

Rapoport, A. (1976) Environmental cognition in cross-cultural

perspective, in **G. T. Moore** and **R. G. Golledge** (eds)
Environmental Knowing, Dowden, Hutchinson & Ross,
Stroudsburg, pp. 220–34.

Rapoport, A. (1977) *Human Aspects of Urban Form*, Pergamon
Press: Oxford.

Rapoport, A. (1982) *The Meaning of the Built Environment: A
Nonverbal Communication Approach*, Sage: Beverly Hills.

Rapoport, A. and **Kantor, R. E.** (1967) Complexity and ambiguity
in environmental design, *Journal of the American Institute of
Planners* **23**, 210–21.

Relph, E. (1976) *Place and Placelessness*, Pion: London.

Relph, E. (1981a) Phenomenology, in **M. E. Harvey** and **B. P.
Holly** (eds) *Themes in Geographic Thought*, Croom Helm, London,
pp. 99–114.

Relph, E. (1981b) *Rational Landscapes and Humanistic Geography*,
Croom Helm: London.

Rengert, G. (1980) Spatial aspects of criminal behaviour, in **D. E.
Georges–Abeyie** and **K. D. Harries** (eds) *Crime: A Spatial
Perspective*, Columbia University Press, New York, pp. 47–57.

Reppetto, T. A. (1976) Crime prevention and the displacement
phenomenon, *Crime and Delinquency* **22**, 166–77.

Robertson, I. M. L. (1984) Single parent lifestyle and peripheral
estate residence, *Town Planning Review* **55**, 197–213.

Robinson, J. P., Converse, P. E., and Szalai, A. (1972) Everyday
life in twelve countries, in **A. Szalai** (ed.) *The Use of Time*,
Mouton, Hague, pp. 113–44.

Robinson, M. E. (1982) Absolute and relative strategies in urban
distance cognition, *Area* **14**, 283–6.

Robson, B. T. (1969) *Urban Analysis*, Cambridge University Press:
Cambridge.

Rohe, W. M. (1982) The response to density in residential
settings: the mediating effects of social and personal variables,
Journal of Applied Social Psychology **12**, 292–303.

Roistacher, E. A. and **Young, J. S.** (1980) Working women and
city structure: implications of the subtle revolution, *Signs* **5**(3)
Supplement, S220–5.

Roncek, D. W. (1981) Dangerous places: crime and residential
environment, *Social Forces* **60**, 74–96.

Rosow, I. (1967) *Social Interaction of the Aged*, Free Press: New
York.

Ross, M. B., Layton, B., Erickson, B. and **Schopler, J.** (1973)
Affect, facial regard and reactions to crowding, *Journal of
Personality and Social Psychology* **28**, 69–76.

Rowles, G. D. (1978) *Prisoners of Space? Exploring the Geographical
Experience of Older People*, Westview Press: Boulder.

Russell, J. A. and **Ward, L. M.** (1982) Environmental psychology, *Annual Review of Psychology* **33**, 651–88.

Rutter, M. *et al.* (1974) Attainment and adjustment in two geographical areas. III, *British Journal of Psychiatry* **125**, 520–33.

Saarinen, T. F. (1973) The use of projective techniques in geographic research, in **W. H. Ittelson** (ed) *Environment and Cognition*, Seminar Press, New York, pp. 29–52.

Sack, R. D. (1983) Human territoriality: a theory, *Annals of the Association of American Geographers* **73**, 55–74.

Sadalla, E. K. and **Magel, S. G.** (1980) The perception of traversed distance, *Environment and Behaviour* **12**, 65–80.

Sadalla, E. K. and **Staplin, L. J.** (1980) The perception of traversed distance: intersections, *Environment and Behaviour* **12**, 167–82.

Saegart, S. and **Hart, R. A.** (1978) The development of environmental competence in girls and boys, in **M. Salter** (ed.) *Play: Anthropological Perspectives*, Leisure Press, West Point, New York.

Saegert, S. and **Winkel, G.** (1981) The home: a critical problem for changing sex roles, in **G. R. Wekerle** *et al.* (eds) *New Space for Women*, Westview Press, Boulder, pp. 41–63.

Sagan, C. (1977) *The Dragons of Eden: Speculations on the Evolution of Human Intelligence*, Random House, New York.

Samuels, M. S. (1978) Existentialism in human geography, in **D. Ley** and **M. S. Samuels** (eds) *Humanistic Geography: Prospects and Problems*, Maaroufa Press, Chicago, pp. 22–40.

Sanchez–Robles, J. C. (1980) The social conceptualization of home, in **G. Broadbent, R. Bunt** and **T. Llorens** (eds) *Meaning and Behaviour in the Built Environment*, Wiley, London, pp. 113–33.

Sarkissian, W. (1976) The idea of social mix in town planning, *Urban Studies* **13**, 231–46.

Sarkissian, W. and **Doherty, T.** (1984) *Living in Public Housing*, New South Wales Housing Commission: Sydney.

Scargill, D. I. (1979) *The Form of Cities*, St Martin's Press: New York.

Schmid, C. F. (1960) Urban crime areas, *American Sociological Review* **25**, 527–42 & 655–78.

Schmidt, D. E., Goldman, R. D. and **Feimer, N. R.** (1979) Perceptions of crowding: predicting at the residence, neighbourhood, and city levels, *Environment and Behaviour* **11**, 105–30.

Schmitt, R. C. (1963) Implications of density in Hong Kong, *Journal of the American Institute of Planners* **29**, 210–17.

Schmitt, R. C. (1966) Density, health, and social disorganization, *Journal of the American Institute of Planners* **32**, 38–40.

Schneider, M. (1975) The quality of life in large American cities: objective and subjective social indicators, *Social Indicators Research* **1**, 495–509.

Schutz, A. (1967) *Phenomenology and the Social World* (trans. G. Walsh and F. Lehnert), Northwestern University Press: Evanston.

Seamon, D. (1979) *A Geography of the Lifeworld: Movement, Rest and Encounter*, Croom Helm: London.

Seamon, D. (1984) Philosophical directions in behavioural geography with an emphasis on the phenomenological contribution, in **T. F. Saarinen** *et al.* (eds) *Environmental Perception and Behaviour: An Inventory and Prospect*, Research Paper No. 209, Department of Geography, University of Chicago, pp. 167–78.

Selye, H. (1956) *The Stress of Life*, McGraw-Hill: New York.

Sennett, R. (1977) *The Uses of Disorder: Personal Identity and City Life*, Allen Lane: London.

Shaw, C. R. and **McKay, H. D.** (1942) *Juvenile Delinquency and Urban Areas*, University of Chicago Press: Chicago.

Shepherd, I. D. H. and **Thomas, C. J.** (1980) Urban consumer behaviour, in **J. A. Dawson** (ed.) *Retail Geography*, Croom Helm, London, pp. 18–94.

Sherrod, D. R. (1974) Crowding, perceived control, and behavioural after-effects, *Journal of Applied Social Psychology* **4**, 171–86.

Shlay, A. B. (1985) Castles in the sky: measuring housing and neighbourhood ideology, *Environment and Behaviour* **17**, 593–626.

Short, J. F. and **Nye, F. I.** (1957) Reported behaviour as a criterion of deviant behaviour, *Social Problems* **5**, 207–13.

Siegel, A. W. (1977) Finding one's way around the large-scale environment: the development of spatial representations, in **H. McGurk** (ed.) *Ecological Factors in Human Development*, North Holland, Amsterdam.

Siegel, A. W. (1981) The externalization of cognitive maps by children and adults: in search of ways to ask better questions, in **L. S. Liben** *et al.* (eds) *Spatial Representations and Behaviour Across the Life Span*, Academic Press, New York, pp. 167–94.

Siegel, A. W. and **White, S. H.** (1975) The development of spatial representations of large scale environments, in **H. W. Reese** (ed.) *Advances in Child Development and Behaviour Vol. 9*, Academic Press, New York, pp. 9–55.

Siegel, A. W. *et al.* (1979) The development of cognitive maps of large- and small-scale spaces, *Child Development* **50**, 582–5.

Sim, D. (1983) The conditions in England's inner cities on the eve of the 1981 riots: comment, *Area* **15**, 314–16.

Simmel, G. (1905) The metropolis and mental life, in **P. Sennett** (ed.) (1969) *Classic Essays on the Culture of Cities*, Appleton-Century-Crofts, New York.

Simon, H. A. (1957) *Models of Man*, Wiley: New York.

Smith, C. D. (1984) The relationship between the pleasingness of landmarks and the judgement of distance in cognitive maps, *Journal of Environmental Psychology* **4**, 229–34.

Smith, C. J. (1980) Neighbourhood effects on mental health, in **D. T. Herbert** and **R. J. Johnston** (eds) *Geography and the Urban Environment: Progress in Research and Applications, Vol. 3*, Wiley, London, pp. 363–415.

Smith, C. J. and **Patterson, G. E.** (1980) Cognitive mapping and the subjective geography of crime, in **D. E. Georges–Abeyie** and **K. D. Harries** (eds) *Crime: A Spatial Perspective*, Columbia University Press, New York, pp. 205–18.

Smith, D. M. (1973) *The Geography of Social Well-being in the United States: An Introduction to Territorial Social Indicators*, McGraw-Hill: New York.

Smith, N. (1979) Toward a theory of gentrification: a back to the city movement by capital, not people, *Journal of the American Institute of Planners* **45**, 538–48.

Smith, P. F. (1974) *The Dynamics of Urbanism*, Hutchinson: London.

Smith, P. F. (1977) *The Syntax of Cities*, Hutchinson: London.

Smith, S. J. (1981) Humanistic method in contemporary social geography, *Area* **13**, 293–8.

Smith, S. J. (1984) Crime and the structure of social relations, *Transactions of the Institute of British Geographers* **9**, 427–42.

Sommer, R. (1974) Looking back at personal space, in **J. Lang** *et al.* (eds) *Designing for Human Behaviour: Architecture and the Behavioural Sciences*, Dowden, Hutchinson & Ross, Stroudsburg, pp. 202–10.

Spencer, C. and **Darvizeh, Z.** (1981) The case for developing a cognitive environmental psychology that does not underestimate the abilities of young children, *Journal of Environmental Psychology* **1**, 21–31.

Spencer, C. and **Dixon, J.** (1983) Mapping the development of feelings about the city: a longitudinal study of new residents' affective maps, *Transactions of the Institute of British Geographers* **8**, 373–83.

Spencer, C. and **Weetman, M.** (1981) The microgenesis of cognitive maps: a longitudinal study of new residents of an urban area, *Transactions of the Institute of British Geographers* **6**, 375–84.

Stea, D. (1976) Program notes on a spatial fugue, in **G. T. Moore** and **R. G. Golledge** (eds) *Environmental Knowing*, Dowden, Hutchinson & Ross, Stroudsburg, pp. 106–20.

Stea, D. and **Downs, R. M.** (1970) From the outside looking in at the inside looking out, *Environment and Behaviour* **2**, 3–12.

Steinitz, C. (1968) Meaning and the congruence of urban form and activity, *Journal of the American Institute of Planners* **34**, 233–48.

Stimpson, C. R. *et al.* (eds) (1981) *Women and the American City*, University of Chicago Press: Chicago.

Stokols, D. (1972) On the distinction between density and crowding: implications for future research, *Psychological Review* **79**, 275–7.

Stokols, D. (1976) The experience of crowding in primary and secondary environments, *Environment and Behaviour* **8**, 49–86. Copyright © Sage Publications Inc., Beverly Hills, Ca., USA.

Stokols, D. *et al.* (1983) Residential mobility and personal well-being, *Journal of Environmental Psychology* **3**, 5–19.

Sumner, G. (1906) *Folkways*, Ginn: Boston.

Sundeen, R. A. and **Mathieu, J. T.** (1976) Fear of crime and its consequences among elderly in three urban communities, *Gerontologist* **16**, 211–9.

Suttles, G. D. (1972) *The Social Construction of Communities*, University of Chicago Press: Chicago.

Szalai, A. (ed.) (1972) *The Use of Time: Daily Activities of Urban and Suburban Populations in Twelve Countries*, Mouton: Hague.

Taylor, R. B. (1983) Neighbourhood physical environment and stress, in **G. W. Evans** (ed.) *Environmental Stress*, Cambridge University Press, Cambridge, pp. 286–324.

Taylor, S. (1938) Suburban neurosis, *Lancet* **1**, 759–61.

Thompson, D. L. (1963) New concept: subjective distance, *Journal of Retailing* **39**, 1–6.

Tilden, F. (1967) *Interpreting our Heritage*, University of North Carolina Press: Chapel Hill, N.C.

Timms, D. W. G. (1976) Social bases to social areas, in **D. T. Herbert** & **R. J. Johnston** (eds) *Social Areas in Cities Vol. I: Spatial Processes and Forms*, Wiley, London, pp. 19–39.

Toffler, A. (1971) *Future Shock*, Pan: London.

Tonn, B. E. (1984) A sociopsychological contribution to the theory of individual time-allocation, *Environment and Planning A* **16**, 201–23.

Tönnies, F. (1887) *Community and Society* (1963 edn, trans. C. P. Loomis), Harper: New York.

Tuan, Y-F (1971) Geography, phenomenology, and the study of human nature, *Canadian Geographer* **15**, 181–92.

Tuan, Y-F (1973) Ambiguity in attitudes toward environment, *Annals of the Association of American Geographers* **63**, 411–23.

Tuan, Y-F (1974) *Topophilia: A Study of Environmental Perception, Attitudes and Values*, Prentice-Hall: Englewood Cliffs.

Tuan, Y-F (1976) Humanistic geography, *Annals of the Association of American Geographers* **66**, 266–76.

Tuan, Y-F (1978) Sign and metaphor, *Annals of the Association of American Geographers* **68**, 363–72.

Tuan, Y-F (1980a) The significance of the artifact, *Geographical Review* **70**, 462–72.

Tuan, Y-F (1980b) Rootedness versus sense of place, *Landscape* **24(1)**, 3–8.

Tuan, Y-F (1982) *Segmented Worlds and Self: Group Life and Individual Consciousness*, University of Minnesota Press: Minneapolis.

Tversky, A. and Kahneman, D. (1974) Judgment under uncertainty: heuristics and biases, *Science* **185**, 1124–31.

Unwin, K. (1975) The relationship of observer and landscape in landscape evaluation, *Transactions of the Institute of British Geographers* **66**, 130–4.

Van Vliet, W. (1984) Vandalism: an assessment and agenda, in C. Levy-Leboyer (ed.) *Vandalism: Behaviour and Motivations*, Elsevier, Amsterdam, pp. 13–36.

Von Rosenbladt, B. (1972) The outdoor activity system in an urban environment, in A. Szalai (ed.) *The Use of Time*, Mouton, Hague, pp. 335–55.

Walmsley, D. J. (1974a) Emotional involvement and subjective distance: a modification of the inverse square root law, *Journal of Psychology* **87**, 9–19.

Walmsley, D. J. (1974b) Positivism and phenomenology in human geography, *Canadian Geographer* **18**, 95–107.

Walmsley, D. J. (1976) Territory and neighbourhood in suburban Sydney, *Royal Australian Planning Institute Journal* **14**, 66–9.

Walmsley, D. J. (1978) Stimulus complexity in distance distortion, *Professional Geographer* **30**, 14–9.

Walmsley, D. J. (1980) Welfare delivery in post-industrial society, *Geografiska Annaler* **62B**, 91–7.

Walmsley, D. J. (1982a) Personality and regional preference structures: a study of introversion-extraversion, *Professional Geographer* **34**, 279–88.

Walmsley, D. J. (1982b) Mass media and spatial awareness, *Tijdschrift voor Economische en Sociale Geografie* **73**, 32–42.

Walmsley, D. J. and **Lewis, G. J.** (1984) *Human Geography: Behavioural Approaches*, Longman: London.

Walmsley, D. J. and **McPhail, I. R.** (1976) *The Geography of Hospital Care in New South Wales: A Case Study of Coffs Harbour*, Research Series in Applied Geography No. 44, University of New England, Armidale.

Walmsley, D. J. *et al.* (1982) Variability in crime rates: a study of the New South Wales North Coast, *Australian Journal of Social Issues* **17**, 220–9.

Wapner, S., Kaplan, B., and Cohen, S. B. (1980) An organismic-developmental perspective for understanding transactions of men and environments, in **G. Broadbent, R. Bunt** and **T. Llorens** (eds) *Meaning and Behaviour in the Built Environment*, Wiley, New York, pp. 223–52.

Ward, C. (ed.) (1973) *Vandalism*, Van Nostrand: New York.

Warren, R. B. and **Warren, D. I.** (1977) *The Neighbourhood Organizer's Handbook*, University of Notre Dame Press: Notre Dame, Indiana.

Washburn, S. L. (1972) Aggressive behavior and human evolution, in **G. V. Coelho** and **E. A. Rubinstein** (eds) *Social Change and Human Behaviour*, NIMH, Washington, pp. 21–39.

Watson, M. K. (1978) The scale problem in human geography, *Geografiska Annaler* **60B**, 36–47.

Webber, M. M. (1963) Order in diversity: community without propinquity, in **L. Wingo** (ed.) *Cities and Space*, Johns Hopkins Press, Baltimore, pp. 23–56.

Webber, M. M. (1964) The urban place and the non-place urban realm, in **M. M. Webber** *et al.* (eds) *Explorations in Urban Structure*, University of Pennsylvania Press, Philadelphia, pp. 79–153.

Webber, M. M. (1968) The post-city age, *Daedalus* **97**, 1093–9.

Weinreich, U. (1968) Semantics and semiotics, in **D. L. Sills** (ed.) *International Encyclopedia of the Social Sciences, Vol. 14*, Macmillan, New York, pp. 164–9.

Wekerle, G. R. (1980) Women in the urban environment, *Signs* 5(3) Supplement, *S*188–214.

Wekerle, G. R. (1981) Introduction, in **G. R. Wekerle** *et al.* (eds) *New Space for Women*, Westview Press, Boulder, pp. 125–7.

Wekerle, G. R., Peterson, R. and **Morley, D.** (1981) Introduction, in **G. R. Wekerle** *et al.* (eds) *New Space for Women*, Westview Press, Boulder, pp. 1–34.

Wellman, B. (1978) *The Community Question: The Intimate Networks of East Yorkers*, Centre for Urban and Community Studies, University of Toronto: Toronto.

Wener, R. E. and **Kaminoff, R. D.** (1983) Improving environmental information: effects of signs on perceived crowding and behaviour, *Environment and Behaviour* **15**, 3–20.

West, D. J. (1982) *Delinquency: Its Roots, Careers, and Prospects,* Heinemann: London.

Wheatley, P. (1971) *The Pivot of the Four Quarters,* Aldine: Chicago.

Wheeler, J. O. (1968) Work-trip length and the ghetto, *Land Economics* **44**, 107–12.

Wild, R. A. (1981) *Australian Community Studies and Beyond,* Allen & Unwin: Sydney.

Williams, P. (1984) Economic processes and urban change: an analysis of contemporary patterns of residential restructuring, *Australian Geographical Studies* **22**, 39–57.

Wirth, L. (1938) Urbanism as a way of life, *American Journal of Sociology* **44**, 1–24.

Wolpert, J. (1965) Behavioural aspects of the decision to migrate, *Papers and Proceedings of the Regional Science Association* **15**, 159–72.

Wood, D. and **Beck, R.** (1976) Talking with Environmental A, an experimental mapping language, in **G. T. Moore & R.G. Golledge** (eds) *Environmental Knowing,* Dowden, Hutchinson & Ross: Stroudsburg, pp. 351–61.

Wright, F. L. (1958) *The Living City,* Horizon Press: New York.

Wright, G. (1981) *Building the Dream: A Social History of Housing in America,* Pantheon: New York.

Young, W. (1984) Modelling residential location choice, *Australian Geographer* **16**, 21–8.

Young, M. and **Willmott, P.** (1957) *Family and Kinship in East London,* Routledge & Kegan Paul: London.

Zajonc, R. B. (1980) Feeling and thinking: preferences need no inferences, *American Psychologist* **35**, 151–75.

Zimbardo, P. G. (1969) The human choices: individuation, reason and order versus disindividuation, impulse and chaos, in **W. J. Arnold** and **D. Levine** (eds) *Nebraska Symposium on Motivation,* University of Nebraska Press, Lincoln.

Zimring, C. M. (1981) Stress and the designed environment, *Journal of Social Issues* **37**, 145–71.

Zimring, C. (1983) The built environment as a source of psychological stress: impacts of buildings and cities on satisfaction and behaviour, in **G. W. Evans** (ed.) *Environmental Stress,* Cambridge University Press, Cambridge, pp. 151–78.

Zube, E. H. (1974) Cross-disciplinary and inter-mode agreement on the description and evaluation of landscape resources, *Environment and Behaviour* **6**, 69–89.

Zube, E. H., Sell, J. L. and **Taylor, J. G.** (1982) Landscape perception: research application and theory, *Landscape Planning* **9**, 1–33.

Author Index

Subject Index